THE PROTESTANT ETHNIC
AND THE SPIRIT OF CAPITALISM

THE PROTESTANT ETHNIC
AND THE SPIRIT OF CAPITALISM

REY CHOW

COLUMBIA UNIVERSITY PRESS / NEW YORK

Columbia University Press
Publishers Since 1893
New York   Chichester, West Sussex
Copyright © 2002 Columbia University Press

Library of Congress Cataloging-in-Publication Data

Chow, Rey.
    The protestant ethnic and the spirit of capitalism / Rey Chow.
        p.   cm.
    Includes bibliographical references and index.
    ISBN 978-0-231-12420-1 (cloth: alk. paper)—
    ISBN 978-0-231-12421-8 (paper: alk. paper)

    1. Ethnicity—Political aspects—United States. 2. Ethnicity—
Religious aspects—Protestant churches. 3. Capitalism—United States.
4. Postcolonialism—United States. 5. Cross-cultural orientation—
United States. 6. United States—Ethnic relations. I. Title.

GN560.U6 P76 2002
305.8—dc21
                                                    2002019492

Columbia University Press books are printed on permanent
and durable acid-free paper.
Printed in the United States of America
Designed by Lisa Hamm

Contents

Preface

This book continues the work in cultural politics in which I have been engaged now for a decade. Its focus is the question of ethnicity in late capitalist Western society, where cross-cultural and cross-ethnic transactions have become not only a daily routine but also an inevitability. Unlike works that deal with this subject in some social science disciplines (many of which I hold in great respect and cite in my discussions), my approach is neither purely sociological nor empirical (there are no surveys, statistics, or interviews). Rather, it consists of examinations of critical and theoretical, as well as literary, issues as they pertain to the ethnic as such; it foregrounds the politics of representation throughout these examinations; and it offers argumentative reassessments of various epistemological, disciplinary, and cross-cultural frameworks in which ethnicity is at stake in the contemporary world.

As an introduction, I revisit Michel Foucault's description of the emergence of Man in the post-Enlightenment age, looking in particular at those areas of Foucault's texts in which the questions of race and ethnicity emerge suggestively, albeit ambiguously. By retracing the logic of Foucault's ruminations on biopower and by pushing that logic toward the realm of postcolonized race and ethnicity, I argue that the systematic pursuit and enforcement of *life* in modernity must be recognized as the backdrop to our controversial situations of racial and ethnic violence. In the first chapter, I put forth one of the key ideas in the entire book, namely, that the notion of ethnicity as it is currently used is theoretically ambivalent, confusing, indeed self-contradictory. Although the term "ethnic" used to be deployed, before the nineteenth century, for boundary-setting purposes (by Jews and Christians to refer to gentiles and heathens), the modern use of the term tends to be universalist and inclusionary in that everyone is now considered to be ethnic in the sense of belonging to one or another grouping. Such an attempt at universalism and inclusionism, however, has also meant a disavowal of, and consequently an inability to account for, the hostility and intolerance that accompany ethnic struggles. A more satisfactory understanding of the politics of ethnicity may be reached, I contend, if we analyze the ways in which such politics partakes of the Protestant work ethic that Max Weber identified as the spiritual side of capitalism's commodifying rationale. Although my interest is more in the literal sense of "protestant"—as pertaining to one who protests—than in the restricted historical sense of the religious followers of the Protestant Reformation, my arguments will show that our contemporary culture of protest, too, needs to be seen within the framework of a prevalent work principle. As do some of Weber's interpreters, what I consider most decisive about his theory is the effective structural collaboration he pinpoints between the power of subjective belief (in salvation) as found in modern, secularized society and capitalist economism's ways of hailing, disciplining, and rewarding identities constituted by certain forms of labor. The charged figure that results from this collaboration, one whose features I have only begun to trace in this book, is what I call the protestant ethnic.

Chapters 2 through 5, each with its own theoretical slant and focusing on a different set of texts, are devoted to what to me is the heart of the matter: the vicissitudes of cross-ethnic representational politics. Stereotyping as a dangerous yet unavoidable event in intercultural encounters; coercive mimeticism and its institutional apparatuses of interpellation; autobiographical writing and its collectively narcissistic sense of abjection; the rise of femininity as a form of racial power in an uneven multiethnic world: these are the arenas in which I delineate a series of independently complex yet mutually implicated critical debates. A concern that runs through the chapters is the controversial status of poststructuralist theory—how it has irrevocably radicalized cultural as well as textual studies but meanwhile has tended to remain iconophobic, to essentialize non-Western others' differences in the form of timeless attributes, to conflate the mobility or instability of the sign with existential freedom, and to confine the practice of critically nuanced thinking within specific ethnic parameters. Finally, by way of a postscript, I discuss the typical situation in which ethnic authors, artists, and intellectuals who have become successful internationally tend to be condemned for selling out to white culture by critics within their own ethnic communities. I suggest understanding this as a complex of what may be called postcolonial ethnic *ressentiment*, a kind of self contempt that is historically generated by the unequal and often humiliating contact with the white world but ends up, ironically, being directed against those who, ethnically speaking, are closest to one.

The composition of this book began several years ago, when I was teaching in southern California. In a state that is, to all appearances, more progressive than others on the matter of racial and ethnic diversity, I was haunted by an uneasiness: how is it that it is here, I found myself asking, that I seem to be noticing and encountering such insidious forms of racism, oftentimes from those who profess to be the friends, indeed the political allies, of racial and ethnic minorities? This question made it necessary for me to reflect on the economic and social relations between ethnicity as such and the popular discourses of liberalism, and especially to grasp the manner in which liberalism tends to couch its operational logic in, indeed to capitalize on, social inequity. As long as minorities' rights to speak and to be are derived from and vested in the enabling power of liberalism, it appears, and as long as these minorities are clearly subordinate to their white sponsors, things tend to remain unproblematic for the latter. Should the reality of this power relation be exposed and its hierarchical structure be questioned, however, violence of one kind or another usually erupts, and naked forms of white racist backlash quickly reassert themselves. In a land where ethnic minorities are so highly visible and significant in number, it is perhaps especially important that such classic structures of subordination remain in force, alternating between their benevolent and their violent modes as circumstances require. To this extent, this book is an attempt to probe some of the workings of such structures and their manifestations, though the implications that may be drawn go, I believe, considerably beyond the small corner of southern California in which I resided.

Several groups of people need to be acknowledged for their direct and indirect contributions to the completion of this book. Leonard Tennenhouse deserves special mention for his generously responsive readings of many pieces of my work and for making them seem more interesting than is ever intended by my conscious and unconscious minds combined. Nancy Armstrong, Chris Cullens, John Frow, Harry Harootunian, Marc Katz, Dorothy Ko, John Ma Kwok-ming, Dorothea von Mücke, and James Steintrager helped sustain my faith in intellectual work by providing, with their own writings, admirable examples of scholarly erudition and critical intelligence. I am greatly indebted to Robyn Wiegman and Smaro Kamboureli for their constructive feedback on earlier versions of the manuscript: my own flaws and shortcomings aside, this book became a better one because of them. Jennifer Crewe, as always, is the wonderfully enabling editor who made the book happen. To Austin Meredith, my companion, my coconspirator, and my home, I owe . . . everything.

Sections and earlier versions of some of the chapters were previously published in the following journal issues: sections of the introduction in *Postcolonial Studies* 1, no. 2 (1998): 161–69; sections of chapters 2 and 3 in *PMLA* 116, no. 1 (2001): 69–74, and *boundary* 2 24, no. 2 (1997): 21–45, and 25, no. 3 (1998): 1–24; an early version of chapter 4 in *Traces* 2 (2001): 53–77; an early version of chapter 5 in *differences* 11, no. 3 (1999–2000): 137–68. They have all been modified, revised, and coordinated to form cohesive parts of this book.

THE PROTESTANT ETHNIC
AND THE SPIRIT OF CAPITALISM

From Biopower to Ethnic Difference

The Emergence of Man

Michel Foucault wrote in *The Order of Things* that Man is not an eternal but a rather recent historical phenomenon, who arose with the steady fragmentation of the modern world into individualized compartments of intelligibility known as the disciplines—such as biology, philology, literature, economics, and so forth.[1] The most important point of Foucault's argument is that knowledge itself is not a given but rather an outcome of shifting historical relations of representation. Specifically, these relations involve two parallel, though seemingly paradoxical, sets of developments. The first is an increasing exactitude that accompanies the scientific objectification of the world. Knowledge, in this regard, is a matter of a progressive production of methodological detail, of being able to capture things instrumentally in as precise and meticulous a manner as possible—as measurable data, information, what we now condescendingly refer to as factoids. Simultaneously, however, the linkages between these observable phenomena and the evolving historical conditions that produced them have become increasingly elusive or hidden. As the world becomes more visible and observable, it has also become largely symptomatic. To probe its causes, which are no longer readily understandable, more and more interpretation is needed. But the criteria for such interpretation are themselves far from being continuous or natural; instead, they, too, are constantly being reinvented and reconceptualized. Hence the attempt to render the world as a knowable object is paralleled by increasingly abstract, theoretical processes of explanation and justification—in what may be called the politics of cultural legitimation.

Recent intellectual developments in academic fields such as cultural studies and postcolonial studies have furthered Foucault's arguments by foregrounding a dimension he did not broach in most of his work: that of race and ethnicity. Once this dimension is restored to the picture, the increasing objectification of the world that Foucault so eloquently elucidates can be historicized as part of an ongoing imperialist agenda for transforming the world into observable and hence manageable units, and the intensification of abstract theoretical processes, likewise, must be seen as inseparable from the historical conditions that repeatedly return the material benefits of such processes to European subjectivities. The terms of cultural studies and postcolonial studies, with their frequent foci on race and ethnicity, thus help accentuate the binarism of objectification and theorization introduced by Foucault in the following manner: *some humans have been cast as objects, while other humans have been given the privilege of becoming subjects.* Once we see this, Foucault's point that Man is a recent historical invention begins to make perfect sense— but less because of the emergence of disciplinary knowledge per se than because the objectification-theorization mechanism that is constitutive of disciplinary knowledge is, arguably, best exemplified in historical situations in which "Man" is epistemologically as well as practically divided into subject and object on grounds of racial and ethnic difference (the most prominent instance of this division being "white" and "nonwhite"). If Man is a historical invention, it is because he is a Western invention, which relies for its inventiveness—its originality, so to speak—on the debasement and exclusion of others. And it is these debased and excluded others, the men who were at one time considered not quite Man enough—not only because they had been banished to the European madhouses, prisons, and hospitals that Foucault investigated but also because they happened to be living as subordinates within the European colonial apparatus, as colonized natives, underclasses, laborers, migrants—who are now swarming around the disciplinary boundaries between subject and object. In the presence of these other men, Western Man is now (to borrow Heidegger's famous verb for being) *thrown* back to his proper place in history, where he, too, must be seen as an object.

In his other works, Foucault would continue to revisit the modern (Western) invention of Man by elaborating on the various institutional practices and discourse networks that have been produced around it. (His books on discipline and punishment and on the history of sexuality are the best cases in point here, but the books before *The Order of Things*, such as those on the birth of the clinic and on madness and civilization are also characteristic of such elaboration.) In these other works, the emphasis is not so much on the epistemic dislocation of Man from nature into history (as is the case in *The Order of Things*) as on the systemic techniques—scientific, administrative, and political—that accompany His historical emergence. Interestingly, as in his arguments in *The Order of Things*, Foucault could not really tackle these techniques without eventually running up against the problem of race. The racial implications of his historical analyses demand articulation even when he is not directly addressing them.

Toward the end of volume 1 of *The History of Sexuality*, Foucault moves into what is arguably the most crucial—what he himself calls "the fundamental"—part of the book: a discussion about biopower.[2] His analyses of the various institutional practices devised in European society since the Enlightenment for handling human sexuality lead him finally to the conclusion that such practices are part of a biopolitics: a systematic management of biological life and its reproduction. In the following, I would like to propose that Foucault's discussion of biopower can be seen as his approach, albeit oblique, to the question of the ascendancy of whiteness in the modern world. (See, in particular, his pertinent remarks on ethnology's relation to the human sciences in the last chapter of *The Order of Things*.) What is thought-provoking is that although Foucault adheres to the universalistic vocabulary of "Man" and "humanity"—by asking, for instance, in what ways humanity as such, once conjured, continues to grow and expand, both empirically and abstractly—the dialectical critical logic he follows does not permit such universalism to be invoked without being simultaneously ruptured from within. As in the case of his demonstrating how all positive phenomena of orderliness, discipline, and control are underpinned by, or concomitant with, a certain violence, and as in the case of his demonstrating that power lurks in the very mechanisms of resistance to power, so does he make it clear that the very continuum of the concept of "Man" or "humanity" itself is fragmented precisely by its enthusiastic enforcement. If biopower is about the growth and expansion of Man, we are led to ask, what forms of violence—physical but also cultural—accompany this growth and expansion, and how is such violence rationalized, sustained, and normalized?

To respond to this question, it is necessary to backtrack a little and ask how Foucault's analyses of sexuality shift theoretically into the notion of biopower in the first place. To put it somewhat differently, it is necessary to retrace some of his steps (which are, admittedly, already familiar to many readers) in order to speculate on the not-entirely-explicit connection.

The first major step, of course, involves overthrowing naturalistic assumptions about sexuality and linking it rather to discourse—to what we may arguably also call culture—and only thus to power. This conceptualization of sexuality as something grounded in human discourse networks is the rationale behind Foucault's fundamental critique of (the modern, Freudian legacy of) the "repressive hypothesis," a hypothesis that, for Foucault at least, is problematic because it attributes to sex the status of a natural truth that demands liberation from the bonds of social laws. Foucault's most remarkable point, however—one that is not quite emphasized enough by his readers—is that the repressive hypothesis, along with its discursive productivity, is what amounts to a kind of preaching, premised as it is on the ultimately *religious* belief in a better, brighter future: "It appears to me that the essential thing is . . . the existence in our era of a discourse in which sex, the revelation of truth, the overturning of global laws, the proclamation of a new day to come, and the promise of a certain felicity are linked together. Today it is sex that serves as a support for the ancient form—so familiar and important in the West—of preaching" (7). Foucault's aim, remember, is not to ask, why we are repressed? but rather to explore how we come to believe that we are: "The question I would like to pose is not, Why are we repressed? But rather, Why do we say, with so much passion and so much resentment against our most recent past, against our present, and against ourselves, that we are repressed? By what spiral did we come to affirm that sex is negated? What led us to show, ostentatiously, that sex is something we hide, to say it is something we silence?" (8–9). Only when we highlight Foucault's point about repression in this manner—that is, as a kind of religious belief in an otherwise secular context—does his conclusion, namely, that repression has led not so much to suppression as to a proliferation of discourses, make sense. For only belief—and, furthermore, belief in the possibility of liberation and betterment—holds the capacity for productivity with infinite potential. Taken to its logical conclusion, the repressive hypothesis amounts to a kind of liberation theology, which couches itself in the various secularized institutional mechanisms of classification, surveillance, examination, training, and so forth. Even the recognition of sexual perversions, the tendencies that supposedly depart pathologically from so-called normativity, is now simply part of an organized, panoptic structure of supervision and management, which, in turn, gives rise to multiple forms of research activity, scientific finding, medical and penal correction, and social remedy. The belief in repression—and, with it, in liberation—is thus a force field that, in the multiple etymological senses of the word, *generates*: it begets and begins things, gives them life, enables their continuity, authenticates them with a history.

From Sexuality to Biopower

This generative nature of the repressive hypothesis—in the sense of a negative idea turning itself around into a code for infinite potency, of blockage or prohibition becoming potential and possibility—constitutes the special connection between Foucault's well-known thesis about sexuality, on the one hand, and biopower, on the other. To this extent, sex and its discourses are essential, but by no means exclusive, components that help establish the discursive field, the grid of intelligibility, for Foucault's overall ruminations about the historical change in status in the human species' relations to life and death. As he writes, this change was in part brought about by the economic, agricultural, and other resources that had developed in the past few centuries in the West. As the threats traditionally posed by death were eased by advancements in various spheres of human activity, a newer control over life emerged. Coupled with developments in political spheres, the newly enhanced possibility of survival led to the historically unprecedented explosion of biopower. If the discussions about sexuality are rethought from the vantage point of the latter part of *History of Sexuality*, volume 1, then, they can be seen as simply a step—albeit an indispensable one—in Foucault's attempt to come to terms with something much broader and more elusive, what he would eventually call, in that remarkable phrase, "the entry of life into history" (141). To cite his words at some length:

> What occurred in the eighteenth century in some Western countries, an event bound up with the development of capitalism, was a different phenomenon having perhaps a wider impact than the new morality; this was nothing less than the entry of life into history, that is, the entry of phenomena peculiar to the life of the human species into the order of knowledge and power, into the sphere of political techniques. . . . Western man was gradually learning what it meant to be a living species in a living world, to have a body, conditions of existence, probabilities of life, an individual and collective welfare, forces that could be modified, and a space in which they could be distributed in an optimal manner. . . . If one can apply the term *bio-history* to the pressures through which the movements of life and the processes of history interfere with one another, one would have to speak of *bio-power* to designate what brought life and its mechanisms into the realm of explicit calculations and made knowledge-power an agent of transformation of human life. (141–43)

In retrospect, the sustained failure on the part of scholars to read the history of biopower that Foucault was attempting to write by writing about sexuality is disappointing but not entirely incomprehensible. It is perhaps the habitual tendency in the West to privilege sexuality in the narrow sense—as having to do with sexual intercourse, sex acts, and erotics—that has led to this failure, this systematic and collective blindness. Seen in the light of biopower, sexuality is no longer clearly distinguishable from the entire problematic of the reproduction of human life that is, in modern times, always racially and ethnically inflected. Race and ethnicity are thus coterminous with sexuality, just as sexuality is implicated in race and ethnicity. To that extent, any analytical effort to keep these categories apart from one another may turn out to be counterproductive, for it is their categorical enmeshment—their categorical miscegenation, so to speak—that needs to be foregrounded.

The ascendancy of life over death, naturally, has profound consequences. On the one hand, as Foucault's own work amply indicates, the disciplining of the individual human body, including its anatomy, its energies, its habits, and its orientations, has become something of economic, scientific, and political significance. On the other hand, it has also become necessary to regulate and administer humans as a species, as a global population, by calculating and manipulating the effects of all their activities. What is generated in the process of material improvements is therefore not only more biological life but also the imperative to live—an ideological mandate that henceforth gives justification to even the most aggressive and oppressive mechanisms of interference and control in the name of helping the human species increase its chances of survival, of improving its conditions and quality of existence.[3] In this light, the systematic genocidal campaigns mounted by a political state such as Nazi Germany must, Foucault suggests, be seen as consistent with the emergence of biopower in modernity. To the extent that the purity of blood—and of race defined in terms of genetic heritage—is the primary reason used for the extermination of those who are branded as unclean, racial discrimination is a logical manifestation of biopower, the point of which, it should be emphasized, is not simply to kill but to generate life, to manage and optimize it, to make it better for the future of the human species: "If genocide is indeed the dream of modern powers, this is not because of a recent return of the ancient right to kill; it is because power is situated and exercised at the level of life, the species, the race, and the large-scale phenomena of population" (137).

From Biopower to Racism

As critics have often pointed out, despite their perceptiveness and critical astuteness, Foucault's analyses remain by and large Eurocentric—a feature that, until recently, his readers tended willingly to overlook. For instance, although the implications of his discussion of biopower and its institutional implementation could easily have taken him beyond the confines of European territories into Europe's colonized lands overseas, where such implementation became a systematic effort to subjugate and exploit local native populations, in the bulk of his work Foucault did not exactly push beyond those limits. This point is taken up by Ann Laura Stoler in her magisterial study *Race and the Education of Desire*.[4] Stoler poses the question in this manner: "What is striking is how consistently Foucault's own framing of the European bourgeois order has been exempt from the very sorts of criticism that his insistence on the fused regimes of knowledge/power would seem to encourage and allow. . . . Why have we been so willing to accept his story of a nineteenth-century sexual order that systematically excludes and/or subsumes the fact of colonialism within it?" (5–6). Throughout her discussion, Stoler emphasizes the contradictory impulses in Foucault's work—his ambiguity about racism, his Eurocentric historiography, and the conspicuous absence of a consideration of the impact of European colonialism on the historical emergence of the European bourgeois order. Offering a carefully researched account of some of Foucault's less well known writings (for the English-speaking public), the Collège de France lectures given in 1976 (when volume 1 of *The History of Sexuality* was in press; see chapter 3 of her book), Stoler is able to show how the last of these lectures, clearly dovetailing and overlapping with the final section on biopower in *The History of Sexuality*, volume 1, articulates with somewhat greater clarity the connection Foucault attempted to establish between biopower and race, especially in terms of the technologies deployed by the modern state for purposes of social normalization.

Stoler recapitulates the seemingly paradoxical but crucial question about the biopolitical state raised by Foucault: how can a belief in life lead to mass murder, to the extreme cases of large-scale, organized destruction of life in modern times? Whereas in volume 1 of *The History of Sexuality* he still seems to concentrate on the technical details—the bureaucratic, institutional, and disciplinary instances of the exercise of (bio)power—in the lecture he argues that an additional explanation by way of race and racism needs to be supplied:

> From [the examples of the death penalty and the atomic bomb], Foucault returns to the problem of racism and to a basic paradox of a biopolitical state: how does this disciplinary and regulatory power over life permit the right to kill, if this is a power invested in augmenting life and the quality of it? . . .
>
> For Foucault, this is the point where racism intervenes. . . . What does racist discourse do? For one, it is "a means of introducing . . . a fundamental division between those who must live and those who must die" (TM: 53). It fragments the biological field, it establishes a break (*césure*) inside the biological continuum of human beings by defining a hierarchy of races, a set of subdivisions in which certain races are classified as "good," fit, and superior.
>
> More importantly, it establishes a *positive* relation between the right to kill and the assurance of life. It posits that "the more you kill [and] . . . let die, the more you will live."
>
> (84; emphasis in the original)[5]

Let me attempt to reformulate Foucault's argument in a somewhat different manner. When life becomes the overarching imperative, his argument implies, all social relations become subordinate to the discursive network that has been generated to keep it going, so much so that even a negative, discriminatory fact such as racism is legitimated in the name of the living. Rather than straightforwardly assuming the form of a callous willingness to kill, therefore, racist genocide partakes of the organization, calculation, control, and surveillance characteristic of power—in other words, of all the "civil" or "civilized" procedures that are in place primarily to ensure the continuance of life. Killing off certain groups of people en masse is now transformed (by the process of epistemic abstraction) into a productive, *generative* activity undertaken *for* the life of the entire human species. Massacres are, literally, vital events.[6]

If Foucault thereby shows how murder (a negative act) can be legitimated by a valorization of life (a positive idea), his logic may, I think, also be turned around to demonstrate that the valorization of life itself, by the necessity of practice, can give rise to processes of discrimination, hatred, and, in some extreme cases, extermination. In other words, if the notion of legitimation shows how murder can, indeed, make sense as part of a positive idea, the reversal of Foucault's logic shows that the material process of enforcing a positive idea inevitably derails it into something destructive and unjust. It is, of course, always possible to explain this derailment economically: since an infinite valorization of life cannot possibly be sustained on the basis of finite resources, various forms of disciplinary and regulatory controls must be introduced in order to handle population increases, thereby resulting in a hierarchical situation in which resources are assigned to the privileged few rather than distributed equally among all, etc. Yet this type of explanation—which sees unequal economic distribution as the primary source of social injustice—does not seem adequate to account for the persistence of racism, especially in places where there is actually sufficient wealth, where the democratization of resources seems to some degree to have been achieved. How, in other words, is one to account for an environment in which one may be allowed to stay alive, may be told that all is equal, may be given access to many things, only then to realize that an insidious pattern of discrimination continues systematically to reduce one to a marginal position vis-à-vis mainstream society? Such an environment, which is characterized by a schism between the positively proclaimed values of life, on the one hand, and an affective dis-ease felt by those who sense they are nonetheless the targets of discrimination, on the other, cannot be addressed purely on economic grounds. The schism in question is not simply a matter of lies versus truths, or false ideology versus lived reality. It is rather, if we follow Foucault's thinking, symptomatic of the generative functioning of biopower itself. To illustrate this, some examples may be useful.

From Genocide to Benevolence: The Liberalist Turn

How do biopower and its system of subjugation work in various types of political regimes?

While the obvious example in response to this question is the Nazi state, in his lecture Foucault proceeded to argue that the collaboration between the right to kill and biopower exists in *all* modern states, be they fascist, capitalist, or socialist. In the last case, he went as far as saying that the practice of socialism that insists on the management of life by a collective body, which is given the right to discipline, punish, and execute its members, also partakes of a racist principle: "Each time that socialism has had to insist on the problem of the struggle, of the struggle against the enemy, of the elimination of the adversary inside capitalist society . . . racism has revived . . . a racism that is not really ethnic but biological" (TM 60, quoted on 87). As Stoler comments, Foucault's indictment, a pessimistic one that no one wanted or bothered to take up (at least at the time he wrote it), was that "racism was intrinsic to the nature of all modern, normalizing states and their biopolitical technologies" (88).

I believe that Foucault's notion of biopower also offers an effective means of deconstructing the measures of benevolence in the classic colonial situation, in which it is not always necessary to go to the extreme of extermination in order to accomplish the task of control and subjugation. This is the juncture at which, as is especially evident in capitalist society, the role played by culture—indeed, of cultural tolerance—must be understood to be working in tandem with biopower.

Consider the example of British Hong Kong before its return to China in 1997. It is instructive to remember how the predominant native/local culture—the Chinese—was handled by the British administration in comparison with the colonizer's—the British (and, by extension, Western European cultures in general)—in colonial Hong Kong. To say that Chinese culture had been made unavailable, or simply wiped out or disallowed, would be inaccurate. (For instance, in what comes across as a gross simplification of how colonialism, especially British colonialism, worked, many intellectuals from the People's Republic of China assume mistakenly to this day that only the English language was used in Hong Kong schools during the colonial period.) Instead, what needs to be emphasized is that Chinese culture was never eradicated *tout court* but always accorded a special status—and that this was actually the more effective way to govern. During the era when I was in secondary school (1970s), for instance, English was the mandatory medium of instruction in Hong Kong's Anglo-Chinese schools (there were also Chinese schools where Cantonese was the medium of instruction), but Chinese language and literature and Chinese history were also possible subjects (for public examinations). The native culture, in other words, continued to be taught (all the way to university and postgraduate levels) and allowed a certain role in the colonized citizens' education. Rather than being erased, its value became specialized and ghettoized over time precisely through the very opportunities to learn it that were made available. Albeit not a popular one, the study of Chinese remained an option. It was in this manner that British colonialism avoided the drastic or extremist path of cultural genocide (which would have been far too costly) and created a socially stable situation based on the pragmatist hierarchization of cultures, with the British on top and the Chinese beneath them. To study, to be invested in, Chinese culture was never against the law but was simply constructed as a socially inferior phenomenon. Racism was, indeed, very much in operation, but it was a racism that had turned race and culture into *class* distinctions so that, in order to head toward the upper echelons of society, one would, even (and especially) if one was a member of the colonized race, have no choice but to collaborate with the racist strategies that were already built into the stratification informing the distribution and consumption of knowledge as well as its compensation. It is in this manner that racism, as Albert Memmi writes, functions as a "consubstantial part of colonialism" and "lays the foundation for the immutability of [colonial] life."[7]

The British colonial practice of cultural tolerance, in turn, sheds light on the liberalist claims about ethnic diversity and difference that permeate the climate of multiculturalism in contemporary North America. The official story, in the North American context, is that the new social ethics emphasizing affirmative action, diversity, equal opportunity for minorities, and so forth is intended to correct a previously erroneous, because racially unjust, situation, in which minority peoples were targets of discrimination. Indeed, as Robyn Wiegman has argued, the liberalism currently attached to whiteness in North American society is characterized, first and foremost, by a conscious disaffiliation from the more overt and brutal forms of racial violence, such as segregation and white supremacism: "The hegemonic formation of white identity today must be understood as taking shape in the rhetorical, if not always political, register of disaffiliation from white supremacist practices and discourses."[8] But if we remember that, in Foucault's analysis, the positive momentum of biopower is gathered precisely by (repressively) subjugating bodies and controlling populations (through the surveillance of birthrate, longevity, public health, housing, and migration [*History of Sexuality*, 1:140]), it becomes necessary to rethink this official story of benevolent tolerance on the part of supposedly reformed white societies also in terms of mechanisms of regulation and administration, whereby the privilege of whiteness, as Wiegman points out, is simply reconstituted and reinvested in a different way:

> Indeed, we might say that even as liberal whiteness has overseen the rise of "diversity" in the popular public sphere, the nation-state's capitulation to capitalism—in the deaths of welfare and affirmative action, on the one hand, and the heightened regulation of immigrant populations and borders, on the other—has extended the material scope of white privilege. While the histories of these issues are complicated, it is nonetheless significant how seemingly "benign" is the popular cultural rhetoric of whiteness today and how self-empowering are its consequences. Or, to put this in another way, seldom has whiteness been so widely represented as attuned to racial equality and justice while so aggressively solidifying its advantage.[9]   (121)

To see this—that is, to see how benign tolerance remains cathected to advantage—we need to recall the fundamental change in the conceptualization of race in modernity, something already discussed in substance by critics. Etienne Balibar's essay "Is There a Neo-Racism?" is instructive at this juncture. From the previous (nineteenth-century) association of race with nature, and of racism with a kind of uncrossable, untransgressible boundary based on bloodlines, Balibar writes, race and racism work rather differently in the period after the Second World War. From biology, the problematic of racism has been displaced onto the realm of culture, so that it is the insurmountability of cultural identity, or cultural difference, that has become the justification for racist, discriminatory conduct. "Biological or genetic naturalism is not the only means of naturalizing human behaviour and social affinities. . . . *Culture can also function like a nature*, and it can in particular function as a way of locking individuals and groups a priori into a genealogy, into a determination that is immutable and intangible in origin."[10] Ironically, as Balibar explains, this trend toward culturalist or differentialist racism is in part encouraged by the postwar phenomenon of anthropological culturalism, which is oriented, with the best of intentions, toward the need to recognize the diversity and equality of all cultures. Keeping in mind Foucault's insights, it is now possible to describe the well-intentioned, liberalist telos of anthropological culturalism itself as inherent to the expansionist logic of biopower. The discourses of tolerance, acceptance, and understanding that are crucial to anthropological culturalism are, in this light, part and parcel of the multiplication and democratization of networks having to do with classified lifeworlds, populations, demographic movements, ethnic differences, dispositions of particular social groups, and so on in late capitalist society, in which racial or racialized discourse is not necessarily "opposed to emancipatory claims; on the contrary, it effectively appropriates them."[11]

Perhaps it is only by clarifying this connection with biopower that we can begin to understand why the increase and acceleration of racial and ethnicist violence tend to happen in places where, paradoxically, there is the most talk about and awareness of racial, ethnic, and cultural diversity. Consider the situation in California, where the furor over affirmative action and the raised consciousness about minorities are supposedly events that have potential impact on the entire United States: when white supremacist Buford Furrow decided to open fire in the summer of 1999, he chose Jews and Asians as his targets. Was this a mere coincidence? At the outbreak of violence, the American public's typical response is one of shock and disbelief—"How could something like this have happened in our midst?" As Wiegman demonstrates, such disavowal has been made possible by the peculiar formation of the contemporary, politically correct white subject, who imagines that he has already successfully disaffiliated from his culture's previous, more brutal forms of racism. Yet it is precisely such disavowal, such displacement of violence to another space (other than ours, other than our own nice arena) that continues systematically to perpetuate violence. In this disavowal of violence in our midst—in this particular form of splitting undergone by the white subject—persists an implicit class hierarchy, an "us" versus "them," that once again designates as the enemy, the *de-generate* other, those whose actions we are quick to discredit as "not ours" (and who therefore deserve to be expunged and discriminated against with contempt). What is virtually impossible to acknowledge is that the likes of Furrow are not exactly madmen but rather normal people—like most of us—who at critical moments simply unmask.

In the realm of racial and ethnic difference, the generative nature of biopower can thus be defined as follows: liberally intended, discourse bound, culturally produced and transmitted. This biopowerful capacity (on the part of our discourse networks) to mutate, split, grow, reproduce, adapt, and multiply—in the form of a second-order nature, one that is without limits—suggests that alongside the very real and horrendous events of actual physical violence that happen daily around the world (rape, warfare, racial conflicts, murder, genocide), there also persists another kind of violence, one that will, moreover, always pose as a liberalist alibi against violence. To the extreme acts of violence, this liberalist alibi will mount a morally self-righteous opposition with its many discourses of rights: "the 'right' to life, to one's body, to health, to happiness, to the satisfaction of needs, and beyond all the oppressions or 'alienations,' the 'right' to rediscover what one is and all that one can be"[12]—which have become the issue of political struggles in modernity. Humane, genteel, philanthropic, ever-expanding, ever-eager for a bigger and brighter future, this liberalist alibi is itself generating endless discourses of further differentiation *and* discrimination even as it serves as enlightened correction/civilized prohibition against physical and brutal violence, and it is the glaring schism produced by its unstoppable positive discourses on life that needs to be confronted as the basis of racial and ethnic unrest in the contemporary world today. What needs to be confronted is not racial violence as an exception, a kind of scapegoating, but rather racial violence as a systemic function, one that is internal to the workings of the social body:

Scapegoat theories posit that under economic and social duress, particular sub-populations are cordoned off as intruders, invented to deflect anxieties, and conjured up precisely to nail blame. For Foucault, racism is more than an ad hoc response to crisis; it is a manifestation of preserved possibilities, the expression of an underlying discourse of permanent social war, nurtured by the biopolitical technologies of "incessant purification." Racism does not merely arise in moments of crisis, in sporadic cleansings. It is internal to the biopolitical state, woven into the weft of the social body, threaded through its fabric.[13]

It seems appropriate to conclude this discussion with a story from the academy, since the latter is, after all, one of the predominant networks for the dissemination of knowledge. When I was the director of the Comparative Literature Program at the University of California, Irvine some years ago, I was once informed by a white graduate student that she had been discouraged by her adviser (a white academic who frequently advocated the need to globalize Western theory) from pursuing postcolonial studies because, this adviser pointed out, she was not a person of color. Although anecdotal information does not really constitute any concrete source of scholarly evidence, stories like this do convey some sense of the reality of which they partake. What is relevant to the discussion at hand is the characteristic mix of a benevolent anthropological culturalism and a pernicious type of discrimination. In representing—or constructing a discourse about—a field such as postcolonial studies as the exclusive domain of peoples of color, what this adviser accomplished was not merely racism *tout court* (in the naked form of a white flight from a colored neighborhood) but rather a racism that was sophisticatedly couched in an enlightened discourse of respect for other peoples' cultural or ethnic differences. This deliberate act of racializing an academic sector amounts, of course, to an imperialist strategy of restricting and sabotaging a field, but it does so by assuming the positive form of benevolent professorial advice to a graduate student, who in fact had a strong and quite legitimate interest in postcolonial issues. If enough of this kind of advice were given and taken, a field such as postcolonial studies would, indeed, become a ghetto, evacuated by white people, its activities reproduced and circulated only among so-called peoples of color. Should that happen, it would in effect have been successfully delegitimated as a viable field of study, while the blame for its loss of credibility could, once again, be comfortably laid at the door of those self-same peoples of color and their acrimonious identity politics. (To my student's credit, she had, entirely on her own initiative, already decided to change advisers by the time she recounted this incident to me.)

This student's story is about *antimiscegenation*, a composite attitude that is hostile not only to the mixings of genes (biology) but also to the mixings of genres, the cross-generations of knowledge (discourse). What it reveals is the familiar pattern of the vicious circle that haunts the emergence of any type of intellectual inquiry that develops in response to patterns of injustice accompanying the globalization of biopower. Even as such inquiry seeks to address historical inequities (by drawing on the politics of ethnicity and identity, for instance, in addition to the many theoretical attempts to transform the boundaries of accumulated knowledge), it may in the end be delegitimated by the very historical conditions, including those of anthropological culturalism and its definitive regard for cultural difference, that propelled it into being in the first place. Such delegitimation, moreover, need never be a complete eradication (or extermination). Rather, like the study of things Chinese in British Hong Kong, it can simply be assigned a socially inferior position, a lower-class status; it can simply be put in its place. The course of knowledge management in this instance runs parallel to the course of biopower: in both cases racism intervenes to produce a division between "us" and "them," between those who must live and those who must die.[14]

The point of this little book, then, is to unravel some of the problems characteristic of the liberalist turns, the well-intentioned disaffiliations from overt racist practices, that often end up reconstituting and reinvesting racism in a different guise. I will proceed with a certain assumption. From Man to biopower, from biopower to ethnic difference, the story goes something as follows: all humans and all discourses are created equal—but some are more equal than others.

CHAPTER 1

The Protestant Ethnic and the Spirit of Capitalism

Transactions of Ethnicity in the Age of Global Capital

In 1997, shortly after President Jiang Zemin's visit to the United States, the People's Republic of China released its most famous dissident, Wei Jingsheng, who went into exile and now lives in the northeastern United States. In 1998, before President Bill Clinton's scheduled visit to China, another well-known Chinese dissident, Wang Dan, was also released and sent to the United States on medical grounds. (Wang is now a graduate student at Harvard.) Soon afterward Clinton became the first U.S. president to visit China since 1989.

Ever since the Tiananmen Massacre of June 4, 1989, the issue of human rights has remained in the forefront of China's relations with the West. There are, of course, multiple dimensions to the definition of "human rights," but when evoked in relation to China by the Western media, the phrase is invariably meant as a reminder of what China is lacking, such as democracy and freedom of speech for its live citizens and basic humane respect for its political prisoners, whose body organs are reportedly being harvested in a massive, lucrative underground international trade. Indeed, Western, especially U.S., journalism has in recent years identified human rights as *the* way to make any mainland Chinese story newsworthy, and any slight displeasure at China is enough to instigate yet another round of wrathful accounts about how utterly barbaric this country still remains. When being rebuffed by Chinese authorities on one occasion during Bill Clinton's historic visit to the People's Republic in the summer of 1998, one American journalist, for instance, vowed to "do the human rights story every day."[1]

In the reports that regularly come to the attention of the U.S. public about the arrest, imprisonment, and maltreatment of political dissidents, about the Chinese government's connivance at and participation in the trading of body parts from executed prisoners, and about the continued prohibition of public discussions of democracy in what has become a thriving capitalist economy in the PRC, one thing looms large with remarkable consistency: the fraught relationship between what seems to be a universal issue (human rights) and the specifics of a local, particular culture (China). The argument often put forth by the Chinese government in its own defense is that human rights in China cannot be the same as human rights in the West. Accordingly, whereas the West asserts its moral claims on the basis of a universalist rhetoric traceable to the European Enlightenment, China is reduced to a reactive position from which it must and can speak only in terms of its own cultural and local specifics, in terms of its own historical differences. This typical discursive scenario amounts to a division of cultural labor on the international scene; it is one that hardly needs to be elaborated but badly needs to be challenged. Instead of viewing one party, the West, as the holder of some absolute, uncompromisable value and the other, China, as a stubborn, wayward resister to all that is reasonable, it would perhaps be more productive, in light of Foucault's notion of biopower, to view the West and China as collaborative partners in an ongoing series of biopolitical transactions in global late capitalism, transactions whereby human rights, or, more precisely, humans as such, are the commodity par excellence.

In exiling its political dissidents in single file, while others continue to be arrested and imprisoned,[2] the mainland Chinese government is, de facto, setting itself up as a business enterprise that deals in politicized human persons as precious commodities, the release of which, as the logic of commodification goes, is systematically regulated—by the rules of demand and supply and by the continued presence of an interested buyer. It is as if, in order to honor its part in the business relationship, China must act in good faith by constantly maintaining a supply of the goods being demanded by the West. As some prisoners are traded off, others need be caught and put away in order to replenish the national stockpile, so that transactions can proceed periodically to the satisfaction of the trading parties concerned. Scandalous though this may sound, the point is that human rights can no longer be understood purely on humanitarian grounds but rather must also be seen as an inherent part—entirely brutal yet also entirely logical—of transnational corporatism, under which anything, including human beings or parts of human beings, can become exchangeable for its negotiated equivalent value.[3] By releasing its political prisoners—who can be seen as a kind of national product—in a regulated manner, the Chinese authorities accomplish the pragmatic goal of forcing Western nations to soften their rhetoric against China and thus of receiving more trading privileges and opportunities over time.

It is important to emphasize that the Chinese are not the only ones to benefit from such releases. Western companies, which eye the Chinese market with candid rapacity but are often inconvenienced by the moral embarrassment of conducting business with a totalitarian regime, also stand to gain substantially from the Chinese government's calculated moves. In other words, the "humane" release of famous dissidents arises, in practice, from the same cold-blooded logic of economic transactions as what only appears to be its opposite, namely, the egregious, abusive trading of organs from slaughtered Chinese prisoners. The two kinds of trades form a diversified but cohesive globalized financial order: when dead, humans are exchanged in the form of replaceable body parts; when still alive, they are exchanged whole—body and soul—for lucrative long-term trading arrangements that benefit the entire nation. The ostensible trade in nonhuman commodities between China and the

West—the clothes, toys, industrial equipment, household accessories, and their like—is concurrently facilitated by this other, unmentionable trade in humans as commodities.

China is, of course, by no means the only country in the world with the habit of abusing human rights. Nonetheless, the unique combination of the trade in both live and dead Chinese in the contemporary situation serves as a crystal-clear example of the politics of ethnicization inherent to the global commodification process, a process in which the specifically Chinese contribution is only part of the problem. With the commodities bearing the distinctive trademark that they are—whether dead or alive, whole or part—victims of their own culture, of being Chinese, the gist of this process is that what is being transacted is so-called ethnicity, which is understood in the sense of an otherness, a foreignness that distinguishes it from mainstream, normative society. Understood in this manner, ethnicity is not simply a static space occupied by ethnics who are, somehow, always already there but, more important, also a relation of cultural politics that is regularly being enacted by a Westernized, Americanized audience with regard to those who are perceived and labeled as ethnic. That is to say, the beliefs, desires, attitudes, and life habits of this audience (the American audience that is watching or reading about China and judging the rights and wrongs of China's various human right issues, for instance) are as complicit in the construction of such ethnicity as "the Chinese" themselves.

To this extent, the struggle for human rights in China is no longer simply a Chinese but, properly speaking, an Americanized Chinese affair whose immediate participants include the U.S. Congress, U.S. business corporations, the U.S. media, Hollywood actors and directors, U.S. human rights activists, and the U.S. electorate, as well as Chinese political leaders, dissidents, and prisoners themselves. The binary oppositional narrative that underlies this transnational affair is a familiar one: only the Chinese—in the form of "they"—remain so barbaric as to be ready to violate human rights, trade human organs, and use their people as bargaining chips; only "they" would do something that is so unthinkable among "us" in the enlightened, law-bound nations of the West. Even when humanitarian sympathy is bestowed on the dissidents, therefore, such sympathy is inseparable from the acute awareness that they are Chinese, that they are marked by a kind of difference that should be ignored (since we are all human beings) but, nonetheless, noticeably helps ennoble "our" cause (of trying to rescue them). The commodified relations of ethnicity, in other words, are underwritten by the conviction that the other is being held captive within his or her own culture whether dead or alive and that such captivity necessitates protest and liberation. This conviction can be seen as a variety of what Foucault calls the repressive hypothesis,[4] with the important distinction that the peculiarly generative capacity of the latter, which (as I discussed in the introduction) specializes in turning a negative, prohibitive idea into a positive, expansive set of possibilities, operates here in biopolitical and cross-ethnic terms. Commercial transactions of ethnic bodies, in this light, become not merely exploitative (as they are often said to be) but also a morally justified course of action that helps free the other and confirm our own moral superiority.

The entrance of the ethnic on the late capitalist global stage is hence a rather dramatic affair. Often appearing in captivity and longing for emancipation, the ethnic-as-commodity cannot simply be understood within the parameters of an older humanism with its existentialist logic but must also be theorized in terms of the forces of an inhuman, capitalistic logic, the roots of which, as Max Weber argues, can be traced back to religion—to the tradition of Protestantism. To chart the complex genealogical affinities among ethnicity, capitalist commodification, and the spiritual culture of protest, it is best to begin with some reminders of the difficult and elusive nature of the word "ethnicity" itself. But before I proceed, let me clarify first of all my use of the words "race" and "ethnicity" throughout this book.

It has often been pointed out that "race" and "ethnicity" are not identical concepts and that a certain distinction between them ought to be maintained. (To some scholars, as the discussion to follow will show, talk about ethnicity is simply a way to avoid dealing with problems of race and racism.) To my mind, however, it may actually be more productive not to insist on an absolute distinction between the two terms at all times, for the simple reason that they are, more often than not, mutually implicated. Their frequent conflation is not the result of mental sloppiness on the part of scholars but rather a symptom of the theoretical fuzziness of the terms themselves, a fuzziness that, moreover, must be accommodated precisely because of the overdetermined nature of the issues involved.

My thinking has been greatly influenced by the remarkable analyses offered by Immanuel Wallerstein and Etienne Balibar in *Race, Nation, Class: Ambiguous Identities*. For Wallerstein, arguing from a classical Marxist perspective, race and racism are what accompany the modality of global capital and labor, while ethnicity is subordinate to race as the form of a local cultural or communal process of socialization that is made visible, for instance, in the organization of households. For Balibar, the terms are coordinated differently: ethnicity, like all ideology, is "fictive," but its very real social functioning is made possible jointly by language acquisition (an open, inclusive process) and racial grouping (a closed, exclusive process).[5] My approach to ethnicity is admittedly more closely affined with the paradigm proposed by Balibar, but the classical Marxist questions of labor and capital, insofar as they help explain the class hierarchies of modern society that, in turn, manifest themselves in racialized or ethnicized divisions, also deeply inform my inquiry. If "ethnic" appears to be given a more prominent place in this book, it is not because I fail to grasp the significance of racism but rather because the term "ethnic" as such avoids replicating the residual biologism that is inerasably embedded in the term "race," situates the problems at hand within culture and representation, marks the discrimination entrenched in dominant ways of thinking and talking about so-called minorities, and allows, finally, for an analysis of the discrimination against "ethnics" that is found within ethnic communities themselves.

Ethnicity: A Universal or Local Category?

Dictionary entries for "ethnicity" often inform one that the word, with its roots in the Greek *ethnos* (meaning nation or people), was used by Jews and Christians to differentiate the "gentile" and "heathen" and that since the nineteenth century, however, "ethnicity" has also been used in a more generic fashion to characterize cultural, linguistic, and racial communities possessing distinctive characteristics.[6] Indeed, the later, modern usage of the term, with its universalist implications (i.e., every person is an ethnic), is what causes some social scientists to suppose that ethnicity is rather too vague a concept to be retained for purposes of rigorous analysis. Max Weber, for instance, attributes to it two main characteristics: ethnicity is, on the one hand, a "subjective" category, pertaining to people's belief in the particular ethnic groups to which they belong, and, on the other hand, a "political" category, pertaining to the manner in which political states often appeal to ethnicity as a way to gain support.[7] From Weber's social scientific perspective, ethnicity appears to be a category with mythic potential (since it is a kind of narrative of belonging) and is therefore manipulable (it is by appealing to people's sense of where and with whom they belong that political states manage to exert control over them). While Weber's definitions are useful in considering the ways ethnicity can be put to practical use for political causes, I believe a critique of the ambivalence embedded in the term in its modern usage is very much in order.

In its modern usage, designating a kind of cultural condition that is descriptive of all human beings, ethnicity has, to all appearances, shifted from its early, religious significance as a term of exclusion and a clear boundary marker (between Jew and gentile, Christian and heathen) to being a term of inclusion, a term aimed at removing boundaries and at encompassing all and sundry without discriminating against anybody.[8] This shift, I suggest, is symptomatic of the transformations inherent in the handling of difference, identity, and violence in the post-Enlightenment West, where liberal theoretical claims (with their transhistorical, transcultural, and transracial tendencies) have been steadily gaining ascendancy.[9] The unambiguous hostility and xenophobia typical of the premodern boundary-marking gesture, which would henceforth be labeled with derogation as ethnocentrism, are now replaced and displaced by what purports to be an open attitude toward ethnic difference. Because we now understand that everyone is ethnic, so this attitude implies, there should be no more violence and no more discrimination; there should only be humanistic tolerance. The modern usage of the term thus seeks to undo the clear, aggressive binarism that legitimates the separation between "us" and "them," between the inside and outside of a community. White cultural groups and persons, it would have us believe, are henceforth to be considered just as ethnic as nonwhites, with the emphasis on the crucial equality marker "just as." Thomas Hylland Eriksen puts it in these terms:

> Virtually every human being belongs to an ethnic group, whether he or she lives in Europe, Melanesia or Central America. There are ethnic groups in English cities, in the Bolivian countryside and in the New Guinea highlands. Anthropologists themselves belong to ethnic groups or nations. Moreover, the concepts and models used in the study of ethnicity can often be applied to modern as well as non-modern contexts, to Western as well as non-Western societies. In this sense, the concept of ethnicity can be said to bridge two important gaps in social anthropology: it entails a focus on dynamics rather than statics, and it relativizes the boundaries between "Us" and "Them," between moderns and tribals.[10]

Yet if everyone is ethnic, no one is. Some may therefore raise the question: is ethnicity chronologically a thing of the past—is ethnicity obsolete?[11] This pacific and progressivist view of ethnicity, however, is obviously not the case in practice, as we observe in the recurrent antagonisms, atrocities, and genocides that take place every day around the world in the name of one version of ethnic difference or another. The massacres in Bosnia, Kosovo, and elsewhere in Eastern Europe after the fall of official communism; the struggles in Africa among various traditional tribal alliances; the continuing exclusion and debasement felt by peoples of color in predominantly white nations such as the United States, Britain, France, Germany, Australia, and Canada; conscious or unconscious anti-Semitic attitudes in the presence or absence of Jews; the battles between Israelis and Palestinians in the Middle East; the conflict between French and British descendants in Quebec, Canada; the persecution of Chinese in Indonesia; the struggles for independence among Tibetans, Uighurs, and other minority groups against the People's Republic of China . . . the list can go on. Instead of serving as the occasion for humanistic tolerance of incommensurabilities—a logic that, if followed properly, should mean that the more incommensurable differences there are, the more tolerant people would become—ethnicity as such has often served as the justification for violence and the annihilation of others and, in some cases, a determined abandonment of peace. Rather than encompassing all and sundry, ethnicity seems to have brought about new, immutable frontiers leading to disaffinities and expulsions hitherto unimaginable.

In addition, far from being regarded as a universalism characterizing white as well as nonwhite groups, "ethnicity" is used customarily in a nation such as the United States to refer to nonwhite groups. Ulf Hannerz calls this "the WASP definition of ethnicity," according to which ethnicity is "a quality which is absent among Anglo-Saxons; which . . . increases among Americans of European descent as you pass over the map of Europe from the northwest toward the southeast; and which is very strong among people of non-European ancestry."[12] This "ethnocentric nonsense" (Hannerz's term) is reflected, for instance, in the institutional compartment of "ethnic studies" in American universities, where "ethnic" as a rule designates nonwhite peoples and their histories rather than, say, English, French, German, or Scandinavian traditions, even though the latter are supposedly also ethnic. This actual—and racialized—use of ethnicity as an object of study that is almost exclusively nonwhite can be seen when Eriksen, the author who mentions the supposed universality of the term as quoted above, proceeds to describe "some typical empirical foci of ethnic studies" by providing the following telltale list:

1. Urban ethnic minorities. This group would include, among others, non-European immigrants in European cities and Hispanics in the United States, as well as migrants to industrial towns in Africa and elsewhere. . . .
2. Indigenous peoples. This word is a blanket term for aboriginal inhabitants of a territory, who are politically relatively powerless and who are only partly integrated into the dominant nation state. Indigenous peoples are associated with a non-industrial mode of production and a stateless political system. . . .
3. Proto-nations (so-called ethnonationalist movements). These groups, the most famous of ethnic groups in the news media of the 1990s, include Kurds, Sikhs, Palestinians and Sri Lankan Tamils, and their number is growing. . . .

4. Ethnic groups in "plural societies." The term "plural society" usually designates colonially created states with culturally heterogeneous populations. . . . Typical plural societies would be Kenya, Indonesia and Jamaica.[13]

The various conceptions of the notion of ethnicity are thus blatantly contradictory, and the efficacy of the term derives, precisely, from its contradictoriness, its irrational nature. A term that is promulgated as universal, descriptive, and neutral (everyone is within or has an ethnicity), "ethnicity" is nonetheless resorted to time and again as a boundary marker, in oblivion of its own modernist mission to undo boundaries. The ethnic is both the universal, the condition in which everyone can supposedly situate herself, *and* the local, the foreign, the outside, the condition that, in reality, only some people, those branded "others," (are made to) inhabit. And it is this wavering, unstable state of the ethnic that enables politicians to manipulate populations by appealing to one version of ethnicity or another, depending on the political agenda at hand.

Moreover, as we know in the case of most boundaries, the dividing line between an inside and an outside is never just that; it always simultaneously carries meanings of hierarchy, of what is superior and what is inferior. Despite its proclaimed universalist intent, ethnicity as it is actually used in modern and contemporary Western, especially North American, society also carries pejorative connotations of a limit and limitation of the group marked "ethnic," a limit and limitation that confines that group to an earlier (temporally arcane) condition of humanity, in which the ethnics are, as it were, still held captive. As I mentioned above (in regard to the general Western view of the Chinese abuse of human rights), ethnicity as a cultural boundary easily transforms into a type of temporal/historical discrimination, which is laced with a self-congratulatory moral righteousness: although "ethnics" are "humans" (like us), they are so only because of our benevolent tolerance and acceptance of their stubborn difference. The assumption behind this manner of thinking goes something like this: properly speaking, these poor people, stuck as they are in their past, have not really reached the level of humanity that we have, but we will let them pass as our supposed equals because, after all, we are more advanced and superior human beings to begin with. To be classified as ethnic by white society, then, is to be granted a radical—indeed, politically avant-garde—kind of *recognition*, which compounds a straightforward discrimination and intolerance—based on clear-cut, hierarchical boundaries—with an inclusionist, liberalist cultural logic. While it often subscribes to exactly the same boundaries as its reactionary counterparts, this liberalist cultural logic meanwhile democratizes these boundaries rhetorically with honorable terms such as "multiculturalism" and "diversity" and practically by way of the proliferation of enclaves and ghettos (within institutions such as government bureaucracies, corporations, universities, and so forth).

Among the world's industrially advanced nations, the United States provides perhaps the best example of this unresolved tension between universalist aspirations and particularistic practices. Werner Sollors, noting a basic ambiguity in the Greek noun *ethnos*, which "was used to refer to people in general, but also to 'others,' " writes that in the term "ethnicity" as it is used in America, "the double sense of general peoplehood (shared by all Americans) and of otherness (different from the mainstream culture) lives on." "In America," he continues, "ethnicity can be conceived as deviation *and* as norm, as characteristic of minorities and as typical of the country. . . . A paradox is at the very root of American ethnicity."[14] But there are, as I will argue in the following, more than etymological reasons for this paradox.

As other theorists have pointed out, the unresolved tension between universalism and particularism in the United States persists largely because, while many nations establish their national identities on the basis of some historical cultural past that is specific to certain ethnic groups, the United States has, by contrast, consciously founded itself on abstract, idealist principles that are supposedly inclusionist and universal—such as a common adherence to democracy, human rights, integration, opportunity, and social justice for all—while the actuality of U.S. society, of course, has never coincided with such principles. As Jon Stratton and Ien Ang write: "The gap between Americanist principles and US social reality is not an unfortunate historical aberration to be corrected in the future . . . but the very *effect* of that hegemonic universalism, which denies the structural centrality of policies of exclusion to the formation of the United States."

Because of this foundational hegemonic universalism, ethnicity is of necessity handled with ambivalence. Stratton and Ang continue: "Ethnic identity or ethnicity—the source of cultural distinctiveness—is defined *outside* the general paradigm of a universal all-Americanness. The phenomenon of the hyphenated American—African-American, Asian-American, Italian-American, and so on—should be understood in this way: as the coupling of two separate identities, one culturally particular, the other presumably ideologically universal." This hyphenated American is, moreover, future-oriented, always looking ahead to the time when the United States will have fully realized its universal ideals—that is, when ethnic particulars, while continuing to exist, no longer really matter (because they have been reduced to the merely picturesque).[15] In other words, even when ethnicity is allowed to play a role in the process, the idealist (or theoretical) construction of the American identity must always disavow its own particularism and the lived antagonisms surrounding ethnicity. For the ideal American, ethnicity is something to be overcome and left in the past.[16]

Significantly, this applies not only within U.S. national boundaries but also outside, whenever the United States deals with ideologically "backward" foreign nations such as China, Iran, Iraq, and the like. These foreign nations must, so the logic goes, be taught to shed their obsolete ethnic habits and be brought forward into the global present of tolerance and good will.

Current Paradigms for Studying Ethnicity

The study of ethnicity would not be adequate without an attempt to foreground critically this self-contradiction that lies at the heart of modern usage and, meanwhile, is frequently denied. Precisely speaking, therefore, ethnicity exists in modernity as a boundary—a line of exclusion—that nonetheless pretends to be a nonboundary—a framework of inclusion—only then to reveal its full persecutory and discriminatory force whenever political, economic, or ideological gains are at stake.[17] Currently, however, the study of ethnicity tends to be caught between two large methodological paradigms, neither of which has, in my view, adequately articulated the conundrum at hand.

The first methodological paradigm tends to follow the notion of ethnicity as a universal condition that can be found throughout human history. Ethnicity is understood in this instance as "culture," and, as Fredrik Barth writes, "we are led to imagine each group developing its cultural and social form in relative isolation, mainly in response to local ecologic factors, through a history of adaptation. . . . This history has produced a world of separate peoples, each with their culture and each organized in a society which can legitimately be isolated for description as an island to itself."[18] When such culture is investigated collectively, it gives rise to the notion that ethnicity is a social invention or construction.[19] When such culture is investigated at the level of individuals, it gives rise to the notion that ethnicity is a matter (to use a currently popular term) of performance: ethnics are imagined, accordingly, as "performing" their various ethnic identities. Either way, the study of ethnicity does not depart significantly from a conventional and purportedly neutral understanding of history, which is assumed to be the result of tradition (pertaining to a group) or of individual talent (pertaining to the idiosyncrasies of the performing subjectivity), or of the two phenomena working together.

The second methodological paradigm, which is usually engaged with the politics of ethnicity, in particular the injustices against ethnic peoples, tends to take an oppositional approach to the universalist assumptions underlying the first paradigm. Instead of subscribing to ethnicity as cultural heritage or as individual performance, it situates ethnicity amid major economic and geopolitical networks of power, such as the movements of transnational corporations, the emergence of strategic areas (such as the Pacific Rim) as both local and global points of interest, the histories of diasporic populations, and so on. These networks of power are then often analyzed in tandem with macro period markers such as modernism, postmodernism, colonialism, postcolonialism, and the like in order to pinpoint the historical significance of the events involved. The theoretical strength of this second paradigm lies in its understanding that ethnicity, rather than being a condition equal to all, has often been a source of oppression—indeed, a liability—to those who are branded "ethnics" and that articulations of ethnicity in contemporary Western society are thoroughly conditioned by asymmetries of power between whites and nonwhites.[20]

Despite the differences in their methodological orientations, however, these two approaches often coalesce in practice to produce what is, strictly speaking, a *theoretical stereotype*: an inviolable human subject as such. If the first paradigm defines this human subject in terms of tradition and individual talent, the second paradigm defines it in terms of opposition and resistance. For the first paradigm, the essence of humanity is always already there, inscribed in ethnic customs and literary and cultural representations; for the second paradigm, the human is what has to be redeemed and reaffirmed through a process of struggle against the evil forces from without.

In both paradigms, what appears to have been omitted is a manner of theorizing in which ethnicity would be understood, structurally, as part of an already biopoliticized economic relation, whereby the very humanity attributed to ethnics is itself firmly subsumed under the process of commodification and its asymmetrical distribution of power rather than outside them. Once ethnicity is conceptually linked to commodification defined in these terms, a different kind of question begins to emerge. No longer would it be sufficient to ask, How does an ethnic subject come to terms with his or her identity? Instead, the very assumptions behind this kind of question would themselves need to be challenged with questions such as: What ideological forces are there, if any, that would enable the individual representative of an ethnic minority to move beyond, or believe she could ever move beyond, the macro sociological structures that have already mapped out her existence—such as, for instance, forces that allow her to think of herself as a "subject" with a voice, as a human person? What makes it possible for her to imagine that her resistance-performance is her ultimate salvation, her key to universal humanity, in the first place?

Ethnicity, in other words, needs to be reconceptualized as a critical issue that would, simultaneously, require us to reexamine the more familiar tools provided by contemporary theory. Emerging at the intersection between residual idealist assumptions about individual subjectivities and ever-intensifying processes of collective commodification (with inevitable effects of dehumanization and depersonalization), ethnicity continues, yet exceeds, the paradigm of the meticulous elaboration of the vicissitudes of the individual subject, on the one hand, and the paradigm of humanistic opposition against the rationalization and systematization of human labor under capitalism, on the other. Any consideration of ethnic subjection would therefore need to include not only the manner in which ethnics have been subjected to and continue to "resist" their dehumanizing objectification but also the psychological mechanism of "calling" (sense of vocation)—what Max Weber calls a "work ethic"—that gives rise, certainly, to compelling feelings of individual resistance but is, arguably, already a dynamic built into the rationalist process of commodification itself.

Ethnicity as Alienated Labor: The Legacy of Lukács

There are, naturally, many ways of thinking about ethnicity that are not necessarily focused on labor. For instance, if ethnicity is understood in the broad, neutral sense mentioned above—as a universal condition that everyone has—it might, indeed, be possible to view ethnicity in terms that are not exclusively labor-oriented. But in actual practice in the contemporary world, whereby ethnicity often designates foreignness (which is, in turn, understood as social inferiority), the linkages between certain types of labor and ethnicity are ineluctable. In the context of the United States and other wealthy nations, one does not have to undertake scientific surveys to see that fundamental necessities of society—the lowly, basic services that help to free up well-educated people for more highly paid jobs—are most frequently provided by "ethnics": Mexicans, Caribbeans, blacks, and Asians in the United States; Turks and Arabs in Germany and France; South and Southeast Asians in Saudi Arabia, Kuwait, Japan, Taiwan, Hong Kong, and so forth. These are either immigrant workers or workers who, despite having obtained residency or citizenship status, continue to be treated as migrants because of their skin color and class status.[21]

However, although ethnicity defined in these terms may be intimately connected to the experience of migration (especially forced migration such as in the case of slavery), my focus is not really the experience of migration per se but rather the process in which certain people *within* a particular society, immigrants among them, become marked as ethnics at the same time that they occupy socially inferior positions as low-level laborers. (To this extent, women may be viewed as among the most palpable ethnics in the capitalist workforce, especially when they are doing underpaid or unpaid domestic work.) The experience of migration, in other words, simply highlights and amplifies the connection between commodified labor and ethnicization—what I would call, more precisely, the *ethnicization of labor*—that takes place in a society even when there are no migrants, even when migrants have become citizens. To my mind, to concentrate, as some contemporary theoretical circles tend to do, inordinately on the empirically mobile experiences of migrancy, immigration, diaspora, exile, and so forth is to neglect this ongoing situation of ethnicity as a systematically produced and perpetuated outside of a given society.[22] (See my more detailed discussion of this point in chapter 4.) I would go even further and say that the fashionable theorizing/fetishizing of such experiences, by accepting as an unproblematic point of departure the positivistic view that ethnics are, indeed, aliens from *elsewhere*, in fact ends up lending support to the concept of ethnicity as an a priori, essentialist condition of foreignness.

The point to note about the relation between ethnicity and labor is therefore not the oft-reiterated one of the existential uprooting of the migrant worker from home (with all the sentimental trappings of this line of argument) but rather that the ethnic as such stands in modernity as the site of a foreignness that is produced from within privileged societies and is at once defined by and constitutive of that society's hierarchical divisions of labor. A laborer becomes ethnicized because she is commodified in specific ways, because she has to pay for her living by performing certain kinds of work, while these kinds of work, despite being generated from within that society, continue to reduce the one who performs them to the position of the outsider, the ethnic. For Immanuel Wallerstein, ethnicization must thus be linked to the racism specific to the operations of modern capitalism with its twin objectives of maximizing profits and minimizing production costs.[23] A workforce that actively contributes labor toward the accumulation of capital yet at the same time receives the least of its rewards—namely, an ethnicized population—is the magic formula that "resolves one of the basic contradictions of historical capitalism—its simultaneous thrust for theoretical equality and practical inequality."[24]

Once it is foregrounded through the commodification of labor, ethnicity becomes much more than what the conventional definition of "specific culture" often imagines it to be. Instead, it stands more precisely as a society's way of projecting onto some imaginary outside elements it deems foreign and inferior. Always a shifting relation, ethnicity is virtually society's mechanism of marking boundaries by way of labor. As Wallerstein writes, such a mechanism is a flexible one, whereby "racism [is] constant in form and in venom, but somewhat flexible in boundary lines": the groups that are thus ethnicized "are always there and always ranked hierarchically, but they are not always exactly the same. Some groups can be mobile in the ranking system; some groups can disappear or combine with others; while still others break apart and new ones are born. But there are always some who are 'niggers.' If there are no Blacks or too few to play the role, one can invent 'White niggers.'"[25]

Understandably, since ethnic labor is frequently underpaid, misappropriated, or unrecognized, the handling of ethnic histories in the United States, in academic fields such as African American studies, Asian American studies, Hispanic studies, and so forth, has conventionally taken the form of a settling of past accounts, a renarrativization of the work that had been contributed by generations of ethnic peoples but was never given due acknowledgment by mainstream society.[26] The discursive, revisionist investigation of ethnicity, in short, has more or less followed the classical premises of Marx's analysis of alienated labor. But it is, I think, the model of class consciousness expounded by Georg Lukács in *The History of Class Consciousness* that stands as the most compelling progenitor of the type of cultural work currently undertaken in ethnic studies.[27] For this reason, it is worth taking a closer look at the implications of Lukács's model.

Lukács, of course, did not deal with ethnicity as such but provided a specific framework for thinking about exploited subjecthood in terms of class. Lukács calls this framework "consciousness." He theorizes consciousness in such a way as to move it—or so he intended—beyond the antinomies (nature/man, subject/object, mind/matter, nature/rationalization, etc.) left unresolved by classical philosophy, which has kept the fragmentation between the subject and the outside world (a fragmentation that is in turn translated into the seeming impenetrability of the outside world as the thing-in-itself) intractable and irreconcilable. For Lukács, consciousness in its ideal form—what he calls class consciousness—would no longer simply be an individual psychological state of awareness; rather, it would be a collective state of awareness that expresses an understanding of history in totality, through a capacity for self-criticism. From the condition of exploitation and subjection under the demeaning forces of capitalism, the proletariat would move through class consciousness to the point at which history—pertaining not only to itself but to all classes—can be transformed and transcended.

Interestingly, Lukács takes as his point of departure not only the classical philosophical preoccupation with consciousness but also Marx's materialist analysis of commodities. Indeed, one may argue that this two-pronged approach to consciousness or subjectivity is ultimately what makes his work so fascinating to read despite its notable blind spots.[28] Rather than relying simply on idealist philosophical terms, Lukács grounds his analysis of consciousness in commodification—that is, in the very economic process of objectification and reification that he defines as "the necessary, immediate reality of every person living in capitalist society" (HCC 197). "Objective reality," that external "thing-in-itself," therefore, takes on a man-made and thus historical significance of universality; this reality, moreover, is the same for the landowning class and the proletariat alike. While the landowning class feels completely at home in it, however, the proletariat feels destroyed and dehumanized (HCC 149). This difference, which Lukács calls "the different position occupied by the two classes within the 'same' economic process" (HCC 150), leads to the latter's critical "standpoint" (HCC 149 ff.) and aspiration toward change. This significantly different evaluation of a reality that has hitherto remained the same for all classes is, then, the gist of class consciousness.

Clearly, for Lukács, the proletarian is a figure of resistance, but what is intriguing about his formulation of this figure is its ambivalence—its attempt to locate him *at once inside and outside commodification*. Lukács's text is revealing in this regard. On the one hand, the proletarian's consciousness is, he writes, "the self-consciousness of the commodity": "Above all the worker can only become conscious of his existence in society when he becomes aware of himself as a commodity. . . . Inasmuch as he is incapable in practice of raising himself above the role of object his consciousness is that *self-consciousness of the commodity*" (HCC 168; emphasis in the original). These statements suggest that it would be virtually impossible to separate the proletarian's consciousness from his reified and commodified existence. On the other hand, against the definitions he himself has provided, Lukács also insists that there is something else, something more to the proletarian's consciousness that distinguishes him from other men:

> It is true . . . that the basic structure of reification can be found in all the social forms of modern capitalism (e.g. bureaucracy.) But this structure can only be made fully conscious in the work-situation of the proletarian. For his work as he experiences it directly possesses the naked and abstract form of the commodity, while in other forms of work this is hidden behind the façade of "mental labour," of "responsibility," etc. . . . *While the process by which the worker is reified and becomes a commodity dehumanizes him and cripples and atrophies his "soul"—as long as he does not consciously rebel against it—it remains true that precisely his humanity and his soul are not changed into commodities.* He is able therefore to objectify himself completely against his existence while the man reified in the bureaucracy, for instance, is turned into a commodity, mechanised and reified in the only faculties that might enable him to rebel against reification. (HCC 171–72; my emphasis)

Lukács's statements oblige one to ask: What are this "humanity" and "soul" that, in the case of the worker, can somehow remain pure from commodification? From where do they emerge? Lukács's answer to these questions would have been, precisely, "labor." As he writes elsewhere, labor, which distinguishes humans from nonhuman animals, "is a vehicle for the self-production of man as man" and a model for "all social practice" and "all freedom." Conversely, the "genuine humanization of man is the necessary ontological consequence of labor."[29] Yet, once we see that the assumptions of the proletarian's capacity for resistance are, in fact, underscored by these idealizations of labor, the fundamental contradiction embedded in Lukács's thought comes to the fore. This is the fact that labor itself—the very source of the proletarian's humanity and soul—has been constructed by Lukács simultaneously as a historical process (what pertains to social practice) and as an a priori, originary condition (what transcends biology and distinguishes man essentially from animals).

Class Consciousness as a Captivity Narrative and the Problem of Ethnicity Recast

This fundamentally problematic status of labor indicates that, in considering the validity of Lukács's model of class consciousness, we cannot simply follow his lead and idealize or essentialize labor and, by implication, idealize or essentialize the proletarian's capacity for resistance. Rather, it is necessary to examine his arguments systematically. In this light, it would be helpful to transpose Lukács's arguments onto some alternative, but nonetheless entirely relevant, frames of reference.

The first of such frames would be that of *temporality*. The proletarian consciousness as given by Lukács can here be understood in terms of a dialectical but *present* moment, whereby two completely different—indeed, opposed—kinds of subjective orders—oppression and liberation, commodity and not-commodity—can somehow coexist. Consciousness as such stands both as the receptor of violence and the critical point of departure from violence, a *now* that is nonetheless capable of becoming not-now, a process of commodification that is also transcendent of commodification. This structure of simultaneity—of the copresence of A and not-A—requires an external source—an outside, so to speak—to make it possible. As evidenced in the long passage just cited above, Lukács would give this mysterious outside the familiar names of "humanity" and "soul." This crucial move, of course, raises precisely the question to which it has, wishfully, already provided an answer: Can "humanity" and "soul" be conceived as outside the temporal (that is, social) order of consciousness? Lukács's answer is, obviously, "yes" because, as I mentioned, "humanity" and "soul" are, for him, constituted by the implicit, ahistorical concept of labor-as-(human)-essence.

Second, reading Lukács's argument as a *narrative*, one must notice a definite teleological tendency. The story of the proletariat is, in this instance, interestingly premised on a linear plot development, from oppression (that is to say, reification and commodification) to self-awakening (the emergence of class consciousness), to ultimate liberation for all of mankind (the achievement of a classless society). The status of the proletarian is that of the wounded—indeed, sacrificed—innocent man who ultimately attains, through his own destruction, salvation for all—in a manner that recalls the Christian cult of Christ.

Third, it would also be possible to reread Lukács's thesis not only as a narrative but also specifically as a *narrative of captivity* that is characteristic of post-Enlightenment, modernist conceptions of violence and counterviolence. In an essay entitled "The Case of the Resistant Captive," Leonard Tennenhouse offers a provocative analysis of the discursive reliance on captivity that is typical of modernist narratives of violence. According to Tennenhouse, modernity, which prides itself on having progressed toward a peaceful, civilized tolerance of difference, must by necessity project the things it imagines to be opposite to itself, such as violence, savagery, and primitivist intolerance, onto a temporal other—the past—only then to be surprised and scandalized time and again by the eruption of such violence, savagery, and intolerance within modern and contemporary social situations. The past, in other words, is perhaps simply the name of a (modernist) process of rationalization in which humanity must first be imagined in some form of captivity (some kind of imprisonment within a condition of barbarism) in order for its putative progress toward a nonoppressive, civilized state to become credible.

What this means is that captivity and emancipation, in fact, belong together inextricably in a binarist correlation, with captivity serving as the indispensable underside to the emancipatory meaning of modern civilization itself. Moreover, if captivity itself is a historical, discursive construct—in what may be termed a modernist imaginary—then the idea of resistance that is hitherto considered such a natural and logical, because "human," response to captivity would also need to be rehistoricized as a modernist invention.[30]

Tennenhouse's analysis of captivity enables us to reframe Lukács's argument about history and class consciousness as a kind of captivity narrative. The proletarian, in this light, is the prototype of a humanity held prisoner in a barbaric state—the capitalist process of commodification—and must struggle to attain a more civilized condition of existence through resistance. With what does the proletarian resist his captivity? If the very source of captivity, namely, commodification, is itself a historical and universal condition, how can the proletarian go beyond it—how can he break free? This is the point at which Lukács, in spite of his historical rigor, resorts to idealist terms such as "soul" and "humanity," insisting that they have not been "changed into commodities." But if "soul" and "humanity" are, indeed, elements that, even while in captivity, can remain somehow outside, free, resistant to bondage, is it because they are beyond history (as one portion of Lukács's argument would suggest)—or is it because they are part of a historical narrativization of modernity-as-emancipation, with its rhetorical dependence on some presumed outside, some divine origin? At the most crucial juncture of his arguments, Lukács has in effect left *reified* precisely the terms on which he bases his entire thesis. "Humanity" and "soul," like the much idealized term "labor," remain ahistorical essences. They can be invoked with passion, but their status cannot be questioned.[31]

And yet, despite its significant moments of self-contradiction, and despite its reliance on elements that must somehow remain unhistoricized in a project otherwise known as "history and class consciousness," Lukács's work remains, I believe, one of the most influential models for imagining consciousness- or subjectivity-in-exploitation. Be they through feminism, postcolonial theory, alternative sexual preferences and lifestyles, or other types of minority discourses, numerous contemporary versions of identity-based critical thinking have, wittingly or unwittingly, been replicating Lukács's modernist narrative with its telos of self-ownership and self-affirmation in both individual and collective senses. Most of all, such critical thinking has frequently resorted to a similarly idealized assumption about humanity and subjectivity, which are imagined as at once historically damaged and essentially beyond damage. The same can also be said about predominant trends in ethnic studies. Insofar as ethnicity is intimately associated with processes of alienated labor, the discursive imaginings of its struggle perhaps come closest to the model of class consciousness laid down by Lukács. The ethnic has, in many ways, been conceived of implicitly as a proletarian, a resistant captive engaged in a struggle toward liberation.

Even more important, the entire process of theorizing ethnicity, perhaps more than any other type of theorization, exemplifies the predicament inscribed in Lukács's modernist narrative precisely because of the ambivalence inherent in the modern use of the term "ethnicity" itself. This ambivalence may now be amplified in this manner: on the one hand, we are supposed to understand that *everyone* is ethnic and that we should tolerate ethnic differences; on the other hand, we also continue to think that *certain* people are still held captive in their specific histories, that is, in ethnic conditions that seem foreign or alien to us. These two conceptually incommensurate views of ethnicity—one universal and the other local—would have to be reconciled through a kind of discursive compensation, whereby feelings of intolerance, precisely the states of mind that cannot be reasoned away, are projected onto some kind of outside, in the form of an ethnic otherness or ethnic past. This would then push the localized, alienated, and thus restricted form of ethnicity into a primitive, barbaric realm from which we, in our enlightened present, can safely remove ourselves.

But this act of distancing, rejecting, and repudiating, an act based ostensibly on progress and liberation, is none other than an act of *ethnicizing* others—as not being like us—in the classical, negative sense: "we, who believe in tolerance, will not tolerate those who are intolerant; we will denounce them as ethnocentric." Ironically, this so-called universalist view of ethnicity can only operate by insisting on a specific boundary, a dividing line between an "us" and "them." What this means is that the ethnicity that vows to tolerate all ethnic differences, too, grounds itself in a fundamental act of intolerance—and, frequently, of violence.

To recapitulate, let me summarize the major points I have attempted to put across in this section:

1. The model of class consciousness as laid down by Lukács, which has been consciously or unconsciously adopted for the theorizing of other kinds of group consciousness, can be understood, through Tennenhouse's argument, as a modernist narrative based on notions of captivity and resistance.

2. The theorizing of ethnicity can, arguably, be considered an exemplary case of such use of the class consciousness model, replete with implications of captivity and resistance.

3. Meanwhile, ethnicity in its modern and contemporary usage is also caught in a conceptual ambivalence between an intended universalism and a recurrent localism—that is, the persistence, within universalist intent itself, of specific boundaries.

4. Because of the ambivalence characteristic of the modernist understanding of the ethnic as such, the progressive articulation of universalist moral claims (such as the universal tolerance of ethnic differences) is, despite itself, implicated in violence; this violence, in turn, reproduces the narratives of captivity and resistance, thus necessitating the appearance of more violence, and so on, ad infinitum.

The Culture of Protest and the Spirit of Capitalism

Since the ethnic is explicitly or implicitly understood as a proletarian from whom work has been stolen and to whom credit must be restored, ethnic existence is habitually not only imagined as captivity-in-resistance but also articulated as a protest—a protest that, in the course of voicing complaint against injury and injustice, demands recognition and compensation for the victims. The progressive emancipation of all and sundry that is typically intended by universalist moral claims is hence supported, discursively, by a concomitant culture of protest. There can be no such universalist claims without implicit or explicit protest; conversely, the act of protesting itself is often underscored by some form of universalist intent, whether or not such intent is overtly announced. However, universalist intent, as I have shown in the case of ethnicity, is itself based on specific boundaries—the intolerance of violence, the intolerance of exploitation, the intolerance of commodification, and so forth—*boundaries, moreover, that must remain intractable* in order for the dream of emancipation to stand. Given that universalist intent seems by necessity to carry its own contradiction, what may be said about its supporting culture, the culture of protest?

This is the juncture at which, instead of making the kind of Lukác-sian move that would simply idealize protest by essentializing it as "human," an alternative reconceptualization might be sought by situating protest itself as an event within, rather than without, capitalist society. Once we accept this alternative, nonessentialist premise, the question of the universalist moralism accompanying protest becomes mind-boggling. For how is it that a quest for salvation for all with such stern, intransigent moral boundaries can emerge from within the boundless, amoral processes of capitalist exploitation?

I believe this paradox about modernist moralism is what lies at the heart of Max Weber's discussion of the Protestant ethic and the spirit of capitalism.[32] Weber traces the origins of the capitalistic work ethic back to religion, to the medieval Reformation movement in Europe, thus providing, as one critic puts it, "insight into the peculiar union of secularity and religiosity in American everyday culture."[33] As is well known, Weber argues that the drive toward material gains that is characteristic of capitalist enterprises cannot simply be seen as the outcome of human greed, which is found throughout history, but should rather be seen as the outcome of a force of internal disciplining peculiar to the secularizing West. This internal disciplining owes its historical origins to the post-Reformation religious belief in "calling," the belief that one is divinely endowed with a life task, a mission, or a field to which one is supposed to devote one's best energies. Calling provides a powerful moral justification for worldly activities, the so-called good works. Because calling is sensorially intangible, the proof of its existence can only be sought in what can be physically observed: being rigorously religious would thus mean not a withdrawal from the world but an involved, disciplined participation in worldly affairs resulting in a large net balance at the end of the page. In such a context, diligence, persistence—indeed, endurance—in face of hardships all become palpable signs of grace, while the incapacity for or unwillingness to work—that is, to create that large net balance—becomes, by comparison, signs of the lack thereof. And, although the religious foundations for work defined in such terms have gradually dissipated in the wake of secularism, the ideological efficacy of these foundations continues, Weber writes, to manifest itself in what he terms "worldly asceticism." Weber emphasizes the decisive point of his own argument in this manner:

To repeat, it is not the ethical *doctrine* of a religion, but that form of ethical conduct upon which *premiums* are placed that matters. Such premiums operate through the form and the condition of the respective goods of salvation. And such conduct constitutes "one's" specific "ethos" in the sociological sense of the word. For Puritanism, that conduct was a certain methodical, rational way of life which—given certain conditions—paved the way for the "spirit" of modern capitalism. The premiums were placed upon "proving" oneself before God in the sense of attaining salvation—which is found in *all* Puritan denominations—and "proving" oneself before men in the sense of socially holding one's own within the Puritan sects. Both aspects were mutually supplementary and operated in the same direction: they helped to deliver the "spirit" of modern capitalism, its specific *ethos*: the ethos of the modern *bourgeois middle classes*.[34]

In the age of godlessness, when all sacraments for purposes of salvation have been radically devalued, the original religious justification for work finds its substitute in human activities themselves. The attainment of what was once believed to be divine grace is now reconceived exclusively in terms of a rationalistic, systematic, results-oriented work ethic, in terms of a drive to do well—that is, make profits. In a country such as the United States, the once privileged status of religious belief, as an animating force giving the devout their firm sense of calling, is thus taken over by capitalism, which, by rewarding the impetus to work hard, simultaneously gives free rein to man's pursuit of pecuniary and worldly interests. Capitalism, in brief, has succeeded Protestantism in granting psychological sanction for hard work. Worldly success within capitalism stands de facto as the secular equivalent of a demonstrated conferral of grace and the assurance of religious salvation. This "fateful combination"[35]—and elective affinity—between (residual) religious belief and (dominant) desacralized economic arrangements in everyday life is, according to Weber, the reason for capitalism's triumph in American society. Work may be spiritualized and idealized, indeed, but this spiritualization and idealization can now take calculable form, as remuneration.

Juxtaposed with Weber's analysis, Lukács's model of an attempt to restore the proprietorship of labor to the worker could be seen as a secularist act of intervention in capitalist appropriation—appropriation not only of the material profit (surplus) generated by alienated labor (as argued in classical Marxism) but also of (the equivalents of) grace and salvation, the nonmaterial rewards that rightfully belong to the worker (or to her soul). Such a juxtaposition would put Lukács's theorization of class consciousness not only in the direct lineage of Protestantism but also in the spirit of capitalism, whereby the drive to work, together with the results such drive is hoped to produce, is taken as the (only perceptible) origin, sign, and evidence of redemption. By reading Lukács against Weber in this manner, we can see for the first time the Janus-faced underpinnings of the narrative of class consciousness with their far-reaching implications for other discourses of minority identity struggles. These underpinnings are not, as Lukács would have it, simply "human" but rather economic as well as theological in construct.

While Lukács, at the crucial moment of having to account for the (subjective) source of the proletarian's resistance—What makes her work? What makes her protest and struggle?—would resort to essentialist terms such as "soul" and "humanity," Weber has provided an implicit theory of subjectivity that is firmly grounded in the material conditions of production and their accompanying social relations. Interestingly enough, Weber is able to enunciate such conditions and relations because he takes the religious basis of the capitalist spirit seriously—because, in other words, he does not dismiss religion as mere airy superstition (that is, mere "suprastructure"). Instead, he shows that even airy superstition can be a form of material support with real sociological consequences. To this extent, Weber's work can, to borrow Fredric Jameson's words, be described as "perfectly consistent with genuine Marxist thinking":[36] unlike many contemporary theorists of subjectivity who discuss so-called psychological concerns in idealist subjective terms (referring only casually and perfunctorily to the economic as such), Weber demonstrates the mutual adaptation between the psychological and the economic, locating what seem to be elusive, subjective matters in the objective, financial workings of capitalism and its religious precedents. Whereas the question asked by Lukács and his successors is, "How does the 'inner' human force, its soul and its humanity, so to speak, resist and protest against the evil of capitalism?" the question Weber asks is rather,

"How does the 'inner' human force—including especially the soulful force of resistance and protest—come about *in* capitalism and further enhance the progress of capitalism?" To this question, Weber provides, provocatively, the notion of calling.[37] Whereas the "soul" and "humanity" in Lukács function as that mysterious something that remains outside the worker's existence as a commodity, Weber would put this very "soul" and "humanity" back in history—an entrepreneurial history, in fact, in which protest and struggle can be part of the route to worldly compensation, advancement, and validation.

Associating Weber's theory with a Nietzschean will to power and with Foucault's technologies of the self, Harvey Goldman offers a succinct description of the uniqueness of Weber's contribution:

> The explanatory heart of *The Protestant Ethic* has less to do with the historical linkage of Calvinism and the spirit of capitalism than with Weber's positing of the existence and action of a unique type of self newly constituted in the Reformation. In effect Weber argued that for capitalism to have developed in the West, there was a need not only for the separation of classes, accumulation, and the circulation and use of money as capital in pursuit of ever-renewed profit, all of which Marx had already recognized. There was also a need for a mode of power found not in techniques or rationality *outside* the self as material preconditions, but a mode of power found and engendered *inside* the self. . . . This power was rooted in ascetic triumph over the natural self and in the need to discharge anxiety about salvation through a search for proof of grace in world mastery for God's purposes. Weber's conclusions are based on the crucial role he ascribes to the idea of calling in modern culture and to the extraordinary powers and "taming of the soul" with which, he claimed, the Calvinist calling endowed what we can call "the first great entrepreneurs."[38]

Whereas in Lukács's model, labor is that original, uniquely human essence that distinguishes humans from animals and has been unjustly appropriated from the worker, for Weber, labor is already a fully cultural event—the historical sign both of a (residual) religious vocation and of a rationalized, systematized economic system. It is labor, regulated either through divine "grace" or through the secularist implementation of discipline and punishment with its institutionalized codes of efficiency, that produces "Man" (his "soul" and "humanity"), *rather than vice versa.* (To this extent, Foucault's *Discipline and Punish* may be seen as an extension of Weber's basic argument to the modern penitentiary system.)

This examination of Weber has considerable implications for our ongoing discussion about ethnicity in modern and contemporary times. These implications may be restated as follows:

1. In order effectively to protest against past injustice, discussions of ethnicity are often compelled to follow, wittingly or unwittingly, the powerful model of class consciousness and struggle laid down by Lukács.
2. Lukács's model leads, nonetheless, to a certain contradiction, whereby the class or group arriving at critical consciousness must somehow inhabit the nonplace of being at once commodity and not-commodity (or "human"), being thoroughly victimized yet still miraculously retaining the capacity ("humanity" and "soul") to fight against such victimization, to transcend commodification.
3. This contradictory narrative structure ultimately places the victim in the (modernist) position of a captive, whose salvation lies in resistance and protest, activities that are aimed at ending exploitation (and boundaries) and bringing about universal justice.
4. For Lukács, this teleological narrative of resistance and protest constitutes the emergence of class consciousness. For Weber, however, precisely this narrative of resistance and protest, this moral preoccupation with universal justice, is what constitutes the efficacy of the capitalist spirit. Resistance and protest, when understood historically, are part and parcel of the structure of capitalism; they are the reasons capitalism flourishes.

I Protest, Therefore I am: The Ethnic in the Age of Global Capital

To return finally to the scenario of China with which I began this chapter, I may now say that in the transactions between China and the

West, the loss/captivity of human rights has, in effect, been staged definitively as ethnicity—the Chinese difference, or Chineseness—an ethnicity that is, moreover, implicitly defined as a kind of alienated or misappropriated labor. In these cross-cultural transactions, the Chinese are, by logic, people who must continue to act as victims—to protest and struggle continually for what has been stolen from them—for the entire world to see.

As it is dramatized currently on the global scene, ethnicity thus occupies an epistemologically fascinating, because uncertain, status. Admittedly, ethnicity continues, as it does in the case of Chinese dissidents, to function in a utopian, Marxist/Lukácsian paradigm of protest and struggle, which is grounded in moral universalisms such as democracy, freedom of speech, and human rights. At the same time, this familiar paradigm seems readily to be transforming into something else, something akin to a systematic capitalist ethos of objectification and reification, whereby what is proclaimed to be human must also increasingly take on the significance of a commodity, a commodified spectacle. Even though it may still appear that ethnicity is underwritten with the modernist narrative of alienated labor and resistant captivity, therefore, it would be more precise, I think, to argue that contemporary articulations of ethnicity as such, much like the articulation of class consciousness, are already firmly inscribed within the economic and ideological workings of capitalism, replete with their mechanisms of callings, opportunities, and rewards. In this context, *to be ethnic is to protest*—but perhaps less for actual emancipation of any kind than for the benefits of worldwide visibility, currency, and circulation. Ethnic struggles have become, in this manner, an indisputable symptom of the thoroughly and irrevocably mediatized relations of capitalism and its biopolitics.[39] In the age of globalization, ethnics are first and foremost protesting ethnics, but this is not because they are possessed of some "soul" and "humanity" that cannot be changed into commodities. Rather, it is because protesting constitutes the economically logical and socially viable vocation for them to assume.

Finally, even more to the point of Weber's argument, those who are eager to stage ethnic struggles are often not only the ethnics themselves. In the China scenario, it is often Westerners—Americans, in particular— who make the most spectacular, productive exhibits of Chinese people, be they dictators or dissidents, political prisoners or traders of human organs. In a manner that is remarkably true to the spirit of Protestantism, such vicarious demonstrations are always made in the name of universal moral principles, even as those who make such demonstrations on behalf of the Chinese often turn out to be people who have specific self-interests, especially commercial interests, in China. In order to understand the enthusiasm and determinism with which U.S. politicians, businessmen, missionaries, media personalities, and academics "do the human rights story" whenever possible—on behalf of the Chinese and all other suffering ethnics in the world—it is incumbent upon us to understand the historical affinity between Protestantism and capitalist entrepreneurship as such, an affinity whose rationale may be ultimately paraphrased as "I protest, therefore I am": the more one protests, the more work, business, and profit one will generate, and the more this will become a sign that one is loved by God. In this boundless capacity for moral self-production, -expansion, and -proliferation, ethnic captivity thus transubstantiates, its lines of flight readily morphing—and merging—into global capital's phantasmagoric flows.[40]

CHAPTER 2

Brushes with the-Other-as-Face:
Stereotyping and Cross-Ethnic Representation

Once ethnicity's relation to capitalism, in particular to labor, has been amplified, its ambivalent ontological status—as at once subject and object—can no longer be evaded. Despite the obvious dehumanization that accompanies the objectification of ethnicity, I believe we would be naive to suppose that, simply with the proper kind of education, we would be able to stop objectifying our others once and for all and begin to treat every human being from now on as an equal ethnic subject. The mechanisms of such objectification remain to be understood in their persistence and ubiquity, often in ways that surprise us. Objectification is, in this instance, inseparable and perhaps interchangeable with representation. In this and the following three chapters, my goal is therefore to examine the specific and ineluctable issue of representation in cross-ethnic situations.

To begin such an examination, it is necessary to distinguish what I am trying to do from two major tendencies in understanding the relationship between ethnicity and representation. This, again, follows from the two types of approaches to ethnicity—the universalist and the oppositional—that I delineated in the previous chapter. The first tendency is that of treating ethnicity as a thematic concern. Though this tendency may yield copious results, it has the unfortunate effect of keeping ethnicity at the level of a more or less realist cultural content, so that, while ethnic details and characters may make interesting stories, they do not necessarily tell us anything new about writing or the act of representation per se. When the ethnic is treated merely thematically as such, analysis pays the price of quickly acquiring tedium, allowing people to dismiss it in terms of the already known or the predictable—"yet another story about Asian Americans in San Francisco"; "yet another story about Eastern European immigrant families in New York," and so forth. At this level, at which readers may safely conclude, "We have heard all this before," the representation of ethnicity becomes an option, variable but known, that may or may not be chosen without affecting the overall structuring principles of representation itself. This leaves intact the elitist notion that so-called great literature, by contrast, is usually unpredictable and exciting because it transcends such tedious, culturally specific content. Even if it has a place in representation, the (sociological) appeal of the ethnic in this instance is, alas, precisely its confining and limiting element—what obstructs it from ever becoming "great" writing, "great" art, or "great" music.

On the other hand, if ethnicity is, as the previous chapter has already shown, an ontologically liminal phenomenon, something whose status is between subject and object, then its representation, too, must involve a way of reading that is much more complex than the thematic approach. *This, however, cannot simply mean placing the ethnic in the role of a resisting agent*, and this is where I distinguish my aim from the second major tendency in the handling of ethnicity and representation. When ethnicity is not being treated thematically, as a content reflected in literature, the overwhelming trend these days among those who equate critical thinking with political activism is to treat it, instead, as some kind of empowered agency "resisting" the conventions of ethnic reflectionism, in a manner that recalls the problems inherent to the resistance paradigm that I have analyzed. The practice of reading ethnic texts on the basis of resistance—be it on the part of the individual protagonist, the ethnic group, subjectivity, or the text itself—has become so rhetorically formulaic that it is often incompetent to bring about any substantive intervention.

The conundrum central to the current trends of handling ethnicity and representation is, in other words, inscribed in the very ambivalent status bestowed on ethnicity by post-Enlightenment modernity. Is ethnicity a core and kernel, with different characteristics in individual cases but nonetheless a truth universal to all; or is it a boundary and a limit, implicated in forces of discrimination and exclusion, and often in violence? Accordingly, when it comes to representing the ethnic, is representation simply a matter of documenting the reality that is ethnicity, or should representation be understood as some kind of ontological performance-cum-resistance, bracketing all realist content, however historical that content may be? In these characteristic ruminations, an argument that is equally responsive to the materiality of ethnicity *and* to the materiality of representation is, somehow, always missing.

It is at this juncture that I would like to introduce a familiar topic, the use of stereotypes, as a way to gauge this undismissable yet persistently elusive relation between ethnicity and representation.

The Inevitability of Stereotypes in Cross-Ethnic Representation

Readers are well acquainted with the fact that stereotypes are almost always spoken of in negative terms, as a wrongful act of misrepresentation. How did this happen? It is crucial to remember that when the word "stereotype" was originally coined in the late eighteenth century, it was meant to describe a mass printing process designed to duplicate pages of type set in fixed casts. The printer's term was then recycled by the American journalist Walter Lippmann in his 1922 book *Public Opinion* to describe the subjective cognitive processes involved in people's behavior toward others. The hallmark of the perfect stereotype, according to Lippmann, is that "it precedes the use of reason; is a form of perception, imposes a certain character on the data of our senses before the data reach the intelligence." Offering some examples of what he means, Lippmann goes on to describe the stereotype as being "like the lavender window-panes on Beacon Street, like the door-keeper at a costume ball who judges whether the guest has an appropriate masquerade. There is nothing so obdurate to education or to criticism as the stereotype. It stamps itself upon the evidence in the very act of securing the evidence." In addition, Lippmann associates stereotypes with what he calls "pictures in our heads."[1]

Two things are immediately noteworthy here. First, a word that was intended to refer to an external state of affairs—a process of mechanical reproduction by means of technology—has, in Lippmann's description, been transformed into a designation for a state of mind, an intersubjective relation with other people.[2] Second, by associating stereotypes with "pictures in our heads," Lippmann also points to the fundamental visualism of such intersubjective relations. The suggestion is that whether conscious or unconscious, the use of stereotypes involves the use of some (mental) images, some pictorial representation of our others.

Whereas Lippmann remains largely descriptive and nonjudgmental in his notion of stereotypes, which he considers to be a means of economizing attention in the rush of modern life and even as a strategy for self-defense and self-respect,[3] many social psychologists have since been using the term pejoratively to refer to incorrect generalizations that are rigid, oversimplified, and biased and that, moreover, are regarded as the results of an inability to process information, of prejudice in judgment, and of ethnocentrism.[4] To cite some book titles, stereotypes are commonly considered to be "images that injure," to be word games that "dehumanize the vulnerable" and "take lives."[5] These days, when the representation of others has become a sensitive issue in cultural politics, stereotypes involving sexual preference, race, age, illness, deformity, and disability are invariably targets of criticism.[6] Above all, they stand as proofs of inexcusably hurtful attitudes toward the many others whose equality with us should be acknowledged rather than denied and whose alterity from us should be respected.

Although I do not want to dispute the findings of the social psychologists, my own interest in stereotypes is quite distinct from theirs. Rather than viewing stereotypes as a problem in cognitive psychology—defined typically as mental structures or reflections—involving intergroup relations,[7] I am primarily concerned with their function as a representational device, a possible tactic of aesthetic and political intervention in situations in which the deployment of stereotypes by dominant political or cultural discourses has long been a fact. I believe it is only by considering stereotypy as an objective, normative practice that is regularly adopted for collective purposes of control and management, or even for purposes of epistemological experimentation and radicalism, and not merely as a subjective, devious state of mind that we can begin to assess its aesthetic-cum-political relevance. To that extent, it may be more useful to return to the original coinage of the word than to adhere to its more contemporary, popular psychological usage: stereotypes are thought-provoking precisely because they are forms of representing (human beings) that involve, as in the case of printing, a deliberate process of *duplication*, a process that, when cast in literary language, may be seen as the equivalent of *imitation*. If stereotypes are, as they are often characterized to be, artificial, exaggerated, and reductive, such qualities must be judged against the background of (the mechanics of) representational duplication or imitation.

Once the attention shifts from cognitive psychology to aesthetic representation, a very different kind of question emerges. No longer is it sufficient to ask how stereotypes injure real human beings. Rather, it becomes necessary to consider exactly how stereotypes duplicate and imitate and what they can tell us about the negative acts that are often attributed to them—injury, violence, and aggression—and the assumptions that support such attributions.

Among contemporary cultural critics, Fredric Jameson is the only one I know of who has unambiguously and unapologetically affirmed the inevitability of stereotypes as something fundamental to the representation of one group by another.[8] The unique stance taken by Jameson on this controversial topic is refreshing, and it deserves a closer examination. Not surprisingly, Jameson's statements about stereotypes are situated in his long discussion of the new field of cultural studies, a field in which representations of our others are a regular and unavoidable practice.[9] He begins with an astonishing reference to Erving Goffmann's classic *Stigma* in order to remind us that what we call "culture" is really "the ensemble of stigmata one group bears in the eyes of the other group (and vice versa)" (OCC 271). In light of the fact that Goffmann's subject is, as indicated in the subtitle of his book, what he calls "spoiled identity"—namely, the inferior sense of self experienced by people such as cripples, deformed persons, criminals, or ethnic outcasts (Goffmann's specific example being Jews), who are considered deviant from normative society because of their peculiar physiological, sociological, or cultural conditions—Jameson's analogy is, to say the least, provocative.[10] The reasons behind this analogy are compelling. Using Goffmann enables Jameson to argue that so-called deviance or "stigma" is actually constitutive of cultural identity itself and that that is how one group is usually perceived by another. In this manner, not only does Jameson make the conventional division between normativity and deviancy irrelevant; he has also turned (the perception of) stigmatization into the very condition, the very possibility, for cross-cultural recognition. It is, then, precisely in a stigmatized state that culture becomes "a vehicle or a medium whereby the relationship between groups is transacted" (OCC 272).

At the same time, Jameson writes, there is nothing natural about such transactions: "The relationship between groups is, so to speak, unnatural: it is the chance external contact between entities which have only an interior (like a monad) and no exterior or external surface, save in this special circumstance in which it is precisely the outer edge of the group that—all the while remaining unrepresentable—brushes against that of the other. Speaking crudely then, we would have to say that the relationship between groups must always be one of struggle and violence" (OCC 272). This little passage is remarkable because it defines cross-cultural contact in the unsentimental terms of a brushing against the other as a mere external surface and underscores the struggle and violence inherent to this process. One finds here not the liberalist, progressivist view that different cultures together form one big multicultural family but a reminder of the uncompromised understanding about human aggressiveness advanced by Sigmund Freud in his *Civilization and Its Discontents.* We recall that what bothers Freud is the widespread, traditional religious belief in universal love, a belief that is epitomized in the Judeo-Christian ideal, "Thou shalt love thy neighbour as thyself" (*Leviticus* 19:18). Against this moralist pinnacle of human civilization, Freud argues that there is a basic antagonism, a fundamental destructiveness, within human beings that will always show up such an ideal as a mere piety and a mass delusion rather than a reachable destination. Consequently, civilization must be understood as a permanent struggle by humankind against itself in an attempt to preserve whatever it has accomplished.[11]

If the popular indictments against stereotyping our others are read in the light of Freud's book, they need to be recognized as the contemporary, secularized reenactments of the religious dictum "love thy neighbor as thyself": "Do not deface your neighbor with false representations; do not refer to her by wicked, demeaning names; do not stereotype her." In terms of the arguments about ethnicity in the previous chapter, such indictments of stereotypes should also be seen as arising from the same modernist, universalist claim about ethnicity as a condition equal to all humans, who must therefore be treated with the same degree of respect (or love) around the world.

Jameson's contrary statements about stereotypes, on the other hand, are as unpious and unflattering as Freud's view of human aggressiveness. Like Freud, he does not think that such acts of violence are ever entirely suppressible. Rather, it is incumbent on us to come to terms with their ineluctability:

> Group loathing . . . mobilizes the classic syndromes of purity and danger, and acts out a kind of defense of the boundaries of the primary group against this threat perceived to be inherent in the Other's very existence. Modern racism . . . is one of the most elaborated forms of such group loathing—inflected in the direction of a whole political program; it should lead us on to some reflection of the role of the stereotype in all such group or "cultural" relations, which can virtually, by definition, not do without the stereotypical. For the group as such is necessarily an imaginary entity, in the sense in which no individual mind is able to intuit it concretely. The group must be abstracted, or fantasized, on the basis of discrete individual contacts and experiences which can never be generalized in anything but abusive fashion. *The relations between groups are always stereotypical insofar as they must always involve collective abstractions of the other group, no matter how sanitized, no matter how liberally censored and imbued with respect. . . . The liberal solution to this dilemma— doing away with the stereotypes or pretending they don't exist—is*

not possible, although fortunately we carry on as though it were for most of the time.   (OCC 274; my emphasis)[12]

In the midst of these statements, perhaps sensing that their absolute nature would no doubt offend the piously minded, Jameson makes a small concession to the "liberal solution" by adding that "what it is politically correct to do under such circumstances is to allow the other group itself to elaborate its own preferential image, and then to work with that henceforth 'official' stereotype" (OCC 274).[13] But the qualifying tone of this remark—"what it is politically correct to do"—has the effect rather of further strengthening his predominant argument that stereotypes are virtually indispensable. Should the politically correct solution be adopted single-mindedly, it would only raise more questions: would everything be all right if we simply let our others tell us what stereotypes to use about them? Does this mean that we should simply divide stereotypes into different categories—the good and safe on one side and the bad and incorrect on the other? How do we differentiate between them in the first place?

In other words, the understanding of stereotypes that Jameson has so succinctly delineated—namely, that it is a matter of the outer edge of one group brushing against that of another, that it is *an encounter between surfaces rather than interiors*—cannot really be foreclosed again by the liberalist suggestion that everyone is entitled to her own stereotypes of herself, which others should simply adopt for general use. Once the inevitability of stereotypes—now clarified as relations conducted around exteriors—is understood, the liberalist solution along the lines of cultural entitlement can no longer be a solution. A chasm has irrevocably opened up between the two ends of Jameson's discussion.

As the politically correct go about attacking stereotypes, what is usually repressed is a paradox in the very act of criticizing stereotyping: namely, that in order to criticize stereotypes, one must somehow resort to stereotypical attitudes and presumptions. For instance, in order to repudiate a certain attitude as racist stereotyping, one would, to begin with, need to have already formed certain attitudes toward that attitude, to have *stereotyped* it or marked it as uniformly possessing a distinguishing set of traits. In other words, any charge that others are stereotyping inevitably involves, whether or not one is conscious of it, one's own participation in the same activity. In Mireille Rosello's words, "there is a stereotype of the stereotype: the stereotype is always bad, simplistic, idiotic." When "attacked as a unit of truth, it takes its revenge by forcing speaking into an act of mimesis."[14] This tendency of stereotypes to force even—perhaps especially—their most severe critics to inhabit or become what they are criticizing points to a fundamental discrepancy in representation—between intention and manner, signified and signifier. Insofar as stereotypes are generalizations that seek to encapsulate reality in particular forms, they are not essentially different from the artificial or constructed makeup of all representations. Where stereotypes differ is in the obviousness and exaggeration of their reductive mode—the unabashed nature of their mechanicity and repetitiveness.

Thus, behind the specific disapproval of stereotypes is, in fact, a general anxiety over the purity of language and speech (or representation) and, with that, an age-old demand for conciseness and correctness, qualities that are perpetually in conflict with the way language and speech actually operate. The demand that stereotypes be eliminated is inevitably the demand for a kind of (boundary and thus ethnicity) cleansing. As in the case of all attempts to cleanse speech, this is also a demand for the kind of violence that is censorship. But more disturbing is the fact that such a demand carries within it an implicit acknowledgment of the dangerous potential residing in that which it wants to eliminate. With stereotypes, I would argue that this dangerous potential is not, as is usually assumed, their conventionality and formulaicness but rather their capacity for creativity and originality. To put it more bluntly still, the potential, and hence danger, of stereotypes is that they are able to conflate these two realms of representational truisms—the conventional and the formulaic, on the one hand, and the creative and the original/originating, on the other—when, for obvious reasons of propriety, they ought to be kept separate.

The best instance of such a conflation is the use of stereotypes by political regimes themselves, whether or not they are recognizably repressive. Anyone who has had any experience with the operations of political regimes knows that the use of stereotypes, especially racial stereotypes, is a regular strategy for constructing a mythic other to be relied on for purposes of war, imperialism, national defense, and protectionism. Examples of such mythic others abound in history—the Jew in the Nazi regime, the Jap in U.S. propaganda during the Second World War, the Africans and South Asians who, even though previously colonized by Great Britain, must be barred from "invading" Great Britain, the Hispanic wetbacks who are said to contribute to the economic malaise of the border states in the United States, and the Arab and Turkish guest workers who are being denied basic legal rights in such European countries as France and Germany. The list can go on and on. As Richard Dyer writes, the most important function of the stereotype is "to maintain sharp boundary definitions, to define clearly where the pale ends and thus who is clearly within and who clearly beyond it. Stereotypes do not only, in concert with social types, map out the boundaries of acceptable and legitimate behaviour, *they also insist on boundaries exactly at those points where in reality there are none.*"[15] When a community, under the leadership of a government, decides to draw a boundary between itself and what is not itself, racial stereotypes are typically deployed as a way to project onto an other all the things that are supposedly alien. In the light of an idealized group identity to be guarded in its purity, such stereotypes (of unwelcome others) are, indeed, demons—bad figures to be exorcised.

At the same time, what the successful use of stereotypes by political regimes has proved is not simply that stereotypes are clichéd, unchanging forms but also—and much more importantly—that stereotypes are capable of engendering realities that do not exist. The fantastic figures of the Jew, the Jap, and the wetback have all produced substantive political consequences, from deportation to incarceration to genocide or ethnic cleansing. Contrary to the charge that they are misrepresentations, therefore, stereotypes have demonstrated themselves to be effective, realistic political weapons capable of generating belief, commitment, and action.

His astute insight into the irreducible nature of stereotypy in cultural relations notwithstanding, Jameson has, it seems to me, stopped short of elaborating the issue of power differentials in the very deployment of stereotypes. Such an elaboration would have helped explain how and why stereotypes can be so controversial and explosive under specific circumstances, while under other circumstances the act of stereotyping can pass for acceptable or even conscionable speech. As Dyer puts it, "it is not stereotypes . . . that are wrong, but who controls and defines them, what interests they serve" (12). For instance, in the United States, there is a much higher intolerance of anti-Jewish than of anti-Islamic representations, to the extent that Bill Clinton could, in his public statements as the U.S. president, repeatedly refer to an Islamic head of state such as Saddam Hussein by his first name without raising eyebrows. (To understand the absurdity of this situation, we need only to imagine what it would be like were Clinton himself to be repeatedly referred to as "Bill" in public speeches made by other government leaders. What is disturbing, nevertheless, is not simply his irreverent use of "Saddam" but also its apparent acceptance by the American public.)[16] Similarly, as Rosemary J. Coombe writes, "It is . . . inconceivable that a vehicle could be marketed as 'a wandering Jew,' but North Americans rarely bat an eyelash when a Jeep Cherokee® passes them on the road or an advertisement for a Pontiac® flashes across their television screens. More people may know Oneida® as a brand of silverware than as the name of a people and a nation."[17] A third instance: The racist rejection of black people is equally common among Asians both in Asia and within the United States, but often it is only white people's stereotypes of blacks that receive media attention. Could this be because it is not only the stereotypes themselves but also the power behind their use that accounts for their perceived atrocity, that really counts as it were—so that the question of who is being stereotyped becomes—in this instance, at least—subordinate to that of who is doing the stereotyping and who is accepting/endorsing it? If this is the case, then doesn't it mean that the phenomenon of stereotyping is far more tricky than hitherto thought, because the perception or awareness of stereotypes—that is, at those times when we happen critically to *notice* such representations—may itself already be following a certain stereotypical pattern, the pattern of focusing predominantly on the powers that be?

In the following, I will read two different instances of the use of stereotypes—one from high theory and very famous and the other from mass culture and much less known—in order to elaborate further the implications of my discussion. Despite their disparate discursive locations, these instances, especially when they are juxtaposed with each other, have much to tell us about how stereotypes are or can be reproduced, the special relation they have with graphicity, the potential cultural transactions they mobilize, and the lingering questions of power that ensue therefrom.

How (the) Inscrutable Chinese Led to Globalized Theory

In contemporary theoretical studies, a significant globalizing move is found in Jacques Derrida's deconstruction of Western logocentrism. Following Western philosophers and critics such as Descartes, Leibniz, Ernst Fenollosa, Ezra Pound, and others in a nuanced series of readings, Derrida replicates the age-old idea of Chinese as an ideographic language in his own groundbreaking critique of phonetic writing: "Nonphonetic scripts like Chinese or Japanese . . . remained structurally dominated by the ideogram or algebra and we thus have the testimony of a powerful movement of civilization developing outside of all logocentrism."[18] This reference is summed up imagistically in the picture of Chinese writing on the cover of the English translation of *Of Grammatology* published before 1998.[19] Because Derrida's idea about the Chinese language is so well known and shared by so many in the West,[20] it does not require further recapitulation, but to complete this part of my discussion let me quote John DeFrancis's succinct criticism of this common (mis)reading of Chinese as an ideographic language: "Chinese characters are a phonetic, not an ideographic, system of writing. . . . There never has been, and never can be, such a thing as an ideographic system of writing. The concept of Chinese writings as a means of conveying ideas without regard to speech took hold as part of the chinoiserie fad among Western intellectuals that was stimulated by the generally highly laudatory writings of Catholic missionaries from the sixteenth to the eighteenth centuries."[21]

Considering the centrality of Derrida's early work for poststructuralist studies in general, and remembering how that work uses Chinese writing as a key metaphor for *contrast* or *difference* from Western phonocentrism, which is the heart of Derrida's critique, the implications of DeFrancis's counterassertions can be staggering. According to DeFrancis's argument, Derrida, like the philosophers and critics before him, might be guilty of a certain practice of orientalism because he attributes imagined, fantastical qualities to the East without paying attention to its actual reality. Indeed, as Gayatri Chakravorty Spivak, Derrida's translator, points out—and she was probably among the very first to do so—the East is preserved in an essentialist, unchanging condition in Derrida's text: "Paradoxically, and almost by a reverse ethnocentrism, Derrida insists that logocentrism is a property of the *West*. He does this so frequently that a quotation would be superfluous. Although something of the Chinese prejudice of the West is discussed in Part I, the *East* is never seriously studied or deconstructed in the Derridean text. Why then must it remain, recalling Hegel and Nietzsche in their most cartological humors, as the name of the limits of the text's knowledge?"[22] Similarly, on noting the logocentric metaphysics that is equally present in the Chinese literary tradition, Han-liang Chang writes: "There is no reason why Derrida's deconstruction of Western mimesis cannot be done to its Chinese counterpart. Thus I am tempted to ask: isn't Derrida, like Leibniz before him, suffering from the same 'European hallucination' that China is of necessity exempt from logocentrism?"[23]

My point in using this familiar example of Derrida, however, is not to take him to task, as others have done, for ignoring the actuality of the Chinese language. Insofar as he appeals to an ahistorical notion of Chinese writing for his philosophizing, Derrida does not, to my mind, depart significantly from the habit of hallucinating China (as difference) that has been characteristic of European writings since the sixteenth century. This much is a foregone conclusion (with implications in multiple directions, the most obvious one being that it recalls traditional readings of women as passive silent objects). What interests me, rather, is how a kind of work that is radical, liberatory, antitraditional—an epochal intellectual intervention in every respect—is itself founded not only on an apparent lack of information about and indifference to the workings of a language that provides the pivot of its critical turn but also on a continual stigmatization of that language through the mechanical reproduction of it as *graphicity*, as predominantly ideographic writing (ironically, when, precisely because of the pressures of globalization, Chinese authorities have for decades been reinforcing the phoneticization and alphabetization of the Chinese language in the People's Republic).[24]

To reinsert this in the terms of my ongoing discussion, it seems that Derrida's move to read across cultures, like those made by many others, involves a moment in which representation becomes, wittingly or unwittingly, stereotyping, a moment in which the other is transformed into a recycled cliché. Whereas stereotypes are usually regarded pejoratively, as a form of entrapment and victimization of the other, the case of Derrida shows that stereotypes can be enabling: without the cliché of Chinese as an ideographic language, as a writing made up of silent little pictures, the radical epistemic rupture known as deconstruction could perhaps not have come into being in the manner it did. Cross-ethnic representation, then, is not just a matter of discovering more and newer routes to and contacts with other cultures, whether by means associated with Christopher Columbus (caravels) or Bill Gates (modems). Instead, it is a process in which the acceleration and intensification of contacts brought by technology and commerce entail an acceleration and intensification of stereotypes, stereotypes that, rather than simply being false or incorrect (and thus dismissable), have the potential of effecting changes in entire intellectual climates—as Derrida's reading of Chinese writing demonstrates.

Contrary to the euphoria of inclusionist, boundary-crossing thinking that characterizes much of the current talk about globalization, what Derrida relies on in his globalizing move is the insistence on a certain conventional boundary between East and West, a rhetorical essentialism whereby the East is typecast as difference, a difference that, moreover, is seen in the apparently self-evident or transparent form of the graphic, the ideogram. Certainly, such contact with the other is a mere brushing against the other as an exterior—but that is precisely the point, isn't it? As Jameson writes, "The stereotype is indeed the place of an illicit surplus of meaning, what Barthes called the 'nausea' of mythologies: it is the abstraction by virtue of which my individuality is allegorized and turned into an abusive illustration of something else, something nonconcrete and nonindividual" (OCC 274). The point, in other words, is not simply to repudiate stereotypes and pretend that we can get rid of them but also to recognize in the act of stereotyping, such as Derrida's reading of Chinese inscription, a fundamental signifying or representational process with real theoretical and political consequences. In our increasingly global, cross-cultural contacts, this signifying or representational process can only become more critical.

If I were to leave off at this point, I would merely have repeated Jameson's argument (that stereotypes serve a necessary representational function) by using Derrida as an example. Let me, instead, push this discussion further by drawing on a sociological parallel, the familiar stereotype of the inscrutable Chinese. Pertinently for the present purposes, this stereotype hinges on a scrutiny by those who are outside the Chinese culture. Retracing the logic of this stereotype, it becomes clear that the failure of such outsiders to comprehend Chinese (facial) expressions—themselves a kind of corporeal writing—is being retroactively projected onto the other as the other's essential quality: inscrutability. As Jameson would put it, at the moment of cultural encounter, the other is thus brushed against on the outer edge, as a mere exterior. This exterior, which, in this case, is literally expressed as an impenetrable (sur)face, nonetheless returns to me (the non-Chinese subject) as my enlightening, my enhanced understanding, my epistemological progress. While the Chinese are inscrutable, I remain lucid; their objectlike obscurity constitutes my subjectivity, my humanity.[25]

Isn't "inscrutable Chinese" also the lesson about all orientalist descriptions, including Derrida's, of the Chinese language as "nonphonetic"?

What is remarkable here is that a cliché, "the inscrutable Chinese," whose workings belong in the banal realm of identity politics, has something significant to tell us about the stereotypical manner in which cross-ethnic representations are conducted by even the most theoretically sophisticated and politically scrupulous. Translated into the context of high theory and philosophy, "inscrutable Chinese" no longer simply signifies the enigmatic exterior of the oriental but also *an entire language and culture reduced to (sur)face, image, and ideogram.* As Stanley K. Abe writes, "The alterity of Chinese writing in relation to romanized scripts is, of course, central, but it is the visuality of the character—the manner in which it is made manifest in highly abstract forms—that most contributes to its enduring effectiveness as a symbol of China."[26] The face of the Chinese person and the face of Chinese writing thus converge in what must now be seen as a composite visual stereotype—*the-other-*

as-face—that stigmatizes another culture as at once corporeally and linguistically intractable.

But whereas "inscrutable Chinese" at the sociological level is often invoked in mockery against Asian people (hence its reputation as a racist or orientalist stereotype), in the case of Derrida, this assimilation of Chinese to the graphic, this stereotyping of Chinese as (archetypal) writing per se, is offered as the highest of compliments. As the other, Chinese writing is greeted by him with idealism and utopianism; on it is bestowed the value of a primitive logic, a pre-Western past in which are to be found the West's many "posts" or futures. Chinese can enjoy this privileged status precisely because it is treated as an exterior that is emptied of its grammar, syntax, sound, history, and actual speakers—all the linguistic elements that would have ontologized it with substance and rendered it a real, temporally present language like Western languages. Strictly speaking, therefore, the silent graphicity of Chinese writing is both inscrutable and very scrutable: though Westerners such as Derrida may not actually be able to read it, they nonetheless proceed to do so by inscribing it with a new kind of theorizing (speculation), a new kind of intelligibility. The inscrutable Chinese ideogram has led to a new scrutability, a new insight that remains Western and that becomes, thereafter, global.

As the practice that specializes in *dislocating* the sign from its referent, deconstruction has therefore depended for its own possibility on the very act that it would henceforth work vigilantly against—the act of presupposing or *locating* (in the other) an unmediated correspondence between sign and referent, the act of positing an immanent, "nonphonetic" or pictorial metaphysics of presence known as the Chinese ideogram (a metaphysics in which "Chinese" equals "ideogram"). I have called this kind of act by its name: stereotyping. Defined in these terms, Chinese writing is first and foremost a stereotype, one that is perpetrated at the threshold of East-West representational relations. Derrida's approach is noteworthy not because he challenges the stereotype but because he stops at its boundary, hails it as a familiar sight/site ("Ah, such inscrutable Chinese!"), and then redirects his gaze steadfastly at the West, in which things acquire a new significance as a result of this hailing of the other. Instead of working through the stereotype of Chinese as (sur)face, image, and ideographic writing and deconstructing it as he does European texts and languages, Derrida simply circumvents it, helping thus to perpetuate—to stereotype to a second degree—the cultural divide between East and West, even as the name "deconstruction" becomes henceforth associated with, among other things, the meticulous dismantling of stereotypes (known in deconstructive vocabulary as "presences"). It is in this sense that we may finally describe Derrida's Chinese writing as a specter, a kind of living dead that must, in his philosophizing, be preserved in its spectrality in order to remain a utopian inspiration. Slavoj Žižek offers an illuminating summary of Derrida's predicament: "Derrida's entire effort is directed into ensuring that the spectre will remain the spectre, into preventing its ontologization—is not Derrida's theory itself, therefore, a conjuration destined to preserve the spectre in the intermediate space of the living dead?"[27]

This sketchy rereading of one of the key moments of contemporary theoretical articulation demonstrates that stereotyping is perhaps not so much a matter of cognitive psychological projection involving individual or collective identities as such as it is an act of essentialist reduction (in our representation of others) that is duplicated even in the most subversive and radical rewritings of culture. Furthermore, although stereotypes are not necessarily visual in the physical sense, the act of stereotyping is always implicated in visuality by virtue of the fact that the other is imagined as and transformed into a (sur)face, a sheer exterior deprived/independent of historical depth. Insofar as Chinese writing is both a visible entity (one can literally see it as an object, as calligraphy) and the figure of graphicity (a "nonphonetic language") to which Chinese civilization is consistently reduced by Westerners, and insofar as Chinese writing can also be read as a kind of face (surface, exterior, and also the face of a person), the notion of inscrutable Chinese is, perhaps, the cross-ethnic stereotype par excellence. In that stereotype lies the violent cross-ethnographizing of an other's language as (pure) image and of an entire people as (mere) face. What distinguishes Derrida's transactions is that he has succeeded in stigmatizing Chinese as writing (or as face) in such a serious, scholarly manner as to be able to put his own stereotyping act under erasure.

The globalizing move of grammatology, which is undertaken in the name of the other but remains faithful to Western origins (a globalizing move, incidentally, that is very different from the one required of colonized peoples, for whom globalization has always meant the evacuation of their native cultures and languages and adoption of Western ones), even as those origins are being deconstructed, has meanwhile given rise to a second-order globalizing in its cross-cultural influence: we would be hard put to find another contemporary figure whose work has as fundamentally altered the course of the literary humanities worldwide as Derrida's has in the past thirty years. The tremendous impact of Derrida's work, an impact that is felt not only in European philosophy and literature but also, thanks in part to the disseminating efforts of Derrida's followers, in studies of subaltern peoples undertaken by scholars working against the legacy of Western imperialism, compels us to ask if his "error" of simplifying and falsifying the other is not, in fact, fundamental to the operations of cross-cultural, cross-ethnic representation. Does the move to globalize perhaps always involve, as Jameson's discussion indicates, a brushing against the other on the outer edge, an edge that is not in existence until the moment of encounter—and from which one can only dart back into the interiority of one's own speech?[28]

Drawing Against Chinese Writing

While Derrida and his contemporaries in Western Europe were inspired by the utopian political alternatives promised by Mao's China in the era after 1949, people who were living directly under Communist Chinese rule experienced Chinese writing very differently. Among those who actually speak, read, and write Chinese, Chinese writing has never been simply the figure of graphicity that it is hallucinated to be by non-Chinese users but always a historical, politicized system in which they need to find their bearings with caution. Indeed, ever since ancient times, Chinese writing has served as the divide between those who are educated (that is, literate) and those who are at writing's mercy because they cannot read. But it is over Chinese writing understood in a broad sense as both the instrument and record of Chinese history, and therefore as a contested terrain of political power—what is to be done (written), who is to do (write) it, how to do (write) it, for whom, and so forth—that conflicts between the state and civilians, mediated by intellectuals, continue to this day.[29] The fight for human rights and for democracy by Chinese dissidents, alluded to in the previous chapter, may thus be seen in terms of an ongoing struggle with Chinese writing as realpolitik, a struggle in which those who hold state power still have the authority to restrain and suppress—to mark, to write off—whoever dares challenge them.

Like repressive political regimes elsewhere in the world, the People's Republic has, since its establishment in 1949, been regularly deploying stereotypes for its own purposes of political control and management. For necessary ideological reasons, foreign enemies such as Great Britain and the United States were from the beginning depicted as ugly imperialists, but what is much more remarkable is the manner in which stereotypes also effected a reorganization of Chinese society from within. During the Cultural Revolution (mid-1960s to mid-1970s), this was achieved in part through the systematic vilification of so-called incorrect classes such as landlords and intellectuals (to give two of the outstanding examples), who would be forced to march in public wearing dunce caps and other humiliating labels before they were, often, executed. What such theatrical displays demonstrated was that positive glorification alone (of workers, peasants, and soldiers, for instance) was not enough to shake up a society: for a cohesive biopolitical reorganization to take shape, the boundaries of that society had to be strategically enforced by negative representational acts, by repeated rituals of exorcism.

In the days before July 1, 1997 (the date when the British Colony of Hong Kong was handed over to the PRC), it was not difficult to see that stereotypes were also the most common ingredients of political speech. Abundantly found in official rhetoric, stereotypes were often invoked as parts of a Chinese nationalistic narrative. For instance, people were constantly reminded of the "demonic" British imperialists who imposed the sale of opium on China and robbed China of Hong Kong Island over a hundred and fifty years before, of the now "pitiful," now "suspect" colonized half-wits that Hong Kong people had been reduced to since then, and finally of the "righteous" image of a mother country who was opening her arms to a prodigal child that had long been led astray by the enemy. Moreover, since Hong Kong had always been regarded as a colony with no identity of its own, its "restoration" was conveniently imagined as the story of a struggle between China and Britain only, a story that, as it draws the clear boundary between the wounded landlord and the illegal thug, persistently erases the substance of Hong Kong's own history and hence its rightful demand for democracy and self-determination. The ongoing discursive feud between Western and Chinese forces over the discursive representation of Hong Kong in the past several decades is aptly summarized by Matthew Turner:

> From the 1950's, . . . studies of Hong Kong culture [by Western anthropologists or district officials with an anthropological eye] were often a substitute for a study of China, then closed to foreigners. For the most part avoiding urban areas, "Chinese-ness" was instead sought out in the New Territories' villages, which were perceived to be remote from the contamination of capitalism and communism. Not surprisingly, such studies foregrounded conservative attitudes and political indifference as the basis of Hong Kong civic culture.
>
> By contrast, Chinese reflections on Hong Kong tended to present the urban society as a degenerate, treaty port culture. Northern émigrés, exiled by war and revolution, were predisposed to see Cantonese culture as backward, conservative and inferior, and despised the "derivative culture" of those who had ingratiated themselves with colonialism. Many saw nothing but squalor, obscenity and greed in the city. This picture of Hong Kong as a backward Chinese culture, perverted by westernization, and debased by commercialism, remains a potent image, from the pre-war period to the modern period.[30]

What Turner's remarks reveal is that in the cultural transactions between East and West, the colony of Hong Kong served both China and the West as the stigmatized other. For Westerners, Hong Kong was a stand-in for the conservative Chinese hinterland; for the mainland Chinese, Hong Kong was a stand-in for the decadent commercial West. To each side, Hong Kong provided a convenient set of cultural specifics or stigmata that was required for the advancement of its own agenda. Hong Kong was thus thoroughly and multiply stereotyped in a political situation over which it had little control but in which it nonetheless had to negotiate tactically its own survival.[31]

It is in this political situation, ever fraught and precarious and over-saturated with stereotypes, that the modes of representation deployed in the works of Larry Feign, a cartoonist who worked in Hong Kong during the 1980s and 1990s, become fascinating.

For an extended period, beginning in 1986, Feign was the author of *Lily Wong*, a continuing series based on an imagined Hong Kong Chinese family. *Lily Wong* was first serialized in the *Hong Kong Standard* and then, beginning in December 1987, in the *South China Morning Post*.[32] Lily, a beautiful and courageous young woman who speaks fluent English as well as Cantonese, has worked on and off as a secretary in different organizations, including the "Department of Prevarication and Obfuscation" in the Hong Kong government. Her boyfriend, Stuart Wright, is an American graphic designer who has been working for a Hong Kong advertising agency called "Pinchbeck Public Relations." Eventually, Ms. Wong gets her Mr. Wright, and the two are married. Though Stuart is deeply in love with his wife, he does not exactly get along with his in-laws, who include Lily's non-English-speaking parents and her good-for-nothing brother, Rudy. The Wong family also has many relatives in the PRC, whom they visit from time to time. At one point, the entire family emigrates to the United States, but then Stuart and Lily, feeling homesick, return to Hong Kong shortly afterward. By the time the comic strip was discontinued in 1995, Lily and Stuart have become parents of a cute baby daughter.

The circumstances of the discontinuation of Feign's strip by the *South China Morning Post* remain mysterious. According to David Feign (Larry's father), the newspaper, even though one of the most profitable in the world, claimed that the firing of Feign was "a cost-saving measure," while "subsequent events proved that it was politically motivated."[33] This view was supported by Martin Lee, chairman of the Democratic Party of Hong Kong. In a letter to the *South China Morning Post* that the newspaper never printed, Lee pointed out that this was certainly a case of the suppression of journalistic freedom, indeed, of humor itself: "Cartoonists are journalists too," Lee writes, "and although humour is not a freedom expressly guaranteed by the Joint Declaration and the Basic Law, political cartoons are clearly a form of expression and as such should be protected as any other form of speech. . . . The jettisoning of

Mr. Feign's daily comic strip raises the question of whether we in Hong Kong will have 'one country, two systems'—but no sense of humour."[34]

In a political context in which people are still liable to being persecuted if not executed for their speech, Lee's analysis of the controversy over Feign's work in terms of the freedom of speech—in this case, the defensibility of journalistic expression—under the rule of law is certainly pertinent. From the perspective of the politics of representation, however, one crucial question remains. This is the question of cultural form (rather than that of speech-as-expression or speech-as-right). Assuming that the *South China Morning Post* was, indeed, acting out of caution in an attempt to protect itself against possible censuring from the then-future Chinese authorities, what exactly is it in Feign's work that aroused so much anxiety? What kind of "speech" could a cartoonist make that might be deemed so disturbing as to warrant suppression even before the official date of Hong Kong's return to China?

For those who know something about events in Hong Kong in recent years, the most outstanding feature of Feign's work is his ability to draw (on) the most banal moments of everyday life. In order to create humor in the midst of banality, Feign specializes in methods that, on first reading, are simply absurd mimicries of widely used conventions. For instance, to those who can read, what is more common than a dictionary or a glossary? Yet under Feign's pen, the dictionary/glossary as a cultural form becomes an economical means of conveying critical insights the complexity of which is best captured in a compact mode, within a single page. Operating with the assumption that everything under the sun can be classified and explained (complete with illustrations and indications of Cantonese pronunciation and part of speech), the dictionaries/glossaries—or shall we say Feigned dictionaries/glossaries—of *Aieeyaaa!* (Hambalan, 1986, 1995) and *Aieeyaaa Not Again!* (Hambalan, 1987, 1995) constitute a literal and suggestive set of *drawings against Chinese writing*. These drawings are not mere repositories of the details of Hong Kong customs, habits, prejudices, and verbal peculiarities; they also reveal, through their condensed snapshots, the conventional logic of the classifying and explanatory mode bursting at its seams, barely able to keep under control the fantastical features and cantankerous creatures of Hong Kong daily life. And yet at the same time, despite the random, bizarre arrangement (of a group of Cantonese expressions in the arbitrary sequence of the English alphabet), these features and creatures are nonetheless poignantly recognizable and realistic. Some examples from these flipbooks are found in figures 1 to 8.

These examples show that Feign is fearless in his use of stereotypes, of which his cartoons supply a bountiful series: the *gwailo* (literally, "ghost man," meaning foreigner or Westerner) falling in love with an Oriental belle; the father-in-law who hates everyone and everything that isn't Chinese; the relatives on the mainland who are bottomless pits for gifts; the brother-in-law who, when he tries to make a living at all, tries to do it by fraud; the British "expats" who dismiss the locals with habitual racist remarks; the Chinese Communist officials who are autocratic, ignorant, and corrupt; the U.S. customers who react with self-righteous indignation to rumored injustice in another country, only to abandon such indignation expediently when it conflicts with their own consumerist interests. . . . For an example of the highly amusing pictorialized narratives surrounding these figures, see figure 9.

Instead of "stereotypes," it is, of course, conceivable to use a seemingly more appropriate term such as "caricature" to describe Feign's work. However, whereas caricature, by virtue of being understood definitively as a distorted or grotesque imitation, can be safely relegated to the category of the unrealistic and be dismissed as *mere* representation, stereotype carries the contentious and unavoidable implications of realpolitik. By duplicating and parodying Hong Kong's political situation in exaggerated and reductive shapes, Feign's work calls attention to the situation precisely as it is: a manipulative and exploitative speech/writing. If stereotypy must be denounced as false consciousness, his drawings suggest, false consciousness is not necessarily the exclusive property of ordinary people—"the masses" onto whom ideological blindness is often conveniently projected—but also, crucially, the property and propriety of those in power. By revealing that the political state, too, is no more than a user of stereotypes, Feign brings to light the fact that stereotypes are not so much about subjective cognitive processes as about power and competition: the injuries, violence, and aggression commonly attributed to stereotypes are not so much the intrinsic qualities of stereotypes themselves as they are the effects of those in power who must, in order to

FIGURE 1 "Cha" (from *Aieeyaaa!* 7)   (Copyright Larry Feign)

DUEN NG JIT

(n.) Dragon Boat Festival: annual commemoration of the drowning suicide of Wat Yuen (屈原) in protest of government wrongdoing. This festival will be prohibited after 1997, since obviously there will be no government wrongdoing.

MIND IF WE JOIN IN?

CCCP

FIGURE 2 "Duen Ng Jit" (from *Aieeyaa!* 26)   (Copyright Larry Feign)

FAAT GWOON

(n.) Court judge: man who wears a long blonde wig, frilly dress and pantyhose in public and sends other men to prison for doing the same thing.

FIGURE 3 "Faat Gwoon" (from *Aieeyaa!* 30)   (Copyright Larry Feign)

FIGURE 4 "Faat Yam" (from *Aieeyaa!* 31)   (Copyright Larry Feign)

GWAI LO

(n.) Literally translates as "ghost chap" and not "white uncivilized hairy-faced heathen barbarian devil" as is commonly believed.

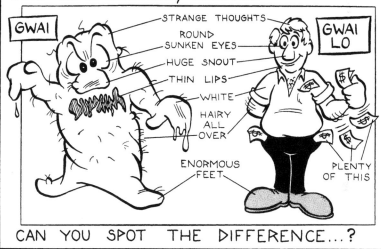

CAN YOU SPOT THE DIFFERENCE...?

FIGURE 5 "Gwai Lo" (from *Aieeyaa!* 46)   (Copyright Larry Feign)

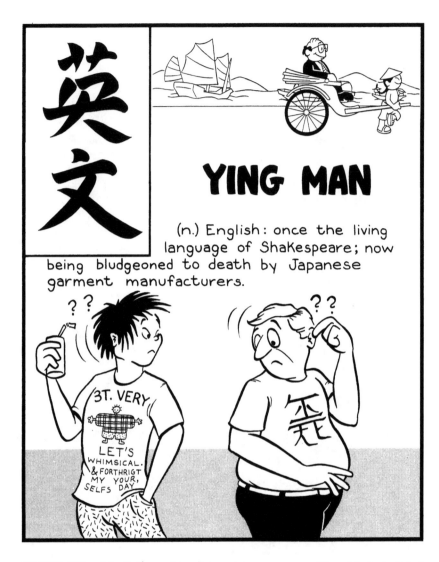

FIGURE 6 "Ying Man" (from *Aieeyaa!* 125)   (Copyright Larry Feign)

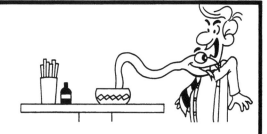

GWAI POH

(n.) Caucasian female; with all the available (and many unavailable) expatriate men busy dating Chinese women, and Chinese men preferring to go out with their own kind, the only date a single gwai poh can look forward to is the date she leaves Hong Kong!

FIGURE 7 "Gwai Poh" (from *Aieeyaa, Not Again!* 41)   (Copyright Larry Feign)

FIGURE 8 "Jung Juk Kei Si" (from *Aieeyaa, Not Again!* 60)

(Copyright Larry Feign)

stamp out competition and preserve their own monopoly, forbid to others the privilege of stereotyping. To this extent, Feign has, precisely through his cartoons, committed the enormity of usurping this privilege from the political state. Hence, perhaps, the anxiety his work provokes: here is someone who openly uses stereotypes without a political license. How dare he?

Technically, how do Feign's stereotypes produce their effects? To answer this question, it is necessary to discuss the function of graphicity in his texts.

First, as in the case of all cartoon strips, the images in Feign's work are narratively significant: they help to move the stories along. It is, however, important to note that his images are not merely illustrations of stories or words whose meanings are already understood. Rather, the images function as a kind of anarchic excess paradoxically because of their graphically pointed nature. By simulating gestures, facial expressions, body movements, and other identifiable traits in bold yet skillfully precise brushstrokes, the images bring to the dialogues a physical dimension, resulting in a visually and epistemologically pronounced effect of transgression whose power is, significantly, nonverbal. In the materiality of the graphic, what is drawn adds quite a bit more—an entire wayward sideshow—to what is spoken or written.

Take the stereotype of the PRC official, for instance. It is when the dwarfish, stubby figure of the PRC official-in-uniform with his shit-eating grin (which is reminiscent of that other cartoon fat cat, Garfield) is juxtaposed with his platitudinous words—words that must have been repeated a thousand times—that the effect of absurdity becomes palpable (see figure 10). The vacant quality of the words and the concrete quality of the graphicization combine to produce an arresting medium of incongruity. If, by its sterility and its formulaicness, the stereotype is a kind of dead body, this dead body is now beaming with life. In this fearless and deliberate play with boundaries—which is not the hackneyed sentimental "border crossing" talk that we encounter so often in contemporary cultural studies but rather a lethal confounding of cliché and creativity, petrifaction and expressivity, death and life—Feign offers one of his most memorable portraits, a portrait of the thoroughly dehumanized party

FIGURE 9 "Christmas in the U.S.A. . . ." (from *Execute Yourself Tonite!* 46–47)

(Copyright Larry Feign)

FIGURE 9 (*Continued*)

cadre, a half-machine, half-animal automaton regularly brimming over with preposterous preprocessed prognostications.

If a sense of the ridiculous is already strongly present in Feign's verbal texts, it is his pictures in their defiant, uninhibited physicality that allow that sense of the ridiculous to emerge fully from the words. Strictly speaking, then, the stereotype in Feign operates in this peculiar intersection between the verbal and the visual, so that it is through being drawn against writing that platitudes appear platitudinous and stereotypes appear stereotypical. By giving the ridiculous words a loaded graphic imprint, Feign's images mark them as postures, turn them into denaturalized signs, and subject them to a critical reading. We may even go so far as to say that his drawings are his way of impersonating those he mocks—for the sake of annihilating them from within with that healthiest of anarchistic explosives, laughter. Through his comic visual narratives, we witness the production of an iconography that is simultaneously the production of iconoclasm: at the same time that they bring human figures to life, Feign's cartoons subvert any idealization of the human image as such in an antirealism that is both aesthetic and political in its implications. Unlike those of official rhetoric, the pictures of Feign's cartoons are images without aura, without a false sense of dignity and importance. In their dehumanized forms, they serve rather as sites of sacrilege, of a profane smashing of the stereotypical, hypocritical sanctification of politics and human relations that is the daily fare of the (writing that is the) political state.

Ethnographer of a "Lifestyle"

Paradoxically, Feign did not begin drawing Hong Kong with political intentions. As he describes it, *Lily Wong* was not at first a political comic strip. "The lives of Lily, her family and her then-suitor Stuart revolved around East-West culture clash and everyday annoyances in Hong Kong," he writes. When the editor at the *South China Morning Post* indicated that he wanted a political comic strip along the lines of Garry Trudeau's *Doonesbury* or Steve Bell's *If . . .* , Feign "compromised with him," and the two agreed that "half the time the comic strip would

SUEN GUI

(n.) Election: of course we'll still have them after 1997... Beijing's policy on Hong Kong's future has always been the embodiment of hypocri— I mean, democracy!

FIGURE 10 "Suen Gui" (from *Aieeyaa!* 106)

cover local politics and the rest of the time it would still be boy-meets-girl and the usual Hong Kong litter, louts and pollution jokes."[35] Feign's reluctance to give up the everyday aspects of his object is an important clue to the understanding of his unique methods. Despite his disclaimer, the "usual Hong Kong litter, louts and pollution jokes," as they appear in his stories, are never very far from the political.

But there is a further dimension to this unmitigated attention to the everyday in the context of Hong Kong. The everyday is poignantly suggestive not only because it is part and parcel of a fashionable postmodernism that relativizes the significance of everything by leveling it as the quotidian. It is also because, in the political discussions deciding Hong Kong's future, the everyday—in its mundane and automatized routines, its mindless repetitions—is virtually *the entirety* of the status that Hong Kong is allowed to have. As Matthew Turner argues, the Sino-British Joint Declaration, while promising to allow Hong Kong to continue its present "capitalist system" after 1997, nonetheless refuses to specify what that system is other than a so-called lifestyle:

> Despite assurances of a "Hong Kong ruled by Hong Kong people," in formal documents the People's Republic assumes that there is no such thing as a "people" of Hong Kong, and indeed the Joint Declaration describes the population in neutral, neutralizing terms such as "inhabitants" or "residents," while local culture is rendered merely as "lifestyle." These words now determine Hong Kong's future: *"Hong Kong's previous capitalist system and lifestyle shall remain unchanged for 50 years"* [Xianggang guoqu de zibenzhuyi zhidu he shenghuo fangshi jiang weichi wushi nian bu bian] (Joint Declaration).[36]

It is important to remember that from an orthodox Marxist perspective, the "capitalist system" encompasses both infrastructure and superstructure, the economic modes of production and the ideological state apparatuses (such as political, legal, and social institutions) that sustain such modes of production. The word "and" (*he*) in the phrase "capitalist system and lifestyle," however, leaves the precise relationship between "system" and "lifestyle" ambiguous. Does the "and" signify an act of supplementary inclusion, so that "capitalist system" and "lifestyle," even if they are not identical things, will *both* be honored? If this (optimistic interpretation) is, indeed, what is intended, one major question remains (for those living in Hong Kong as for the entire world watching Hong Kong's return to China): how could Hong Kong's different "system" and "lifestyle" possibly continue unchanged if they are meanwhile subjected to the ever-pressing idea of "one nation"? Alternatively, does the "and" signify an equivalence between "capitalist system" and "lifestyle"— meaning that Hong Kong's mode of production and superstructure are virtually the same as, are *no more than*, its "lifestyle"—a lifestyle that, in turn, can be equated simply with the routine habits of consumption? As Turner goes on to comment:

> What is the Hong Kong "lifestyle"? A taste for fashion, gossip maga-
> zines and Karaoke? A paradise for consumers and polluters? Or does
> lifestyle suggest something deeper, perhaps the subjective texture of
> identity? Is lifestyle like citizenship, the rights of association and . . .
> forms of representation that underlie civil society, and make it possible
> for citizens to shape policies of common concern? Or is lifestyle like
> fashion, changing from moment to moment? Since no society could
> "remain unchanged for fifty years," how will social change be legit-
> imized? *At the heart of the agreements on Hong Kong's future lies a
> slippery neologism which may be interpreted to mean almost anything.*
> Beijing and London do not suppose lifestyle to be contingent on na-
> tional identity.   (25; my emphasis)

With these remarks, Turner has put his finger on the crux of the matter, namely, a deliberately vague vocabulary in political documentation,
which is designed to guarantee the PRC the largest degree of rhetorical
arbitrariness in governing Hong Kong as it deems appropriate. This
vague vocabulary, moreover, is not only aimed at putting Hong Kong
under control but also indicative of the larger chaos that has characterized the PRC's approach to its own economic reforms during the current
period of modernization. Ironically, despite its morally condescending
attitude toward Hong Kong, Hong Kong's economic success—the result
of dirty capitalism—has in recent years clearly become the PRC's own
developmental model for the future. In a country in which socialism is

still adamantly the official ideology, such aspirations (toward capitalism) must, of course, not be acknowledged openly—unless capitalism itself can somehow be (mis)construed or stereotyped as something unthreatening, as a mere "lifestyle," for instance. On balance, therefore, it is the PRC's own fundamental but inadmissible ambivalence toward capitalism—How to adopt capitalism without acknowledging its centrality? How to become like Hong Kong without giving Hong Kong full credit?—that accounts for the slipperiness of the "and" in the crucial phrase deciding Hong Kong's future. While to all appearances purporting to let Hong Kong retain what it had, this little grammatical conjunction stands in effect as a high-handed act of elision, ensuring that the PRC can, whenever it needs to, obliterate Hong Kong's claim to a political identity of its own precisely on the grounds of (recognizing) Hong Kong's so-called lifestyle.

Even though Feign's cartoons may be seen, then, as so many caricatural portraits of Hong Kong, what stands out is the manner in which his pictorialized narratives alert us to the intimate relation between that decadent, politically indifferent way of living and the perfidious cunning of realpolitik. In Feign's work, even the most banal moment of daily life is just a hairbreadth away from the most alarming issues of racial discrimination, militaristic violence, the denial of human rights, and so forth, so that the physical impurity of the everyday as such is underscored by another kind of impurity: the indistinguishability of the everyday from a ubiquitously dominant discourse in whose interest that everydayness must remain a mere nonpolitical lifestyle. In other words, precisely because of the concerted efforts by both Britain and China to stereotype it and deny it a political identity, Hong Kong's lifestyle, even in its most carefree and leisurely everyday moments, is all the more indivisible from the cruelty and treachery that spill over from the twin legacies of colonialism and totalitarianism. *This* corruption—the corruption between Hong Kong's "litter, louts and pollution jokes" and Hong Kong's political fate—is what constitutes the explosiveness of Feign's drawings. Again and again, we witness in his work the most tragicomic juxtaposition of what are supposedly distinct or opposite categories of events, such as a cartooned home visit to the PRC by a Hong Kong family that leads up to the terrifying scene of an execution (PRC style), which is, meanwhile, hilariously conducted in the manner of a spectacular game show and nicknamed after the longest-standing entertainment program in Hong Kong television history, "Enjoy Yourselves Tonight" (see figure 11). Consider also Feign's depiction of the controversial situation of the large number of Filipinas employed as domestics in Hong Kong's residences. In one strip based on a real-life news event, Feign features a luxury apartment building that posts signs forbidding Filipinas and dogs from using elevators. Rather than stopping short at the safe polarization between oppressors and oppressed, his humor spares no one, not even the lower-class figures of the apartment building guards or even the Filipina maid herself (see figure 12).

If Chinese writing is, for Derrida, the stereotypical image of the other in its exotic alterity, for Feign, it is rather the stereotypical image of the contestable authoritarianism of the Chinese state. In Derrida, the stereotype is left exactly as it is found, as an ideogram and a face without history, a visible object that is to be preserved in inscrutability and spectrality, in the intermediate state of the living dead. In Feign, the stereotype is, by contrast, imploded graphically so as to enable a new order of signification to emerge in its destruction. At the threshold of Hong Kong's return to China, his drawings of Hong Kong's "lifestyle" become acts of defacing the writing that is the smooth functioning of the state. In such defacements, in which stereotypes are called on to blast themselves open, we learn to see afresh the violence of political interests that silently and invisibly imbues even the most ordinary of everyday exchanges.

An instructive example of how such political interests tend to reveal themselves unwittingly in the light of Feign's work was provided at a public event at which I presented a paper on him.[37] As is often the case in the context of Hong Kong's cultural politics, dislike for someone like Feign can be easily justified with a stereotype, namely, that he is a *gwailo* or Westerner, who is presumed to be racist. Indeed, under Hong Kong's fraught historical circumstances, "racist Westerner" is, for many, a tautology. This, then, was the presumption behind a Hong Kong critic's hostile dismissal of Feign on this occasion. After pointing out a biographical detail—that Feign and his family used to live in one of the enclaves for Westerners in Hong Kong, Lantau Island—this critic proceeded to use

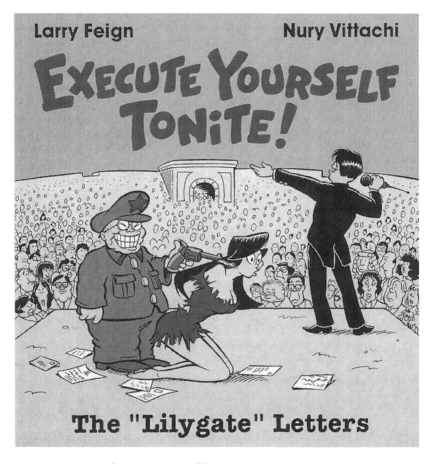

FIGURE 11 Cover of *Execute Yourself Tonite!* (Copyright Larry Feign)

one of Feign's cartoons (figure 6) to expose Feign's "real" political sympathies. This cartoon features the expression "Ying man" (English). Citing Feign's English text, which reads "English: once the living language of Shakespeare; now being bludgeoned to death by Japanese garment manufacturers," this critic's point was that such a derisive description at the expense of Asians could only have come from a *gwailo*, who (as is often the case in a place such as Hong Kong) is lamenting the destruction of a noble European language at the hands of yellow savages. What is this, so the tone of his remarks implied, if not an indication of Feign's pro-Western, anti–Hong Kong bias? Offended by Feign's manner of poking fun at a stereotyped situation (namely, the "sad" fate of postcolonial English), this critic sought to put Feign in his place by resorting to a familiar tactic: by stereotyping him.

Remarkably, however, in taking the moral high ground against Feign as just another racist Westerner, this critic had entirely ignored or was unable to process the other part of the cartoon: the picture of two men looking at each other in mutual bewilderment. The man on the left, a trendy Hong Kong youth with a punk haircut, is wearing a T-shirt printed with nonsensical English; the man on the right, a middle-aged Westerner with a pot belly, is wearing a T-shirt printed with a nonsensical Chinese character. This drawing of a mutually stereotyping cultural encounter undercuts the defensive and hypocritical attitude regarding the purity of the English language as it is expressed in Feign's English text by showing that the "bludgeoning" of the "language of Shakespeare" is only one side of the story—that orientalist representations of the Chinese language (in this case, through a haphazard and fantastical assemblage of lines that together *look like* a Chinese character) are, in fact, an equally customary phenomenon. The humor of the cartoon lies, then, in this unexpected twist to the stereotypical understanding of "English-being-abused-by-barbaric-yellow-people," a twist that can only be grasped when what is verbally written—the English text on the top half of the cartoon—is read against what is drawn below; when the first stereotype (in words) is supposedly illustrated but actually taken apart by the additional stereotype (image) of the Westerner bludgeoning the Chinese language.

In failing to grasp the humor of Feign's composition in this manner, this Hong Kong critic not only proved himself to be unable to deal with the pictorial as such but also—since the pictorial in this instance involves, paradoxically, the ability to read Chinese as well as English writing—unwittingly put himself in the precise stereotypical category in which he attempted contemptuously to put Feign. He proved, ironically by the monolingualism of his own response, that he was acting exactly like the *gwailo* of Hong Kong, who, because of racism, linguistic incompetence, or both, tend to regard the local Chinese language as beneath notice and for whom—the historical bilingualism of Hong Kong's every-

FIGURE 12 "Halt!! Stop or I'll—" (from *Banned in Hong Kong*, 61–63)

(Copyright Larry Feign)

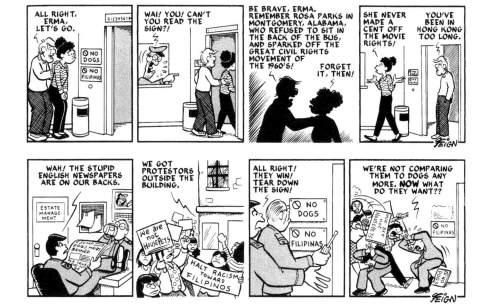

FIGURE 12 *(continued)*

day communications notwithstanding—only what is written and printed in English has status as reality.

Close to the first anniversary of his termination by the *South China Morning Post*, Feign was being honored in Hong Kong by Amnesty International in its first annual Human Rights Press Awards. For the cartoon that had cost him his job, he received first place in the English-language cartoon division and won the only award in the Chinese-language cartoon division. Although the *South China Morning Post* noted the event and listed some award winners, no mention was made of the fact that its own former cartoonist had been among them.[38] As a "document of civilization," the newspaper thus proved itself, in Walter Benjamin's words, "at the same time a document of barbarism." Feign's work, on the other hand, will remain emblematic of the task of the historical materialist—the task of brushing history against the grain.[39]

CHAPTER 3

Keeping Them in Their Place: Coercive Mimeticism and Cross-Ethnic Representation

The reason why men enjoy seeing a likeness is, that in contemplating it they find themselves learning or inferring, and saying perhaps, "Ah, that is he."
— Aristotle, "Poetics"

Mimesis has become that dreaded, absurd, or merely tiresome Other, that necessary straw-man against whose feeble pretensions poststructuralists prance and strut.
— Michael Taussig, *Mimesis and Alterity*

The problem is to keep "in their place," from generation to generation, those who have no fixed place; and for this, it is necessary that they have a genealogy.
— Etienne Balibar, "Class Racism"

Public Zoos and National Allegories: The Epistemic Parameters of a Captivity Narrative

In an essay that explores the historical transformations of Western man's relation with animals, the art historian John Berger points up the fact that the disappearance of animals from modern daily life coincided with the appearance of public zoos.[1] "The zoo to which people go to meet animals, to observe them, to see them," he writes, "is, in fact, a monument to the impossibility of such encounters" (19). Central to Berger's argument are two related issues—the crippling impact cultural marginalization has on those who are being marginalized and, by implication, the self-contradiction inherent to the claims of civic functions (of furthering knowledge and enabling public enlightenment)—that accompany all imperialist establishments, even such apparently innocent ones as the public zoo. For such claims are, as Berger goes on to show, mediated by a kind of gaze that turns what it gazes at—and what it puts on display—into "an image out of focus":

> However you look at these animals, even if the animal is up against the bars, less than a foot from you, looking outwards in the public direction, *you are looking at something that has been rendered absolutely marginal*; and all the concentration you can muster will never be enough to centralise it. Why is this?
>
> Within limits, the animals are free, but both they themselves, and their spectators, presume on their close confinement. The visibility through the glass, the spaces between the bars, or the empty air above the moat, are not what they seem—if they were, then everything would be changed. Thus visibility, space, air, have been reduced to tokens.
>
> The animals . . . become utterly dependent upon their keepers. Consequently most of their responses have been changed. What was central to their interest has been replaced by a passive waiting for a series of arbitrary outside interventions. The events they perceive occurring around them have become . . . illusory. . . . At the same time this very isolation (usually) guarantees their longevity as specimens and facilitates their taxonomic arrangement.
>
> (22–23; emphasis in the original)

All sites of enforced marginalization such as "ghettos, shanty towns, madhouses, concentration camps," Berger concludes, have something in common with zoos (24).

This discussion of animals in zoos offers a disturbingly apt parallel to the topic of this book: the politics of ethnicity in the context of capitalist liberalism.[2] Would it be far-fetched to see in what Berger has said about caged animals—those that are on the verge of disappearance but are nonetheless preserved artificially so as to serve the civic purposes of public education—a suggestive affinity with the predicament in which those who are labeled ethnic find themselves in white capitalist societies? What is particularly memorable about Berger's account is its visual emphasis, its understanding that marginalized existence is a relation of visuality, that is, a relation of the coded manners in which one is being imaged. However well intentioned a newly arrived onlooker may be and however much concentration she may wish to give to those inside the cage, something will, under these circumstances, always seem out of focus. This chapter will be an attempt to elaborate and historicize this condition of out-focusedness.

To begin my elaboration, I will turn again to Fredric Jameson, this time to the much maligned and attacked point that Jameson has made about third-world literature.

In the terms of the discussions I have been offering in this book, Jameson's controversial essay "Third-World Literature in the Era of Multinational Capital"[3] stands as a fine example of the unavoidable pitfalls of cross-ethnic representation. It is important to reiterate the fact that Jameson begins his essay with a conscious and generously intended attempt to articulate the radical difference presented by literary works produced outside the dominant cultural contexts of the capitalist first world. He distinguishes his own approach methodologically from "the strategy of trying to prove that these texts are as 'great' as those of the canon itself" and opts, instead, to pay close attention to the ways in which they differ from such a canon. "Nothing is to be gained by passing over in silence the radical difference of non-canonical texts" (65), he writes, and he goes on to emphasize this point throughout his essay. As a reader interested in writing, he is, understandably, concerned primarily with how the unequal material conditions—economic, political, cultural—between the first and third worlds affect the reading process (66) and thus with how discussions of third-world literature might offer "a remarkable opportunity to rethink our humanities curriculum in a new way—to re-examine the shambles and ruins of all our older 'great books,' 'humanities,' 'freshman-introductory' and 'core course' type traditions" (67).

In trying to chart the third-world difference, Jameson, by necessity, falls back on stereotyping, namely, by observing that whereas first-world literature and culture have been produced with the assumption (accepted in the West) of an incommensurable split between the private and public realms, in the third world, life and writing are "based on the principles of community interdependence" (86)—that is, the private and public are still commensurable—indeed, inseparable—realms of signification. This stereotypical divide between the first and third worlds is what enables him then to make the much debated and criticized statement, which he himself is the first to call a "sweeping hypothesis": "All third-world texts are necessarily . . . allegorical, and in a very specific way: they are to be read as what I will call *national allegories*" (69; emphasis in the original). And, again: "Third-world texts, even those which are seemingly private and invested with a properly libidinal dynamic— necessarily project a political dimension in the form of national allegory: *the story of the private individual destiny is always an allegory of the embattled situation of the public third-world culture and society*" (69; emphasis in the original).

To be precise, one stereotype has been superimposed on another in Jameson's statements. First, there is the stereotype that third-world productions *correspond to* (that is, they repeat or mimic) a predictable notion, the collective. Second, there is the stereotype that third-world productions are *all alike* (that is, they repeat or mimic one another) in their tendency to be about the collective as such. Again, Jameson is the first to acknowledge the orientalist implications and self-contradictory modes of his own argument:

> It is clear to me that *any* articulation of radical difference—that of gender, incidentally, fully as much as that of culture—is susceptible to appropriation by that strategy of otherness which Edward Said, in the context of the Middle East, called "orientalism." It does not matter much that the radical otherness of the culture in question is praised or valorized positively, as in the preceding pages: the essential operation is that of differentiation, and once that has been accomplished, the mechanism Said denounces has been set in place. . . .
>
> Nor can I feel that the concept of cultural "identity" or even national "identity" is adequate. One cannot acknowledge the justice of the general poststructuralist assault on the so-called "centered subject," the old unified ego of bourgeois individualism, and then resuscitate this same ideological mirage of psychic unification on the collective level in the form of a doctrine of collective identity.
>
> (77, 78; emphasis in the original)

These remarks of theoretical qualification notwithstanding, Jameson adheres to the act of stereotyping the third-world text as national allegory, and it is this adherence that has earned him the wrath of many of his fellow critics.[4] Although I tend to disagree with Jameson's conclusions, I think it needs to be pointed out that the mechanism of reading other cultures by stereotyping, a mechanism on which Jameson relies, is by no means unique to him or, as I argued in the preceding chapter, at all avoidable in cross-ethnic representational politics. Jameson's "problem," it would seem, is not that he stereotypes non-Western literatures but that he dares openly assert such stereotyping as a viable method of reading, that he dares put in black and white (with thought-provoking results of analysis) a cognitive operation that normally must remain hushed up even when it is fully adopted. Indeed, to cite but one instance, the "Freud versus Marx" complex that he mentions (69) as a way of differentiating the conditions of cultural production between the first and third worlds is still very much with us, and Jameson's point that, when it comes to third-world texts, "psychology, or more specifically, libidinal investment, is to be read in primarily political and social terms" (72) remains astutely on the mark, from East Asianists' continual insistence on the exceptionalism of the cultures under their scrutiny, to South Asianists' pursuit of subaltern historiography, to other area specialists' investigations of the entanglements of culture and politics in Latin America, the Middle East, or Africa. Meanwhile, how many theorists and critics specializing in Western cultures, who might applaud the moralistic indictments of Jameson's statements, have themselves gone on to study with close attention the Asian, African, and Latin American texts that he has attempted to read with so much interest? Isn't it more often the case that, after joining in such applause, such theorists and critics typically return to their own business as usual, in which the histories of non-Western cultures continue to go unacknowledged?

Nevertheless, although this episode in cross-cultural reading demonstrates that stereotyping is an inevitability, the practice remains subject to criticism. The stereotyping act of reading third-world literary texts as national allegories, we might say, is not unlike the public zoo that Berger uses to describe the predicament of ghettoization and marginalization. This is essentially the gist of the charges made by Jameson's critics, namely, that he does not "see" right, that he does not capture the animals right: "Visitors visit the zoo to look at animals. They proceed from cage to cage, not unlike visitors in an art gallery who stop in front of one painting, and then move on to the next or the one after next. Yet in the zoo the view is always wrong. Like an image out of focus."[5] The question is: can there be an image under such conditions that is truly in focus? Wouldn't it be more accurate to say that, however benevolent and complimentary the visitor might be, the image produced of the animals— in this case, the third-world cultural workers, the ethnics caught in the plight of postimperialist nationalisms—is bound to be out of focus because they are the products of a certain kind of gaze to which they are (pre)supposed to play *as*, to act *like*, to exist *in the manner of* something? This something may be an idea, an image, or a stereotype, but the point remains that the objects under scrutiny are dislocated and displaced to begin with, and subordinated even as they appear as themselves.

A certain moral may hence be drawn. In cross-cultural representation, if conditions are not entirely equal—and they are, of course, never entirely equal—the problematic of stereotyping, which is also the problematic of privileged, prejudiced, out-of-focus viewing akin to that of the visitor at the zoo, will increasingly emerge as what must be read alongside the primary texts themselves. However disputable, the intellectual, cultural positioning of those reading and gazing is now an undismissable component of the picture: just as the zoo visitor's gaze produces the image of the animal she looks at, so, too, is the reading by first-world scholars such as Jameson a critical part of the image—and imagining—of third-world cultural productions. It is this additional awareness, this extra ontological presence—the controversial historical locus from which the zoo visitor's and the Western reader's gazes emanate—that has irrevocably shaped and altered the reception of third-world texts and identities. What are some of the consequences?

Mimeticism and Visuality: Going beyond Poststructuralism

Public zoos and national allegories, taken in this manner, may be understood to constitute, once again, the parameters of a kind of captivity narrative, in which nonwhite ethnicity and its cultural (re)production are continually ensnared in modernity. I believe this narrative can be probed much further through a return to a familiar representational issue, that of mimeticism.

For Plato, the consideration of mimesis was bound up with an implicit visuality—with the image it produces. Mimesis disturbed Plato because the image it produces is duplicitous: by confusing reality and falsehood, such an image charms and gives pleasure, and thus misleads people. (Plato's famous example is the painted picture of a table, which is, to him, twice removed from reality: it is a reflection of the carpenter's table, which is itself an imperfect reflection of the ideal form of the table in the mind of God.) The trickiness of this implicit relation between mimesis and visuality consists in the following: for those who distrust it, mimesis is suspect because it results in an objectified image, yet the image is, ultimately, not the problem; the *act* of imitating, of copying, is. If there is a certain iconophobia involved in the classic Platonic misgiving about mimesis, it is because the image is a byproduct of the process of mimesis. In other words, iconophobia, which is irrefutably present, must be understood as inherent in but subordinate to the phobia about imitation itself.[6]

In contemporary, poststructuralist debates about representation, the precise nature of this relation of mimesis and visuality tends to be sidestepped because the mimetic, whenever it is brought up, is usually relegated to the order of naive referentialism and dismissed *tout court*. As a result of this programmatic rejection of the mimetic as such, mimesis and what comes with it, the image, tend either to be jointly repudiated and discarded or else to have their relation fundamentally severed. In the first instance, in the kind of vigilant textualism inspired by Paul de Man and the early Jacques Derrida, the image tends, it seems, to be conflated with mimetic reflectionism, and image and mimesis are discredited together on account of the illusions of spontaneity they engender. The practice of deconstruction that focuses on textuality is, thus, at once antimimetic and iconophobic. In the second instance, iconophobia is replaced by an apparent euphoria about the image, but only in such a way that the image is now cut off from mimesis altogether and attains an independent life of its own. One thinks here of the work of Jean Baudrillard and the rich varieties of cultural studies that have followed its lead, wherein the image is granted an increasingly sexy, autonomous status to the point that it turns into a simulacrum, a virtual presence that is no longer tied to any original,[7] that is altogether "free of mimetic responsibility,"[8] as it were.

In both of these major poststructuralist tendencies, the culprit that is thoroughly spurned is the act of imitation, which is now considered a bankrupt ideology from which avant-garde theorists feel obligated to disaffiliate themselves. Martin Jay sums up this situation succinctly: "For . . . theorists . . . normally labeled, for better or worse, poststructuralist, a conventional aesthetic privileging of mimesis or what is taken to be its synonym, imitation, is an ideologically suspect recirculation of the ready-made, a false belief in the fixity of meaning and the possibility of achieving full presence, a language game that fails to see itself as such."[9]

While some critics, such as Baudrillard, continue to hold on to the image—albeit only by drastically rewriting the terms of its existence—poststructuralism comes, by and large, to stand for a process of deconstructing essences, origins, closures, reproductionisms, and reflectionisms, a process that firmly keeps its critical distance from any kind of visual, sensuous, or mimetic immediacy. However, in even the most rigorous efforts made by poststructuralists to dissociate themselves from the retrograde crimes of imitative, imagistic correspondence, there nonetheless lingers a fascination with mimeticism as an older—indeed, anthropologically primitive—mode of representation, wherein a magical, immanent resemblance between sign and thing can somehow still be fantasized, imagined, posited. The best example of this nostalgia for mimesis-cum-image, and image-cum-mimesis, a nostalgia that manifests itself in the midst of antimimetic, anti-imagistic poststructuralist critique, is, as I demonstrated in the preceding chapter, Derrida's vision, in his early work, of the Chinese language as (predominantly) ideographic.

This conundrum of an avant-garde writing that so radically dismantles mimesis-as-image, and image-as-mimesis, yet simultaneously (re)locates what it dismantles in cultures considered more ancient and primitive, means that poststructuralist thinking has tended to leave untheorized exactly those cross-cultural representational issues in which mimeticism, often in close affinity with visuality, is still steadfastly in play. The controversial notions of imitating or becoming (like) someone else; of reproducing a language, a practice, or a lifestyle that exists in a different cultural context; of measuring a later text against an earlier one, and so forth—all such notions run deep in the current discussions about identity, disguise, simulation, translation, appropriation, assimilation, passing, and speaking for others. In these hotly debated topics lie the unresolvable implications, first, of the ineluctability of repetition, duplication, and replay (processes that are often visually mediated) between different sets of cross-cultural phenomena; and, second, of the extreme difficulty of evaluating, of assigning appropriate significance to such phenomena when the conditions of exchange remain massively uneven and unequal.

Three Levels of Mimeticism in Postcolonial Cultural Politics

In cross-cultural situations in which the history of colonialism has played a part, mimeticism is further complicated by the fact that it is, often, an existential as well as a representational issue: just as there are texts that are considered to be imitating reality, so, too, are there human beings who are considered to be mimicking others in order to exist as themselves. In both cases, it is easy to understand why mimeticism has such explosive ramifications, for it touches on precisely mutually implicated questions such as: what/who is there first, and what/who is second? What/who is the more authentic? What/who is the copy, the "mere" reproduction? Because both the literary representational and the existential dimensions of mimeticism are intensely and intertwiningly in play, the experience of reading third-world literature, for instance, can no longer be confined purely to one dimension or the other. The question is no longer simply what such literature represents (what reality—national, literary, generic, cultural?) but also to whom such literature refers (the white man? the person of color? the racial and cultural hybrid?). In addition to the question of what is being imitated is now the question of who is imitating whom and how agency should be imagined. Does agency lie with the originator or with the mimic? What kind of agency? Once the extent of these questions is grasped, we will have to recognize that mimeticism is, perhaps, the central problematic in cross-ethnic representation in the postcolonial world.

I would like to propose that there are, in this context, at least three levels of mimeticism working in an overlapping, overdetermined manner at all times. While these levels can, in actuality, never be clearly or entirely separated from one another, for the sake of analysis, let me attempt to describe briefly how each functions.

The first level of mimeticism has to do with the imperative, created by Western imperialism and colonialism of the past few hundred years, of the white man as the original. The economics involved here is familiar to most of us: the white colonizer, his language, and his culture stand as the model against which the colonized is judged; the latter is expected to imitate, to become like her master, while knowing full well that her efforts at imitation will forever remain unsatisfactory. The colonized, her language, and her culture are thus relegated to the position of the inferior, improper copy. The values involved are hierarchically determined and tend to work in one direction only: the original, so to speak, exists as the sole, primary standard by which the copy is judged, but not vice versa; the white man, and the white man alone, is authentic. Condemned to a permanent inferiority complex, the colonized subject must nonetheless try, in envy, to become that from which she has been excluded in an a priori manner. She is always a bad copy, yet even as she continues to be debased, she has no choice but to continue to mimic. She is damned if she tries; she is damned if she doesn't.

The second level of mimeticism complicates the first in that the existential efforts made by the colonized, rather than being dismissed as inadequate, begin to assume a certain complexity. The elaboration of the colonized's state of mind, then, essentially constitutes the main debates in contemporary postcolonial studies. As exemplified by the work of Homi Bhabha, such debates tease out an important feature of the colonized's subjectivity that was previously ignored: the ambivalent wishes and resentments embedded in her identitarian plight. If, as Frantz Fanon writes, for the person of color (in Fanon's case, the black man), "there is only one destiny. And that is white," Bhabha's work has provided a series of attempts to follow up on Fanon's suggestion that "only a psychological interpretation of the black problem can lay bare the anomalies of affect that are responsible for the structure of the complex"[10]—that is, the complex of trying to become white. Bhabha sums up Fanon's critical contributions to the understanding of the colonized subject in this manner: "That familiar alignment of colonial subjects—Black/White, Self/Other—is disturbed . . . and the traditional grounds of racial identity are dispersed, whenever they are found to rest in the narcissistic myths of negritude or white cultural supremacy." In Fanon's work, he writes, "the ambivalent identification of the racist world . . . turns on the idea of man as his alienated image; not Self and Other but the otherness of the Self inscribed in the perverse palimpsest of colonial identity."[11]

By following Fanon, Bhabha elevates the issue of colonized existence to a considerably more sophisticated, because psychologically nuanced, theoretical level. Rather than simply lacking, the colonized is now seen in terms of a *desire* to be white, which exists concurrently with the shame accompanying the inferior position to which she has been socially assigned. In the black man's existential angst, in his inability to control his physical body completely (he is fatefully bound to his skin color and thus to the disdained image it projects) and make it confirm to the model set by his white master, Bhabha has carved out an entire epistemological space that, in turn, makes it possible for various projects theorizing postcolonial subjectivities to emerge. He does this by transforming all the previously hierarchized but immobilized relations between the colonizer and the colonized into a fluid, because vacillating, structure, in which the thoroughly entangled feelings of wanting at once to imitate the colonizer and to murder him become the viable basis for a new kind of analysis, with the tormented psychic interiority of the colonized as its center. Whereas, at the first level of mimeticism, these same feelings would simply relegate the colonized to the position of the irrevocably subaltern, in the kind of analysis Bhabha helps to open up, these feelings stand, instead, as elements of a resilient—indeed, mobile—framework for conceptualizing dominated selfhood.

Although it in no way denies the harsh objective reality of colonialism, then, Bhabha's reading allows for an alternative approach to such reality by focusing on the colonized person as an indeterminate, internally divided subject, a subject that, in the language of poststructuralism, is not self-identical. The redemption of this split subject at the level of a libidinal economy thus marks the critical *humanistic* turn of this second level of cross-ethnic mimeticism, and, as is consistent with such humanism, it is the failure, the incompleteness of the mimetic attempt (a point on which the second level of mimeticism, in fact, concurs with the first) that makes the nonwhite subject theoretically interesting. Consciously or unbeknownst to herself, and vacillating between black and white, the colonized subject is now pluralized and multiplied in a poststructurally informed, neoliberalist manner. No longer rigidly polarized against each other, black and white can now be considered as mutually constituted.

Importantly, insofar as it adheres to the deconstructive strategy of rendering identity opaque with a difference or plurality from within, Bhabha's approach to mimesis is a negative one. His work is staunchly critical of representation defined as analogical consciousness and as visual resemblance; by the terms of my discussion, it is, ultimately, iconophobic.[12] For Bhabha, subjectivity is a matter of resistance against the imagistic framings of identity, a resistance that "eludes the eye, evacuates the self as site of identity and autonomy," and so forth.[13] Meanwhile, insofar as it moves away from the conservative understanding of colonialist ideology as monolithic and invariably dogmatic toward a flexible one in which it is seen as ambi- or multivalent, dialogic, polyphonic, and heterogeneous, Bhabha's postcolonial criticism tends, also, to underscore Mary Louise Pratt's point that "ideology works through proliferation as well as containment of meaning."[14] Is this perhaps the reason this criticism has commanded such popularity in an academic environment already predisposed toward variations, transformations, and novelizations—that is, toward the proliferation of meaning on which the logic of capitalism thrives? In the end, Bhabha's conception of the resistance and subjectivity of the colonized subject does not seem essentially distinguishable from his conception of the productivity of colonial power: in both cases, it is the ambivalences, the contradictions, and the fissures, always already inherent to the dominant modes of articulation, that open things up, so to speak. What is the genuine import of such openings? Whom do they benefit? These questions will no doubt persist.

In the general preoccupation with this second level of mimeticism—a mimeticism that assumes the antistance of resistance but is still, by and large, governed by the white man as the original, with the supposedly important difference that the unsuccessful imitation of the colonized subject is now deemed equally worthy of critical attention—cultural theorists have, to my mind, neglected and perhaps bypassed a third level of mimeticism, namely, the level at which the ethnic person is expected to come to resemble what is recognizably ethnic. This is also the level at which the intimate mutual implications between mimeticism and visuality need yet again to be foregrounded, albeit in a different manner. What makes this third kind of mimeticism intriguing is that the original that is supposed to be replicated is no longer the white man or his culture but rather an image, a stereotyped view of the ethnic: I am referring to the "Asianness," "Africanness," "Arabness," and other similar kinds of nativenesses with which ethnics in North American society, for instance, are often expected to conform. This level of mimeticism can in one way be analyzed, as I have argued elsewhere, by way of the problematic of cultural authenticity and nativism.[15] In the terms of the present discussion, I propose that it be defined as a coercive mimeticism—a process (identitarian, existential, cultural, or textual) in which those who are marginal to mainstream Western culture are expected, by way of what Albert Memmi calls "the mark of the plural,"[16] to resemble and replicate the very banal preconceptions that have been appended to them, a process in which they are expected to objectify themselves in accordance with the already seen and thus to authenticate the familiar imagings of them as ethnics. Coercive mimeticism demands that the ethnic occupy a space in modern Western society that is categorically equivalent to that of the caged animals described by John Berger; it is thus, arguably, the very mechanism that holds together the fabric of this particular captivity narrative. In his provocative remarks on what he calls the fugitive poses and interimages of the Indian in American society, Gerald Vizenor describes the workings of coercive mimeticism as follows:

> The *indian* is a daemon, a modernist simulation of the other in the wicked cause of savagism and civilization. The *indian* daemon is a perverse misnomer, a concoction of aversions, curious notions, and "traditions" in the name of a native absence. The eversion of native stories in translation has been cited as *indian* in cultural studies and histories. That eversion is an inane union of other names, such as *indian* traditions, *indian* shamanism, *indian* values, *indian* humor, *indian* arts, *indian* identity, the *indian* way, *indian* alcoholism, *indian*

scapegoat, and the *indian* tragedy. The *indian* as mythic daemon, and the new *indian* as natural ecologist, are secured in social sciences theses, motion pictures, literature, and in national histories. The *indian* daemon is maintained by the enervation of native reason, and the absence of native differences; the *indian* is the absence of natives in the course of modernity.[17]

The question that remains is how coercive mimeticism is actively put into practice—how does it materialize? If the colonized subject that is being theorized at the second level of mimeticism is a neurotic being permanently shuttling back and forth between black and white but basically still identified with whiteness as the ultimate superior value, what is the condition of the ethnic subject who feels she must try to resemble, to appear as herself—to be ethnic? In the first place, how would such a requirement become internalized or incorporated?

The Interpellation of the Ethnic Subject

For readers acquainted with Louis Althusser's argument in the classic essay "Ideology and Ideological State Apparatuses,"[18] an ethnic person's practice of internalizing a cultural stereotype of herself may conveniently be explained by way of what Althusser calls interpellation. Whereas Althusser's frames of reference are religion and the state—so that the hailing of "Hey, you!" is either from the church, the police, or the various apparatuses of civil society—in the realm of ethnic politics, the "Hey, you!" is, we may argue, issued in the form of what Jameson calls "community interdependence"—that is, the ensconcing of the individual within the confines of her ethnic ghetto. Moreover, the ethnic is being hailed not only from within the ghetto but also predominantly from the outside, by the cultural critics (the zoo gazers) who are altruistically intent on conferring on her and her culture a radical meaning, one that is different from the norm of their own society. As is well known, Althusser's suggestive model of internalization has been criticized on many fronts for its seemingly monolithic nature; such a model, it is often said, deprives the interpellated person of her agency to respond with variation or to reject the call altogether. This line of criticism usually appeals to a subject, a will, or an agency that implicitly preexists (or exists beyond) the act of interpellation, and that, therefore, is more or less at liberty to resist the overpowering stamp it bears.

Slavoj Žižek, on the other hand, has offered a theoretically divergent reading of Althusser's argument. Instead of countering Althusser with the usual critical move premised on a resistive subject or individualist agency, Žižek uses what appears to be the weakness in Althusser's argument to argue for—to complete—the latter's implicit but insufficiently articulated logic.

Žižek's reading depends on the recognition that there is, indeed, something irrational in the subject's interpellation process as described by Althusser. He points out that Althusser somehow could not explain how the subject internalizes her interpellation by ideology—that is, how she becomes this thing that she is hailed as. But whereas others tend to seize this lacuna in Althusser by arguing that this is precisely where the subject may rebel against, elude, or ignore the interpellation (an argument that inevitably returns one to the individual with an agency that exists outside, before, or after the hailing), Žižek uses it, instead, to draw attention to (what he calls) the excessive traumatic kernel, a leftover or residue that, by structural necessity, cannot be fully absorbed by the process of internalization but that, paradoxically, helps the latter finish off its task of suturing the subject: *"This leftover, far from hindering the full submission of the subject to the ideological command, is the very condition of it."*[19] In other words, precisely where there is a gap—precisely where it is mysterious how the interpellated subject accepts and internalizes her hailing by the social apparatus—there also is a leap of faith that enables ideology to patch over the fissure, the hole that gapes between the world and the subject. The internalization of interpellation is none other than such an (irrational and senseless) act of patching over, of stitching together this chasm.

Žižek's way of understanding interpellation provides a distinctively different kind of argument about agency and the politics that surrounds it. For Žižek, interpellation succeeds not because those who are being interpellated cannot see through its manipulation (that is, not because they are filled with false consciousness or misguided by lies) but because there occurs at a certain moment in the interpellative process a necessary leap, which pulls together the otherwise irreconcilable gap between the subject per se and the objective reality to which the subject is hailed to respond. The point of interest—for him, at least—is not whether there exists a resistive subject who may or may not answer the call; rather, it is that, only by answering such a call, only by more or less allowing one's self to be articulated in advance by this other, symbolic realm, can one avoid and postpone the terror of a radically open field of significatory possibilities. If one must speak of resistance, Žižek's argument implies, what the subject always resists is this *terror of complete freedom* rather than the ideological, institutional process of being interpellated. (The latter case, unfortunately, is how most of Althusser's critics have countered his argument—that is, by defining resistance as a resistance against the institutional process of interpellation itself.) From this, it follows that identity—be it civic, religious, institutional, or cultural—is the result not exactly only of an imposition of rules from the outside or only of a resistance against such an imposition; it is also the result of a kind of *unconscious automatization, impersonation, or mimicking,* in behavior as much as in psychology, of certain beliefs, practices, and rituals. It is such automatization, impersonation, and mimicry that, in turn, give that identity its sense of legitimacy and security—and, ultimately, its sense of potentiality and empowerment.

To complete this portion of my argument, let me suggest that ethnic identity in multicultural Western society, too, may be conceived through this irrational process of being interpellated. As Tomo Hattori writes, ethnic identity thus interpellated is "simply the residue of a trauma that cultural nationalism cannot resolve in its encounter with the material political and economic forces of the modern world."[20] The fashionable talk these days of performing ethnicity—Asian, Asian American, Latino, black, and so forth—is in part the mimetic enactment of the automatized stereotypes that are dangled out there in public, hailing the ethnic: "Hey you! You X!" Does the ethnic have a choice of not responding? What happens when she responds? How might she respond? What happens if she does not respond?

I Confess, Therefore I Am

Žižek's completion of Althusser's argument—through his own reading of Lacan—resonates with the argument I have already made in chapter 1. Whereas Žižek explains interpellation in the metaphysical terms of ontological terror, which is something to be avoided at all costs, in Weber's analysis the comparable sociological explanation comes by way of the beneficial rewards of wealth and grace that religiously mediated, capitalist productionism entails. In both accounts, moreover, the implicit or explicit articulation of subjectivity is anchored much less in the (ideological) assumption of the subject's so-called resistance than in an inherently paradoxical, frequently self-contradictory, but nonetheless effective set of give-and-take mechanisms that, once set in motion, makes it possible for the subject to function rationally in the modern world.

Still, how exactly does interpellation, as such, actualize on the plane of representation—how does it happen in the material processes of reading and writing? In Jameson's example, we witness the issuing of a call (to the third-world difference), but how is such a call answered, reciprocated, echoed—and only thus becomes reproducible? Rather than simply being identified as a thematic or as an idea, how is psychological subjection to be discerned in the specificities of form? In other words, if the interpellation of the ethnic subject is, in the end, about the successful internalization and incorporation of a hailing from the outside, how is such interpellation detectable symptomatically in the actual instances of cultural representation? If the answer to this within Weber's sociological framework is the work ethic, what is the equivalent of the work ethic in the (cultural representational) realms of writing and reading? What is the phenomenon symptomatic of a ferocious and well-rewarded productionism in contemporary cultural/ethnic politics?

I would suggest that the pivotal case in point here is the turn toward the self, especially the ethnic self—as a form of production. The Western sense of self, writes James Clifford, hinges on two things: first, property *ownership*, and, second, the *exhibition* of what is being owned.[21] Accordingly, it is objecthood, rather than subjecthood, that defines the self—hence the title of Clifford's essay "Objects and Selves." This point can be used as yet another way of elaborating the problematic of the protestant ethnic. In order to be, this ethnic must both be seen to own her ethnicity and to exhibit it repeatedly. This repeated exhibition nowadays tends to take the form of confession, an act that, in the terms of this discussion, may be renamed *self-mimicry*.

The logic that leads to the contemporary ubiquity of confession is simple (albeit fallacious): if even the most apparently objective discussion of another culture could become suspect of the lack of proper representational delegation, and thus of sexual, racial, or class discrimination,[22] does not that mean that one should refrain from referring to others altogether (in the spirit of "I must not commit the indignity of speaking for others") and, instead, refer only to oneself? Does not that mean that representation should, by necessity, become self-referential?

To a large extent, these (misguided) questions have already been answered in the positive by the overwhelming popularity of self-referential genres, such as autobiographies, memoirs, journals, and diaries, in contemporary cultural politics. Nor is the self-referential turn restricted to these publications only; it is increasingly being favored as well in scholarly venues such as critical essays, forums, conferences, and public lectures. One theoretical explanation for this overwhelming tendency toward self-representation is provided by Jean-François Lyotard's well-known argument about the postmodern condition.[23] Postmodernity, according to Lyotard, is a time when metanarratives—that is, the stories and theories that used to have universal explanatory power—have lost their legitimation; people's experiences and the languages they once had at their disposal to comprehend these experiences have become incommensurate. One outcome of such incommensurability is an increasing relativism in representation, since, with the demise of the justifications provided by metanarratives, all experiences now *seem* to be equally valid. It follows that such relativism would find its appropriate expression in self-referential articulations. By capturing the unique, the solitary, and the particularistic, and by not making general claims, self-referential articulations now seem to many to be the only acceptable type of representation.

And yet, even as we understand the trend of self-referentiality as the result of an epochal transformation of the ethics of representing others—a transformation that questions the politics of "speaking for" that divides representer from represented (a politics that is, incidentally, often criticized by way of a condemnation of stereotypes)—the turn toward the self, together with the accompanying claim that metanarratives no longer exist or hold relevance, is far from being unproblematic.

Historically, the belief that a turn to the self is emancipatory is as old a myth as the Enlightenment. The emergence of the self as such, argues Michel Foucault, is, on the contrary, part of a changing organization of power in Western society: whereas power in the ancient world used to be concentrated among a few persons at the top of society, it is, in modernity, widely distributed among society's members, down to the details of the care and uses of the most private areas of existence. Considered in this light, the self and the so-called freedom that comes with it, a freedom that is always imagined as freedom from power and from domination, are, strictly speaking, effects of power; the free or freed individual as such is already a representation of the changing conceptions of power from an absolute-monarchical to an institutional-disciplinary basis. Foucault sums up this paradoxical situation in this statement: "The 'Enlightenment', which discovered the liberties, also invented the disciplines."[24]

To the extent that self-referentiality has increasingly acquired legitimacy as a resistive, liberatory, and thus corrective form of discourse (aimed at setting us free from the fetters of conventional representation), Foucault is perceptively precise on the predicament we face in the age of raised political consciousness. The trap that many fall into when they turn to self-referential genres as a way out of metanarratives, out of the crime of speaking for others, is that of the age-old realist fallacy, which allows them to attribute to self-referentiality the capacity for an unproblematic representation of reality, in this case, the reality of the self. The fantasy they tend to harbor is that the act of referring only to the self can finally redeem us from the fundamental and contentious binary structure of representation in which one is always (inevitably) speaking of/for something or someone else. Presumed to be direct and unmediated, the act of referring to oneself has taken on the aura of a type of representation that can miraculously transcend the limits of representation, a type of representation that, however trivial and self-aggrandizing it might be, is morally justifiable because it is (thought to be) *non-representational*. Such self-representation is now equated with the expression of truth.

Foucault describes this phenomenon, which he terms confession, in the following manner:

> Western man has become a confessing animal.
>
> Whence a metamorphosis in literature: we have passed from a pleasure to be recounted and heard, centering on the heroic or marvelous narration of "trials" of bravery or sainthood, to a literature ordered according to the infinite task of extracting from the depths of oneself, in between the words, a truth which the very form of the confession holds out like a shimmering mirage. Whence too this new way of philosophizing: seeking the fundamental relation to the true, not simply in oneself—in some forgotten knowledge, or in a certain primal trace—but in the self-examination that yields, through a multitude of fleeting impressions, the basic certainties of consciousness. The obligation to confess is now relayed through so many different points, is so deeply ingrained in us, that we no longer perceive it as the effect of a power that constrains us; on the contrary, it seems to us that truth, lodged in our most secret nature, "demands" only to surface; that if it fails to do so, this is because a constraint holds it in place, the violence of a power weighs it down, and it can finally be articulated only at the price of a kind of liberation. Confession frees, but power reduces one to silence; truth does not belong to the order of power, but shares an original affinity with freedom: traditional themes in philosophy, which a "political history of truth" would have to overturn by showing that truth is not by nature free—nor error servile—but that its production is thoroughly imbued with relations of power. The confession is an example of this. (1:59–60)

In Foucault's analysis, self-referential speaking is not only *not* the individual or unique way out of the errors of representation that it is often imagined to be; it is also the symptom of a collective subjection. To represent, to examine, to confess about oneself incessantly are compulsive acts that imagine the self as a refuge beyond the reach of power—an alibi from speaking (of anything), so to speak—when the self is simply a relaying vehicle for institutional forces of rational systematization at the individual level. In the United States, illustrations of this phenomenon are found abundantly on televised talk shows, which, by staging individual confessions in spectacular public forums, only serve to amplify the fact that in order for the self to make sense, certain kinds of metanarratives must somehow remain in place.

From the perspective of ethnicity and feminism, the logical conclusion from Foucault's analysis is, quite clearly, unappealing and unflattering. It demonstrates that the supposed radicalization performed by race and gender awareness on representation—by the insistence on the marginal, the local, the personal, and the autobiographical, for instance—needs to be modified by an understanding of the symbiotic relation between the radical and power as such. Within this relation, resorting to the self-referential gesture as an ethnic and/or sexual minority is often tantamount to performing a confession in the criminal as well as noncriminal sense: it is to say, "Yes, that's me," to a call and a vocation—"Hey, Asian!" "Hey, Indian!" "Hey, gay man!"—as if it were a crime with which one has been charged; it is to admit and submit to the allegations (of otherness) that society at large has made against one.[25] Such acts of confession may now be further described as a socially endorsed, coercive mimeticism, which stipulates that the thing to imitate, resemble, and become is none other than the ethnic or sexual minority herself. When minority individuals think that, by referring to themselves, they are liberating themselves from the powers that subordinate them, they may actually be allowing such powers to work in the most intimate fashion—from within their hearts and souls, in a kind of voluntary surrender that is, in the end, fully complicit with the guilty verdict that has been declared on them socially long before they speak.

Coercive Mimeticism as Pedagogy: the Example of Chinese Literature

How might this mimeticist understanding of self-referentiality in the contemporary age be extended to the institutional dissemination of knowledge? If ethnics are being interpellated by society at large to confess being themselves, what does this mean in terms of the pedagogical practices of reading texts? How does mimeticism work in the disciplinary consumption of literature, for instance?

Within academic discourse, the flip side to Jameson's first-world assertion of third-world literature as national allegories, I believe, is the tendency, on the part of many ethnic critics, to insist on demonstrating in third-world or non-Western subjects and texts an incontrovertible ethnic truth and essence. Insofar as it complies with the demand that ethnic texts (be made to) yield up their ethnic secrets, this critical tendency, too, amounts to a confessional act in the historical sense mentioned above, albeit not a private or personal one. To give one example, when discussing contemporary Chinese films, some Chinese critics not only affirm Jameson's argument that third-world texts are to be read as national allegories but add, unabashedly, that contemporary Chinese films are but "footnotes" to that argument.[26] I refer to this instance, however, not to chastise these critics but rather to underscore the following point: if ethnic subjects and texts, even when they are not necessarily speaking about their so-called ethnic difference per se, are habitually solicited in this manner by the public in the West and the world at large, can we really be surprised that ethnic critics internalize and reproduce precisely this kind of stereotyping of their culture and thus respond appropriately to their "hailing," as it were? Or would it not be logical to expect that all ethnics, critics and authors included, would unavoidably have to play to such a hailing by confessing to and assuming the ethnic roles—and opportunities—dangled in front of them? Indeed, ethnics' voluntary and involuntary manners of mimicking the ethnicity that is pre-scripted, pre-read, and pre-viewed in their utterances, attitudes, gestures, writings, behaviors, and psychologies must now be seen as part and parcel of the fraught dynamic of coercive mimeticism. And, if it is difficult for the ethnic to become a perfect imitation of the white man, it is even more difficult for her to become a perfect imitation of herself.

To see this, we need first to see the very different treatment white people in Western society receive in relation to their no less performative ethnicity. As Robyn Wiegman argues in her critique of the burgeoning academic discipline known as whiteness studies, the split white subject, that is, the white subject who nowadays endeavors to compensate for the historical "wrong" of being white by taking on politically correct agendas (such as desegregation) and thus distancing himself from his own ethnic history, is seldom if ever accused of being disloyal to his culture; more often than not, he tends to be applauded for being politically progressive and morally superior. However far he chooses to go, a white person sympathetic to or identifying with a nonwhite culture does not in any way become less white.[27] Similarly, a white critic choosing to dedicate himself to the study of a nonwhite literature remains firmly rooted in his own ethnic identity, and no one would dream of faulting him for being insufficiently American, English, French, or German simply because he has become intellectually interested in Africa, Asia, or Native American traditions. As Michelle Yeh points out, "No critic has ever suspected, much less declared, that in drawing on classical Chinese poetry for his imagist poetics, [Ezra] Pound lost his cultural identity as an American poet."[28]

When it comes to nonwhite peoples doing exactly the same thing, however—that is, becoming sympathetic to or identified with cultures other than their own—we get a drastically different kind of evaluation. If an ethnic critic should simply ignore her own ethnic history and become immersed in white culture, she would, needless to say, be deemed a turncoat (one that forgets her origins). But if she should choose, instead, to mimic and perform her own ethnicity in her work—that is, to respond to the hailing "Hey, you!" that is issued from various directions in the outside world—she would still be considered a turncoat, this time because she is too eagerly pandering to the orientalist tastes of Westerners. Her only viable option seems to be that of reproducing a specific version of herself—and her ethnicity—that has, somehow, already been endorsed and approved by the specialists of her culture. It is at this juncture that coercive mimeticism acquires additional significance as an institutionalized mechanism of knowledge production and dissemination, the point of which is to manage a non-Western ethnicity through the disciplinary promulgation of the supposed difference of its literary and cultural tradition. The pedagogy of Chinese literature in the English-speaking world serves as a good example of some of the issues at stake here.

A major assumption that binds the discipline of Chinese studies in the West, for instance, is that of an unproblematic linkage between Chineseness as such and Chinese literary writing. In such linkage, what is Chinese is often imagined and argued as completely distinct from its counterparts in the West, even as such counterparts are presumed and accepted as models or criteria for comparison. This systematically *reactive construction of a fictive ethnicity in literary studies* is,[29] arguably, best demonstrated in the prevalent belief held among some sinologists that ancient Chinese writing is distinguished by a nonmimetic and nonallegorical (as opposed to a mimetic and allegorical) tradition. Such a belief is, of course, fundamentally akin to the humanitarian impulses of post–Second World War anthropological culturalism, whereby it has become imperative, in the wake of the European Holocaust, to recognize and honor the differences among cultures. At this level, sinologists are operating from the same well-intentioned premises that inform Jameson's readings of third-world literatures. Where they part company with Jameson is the particular kind of investment they make in cultural difference. Whereas Jameson would locate that difference in the indistinguishability between private and public and thus in the generally politicized nature of third-world writings, for the sinologists, the assertion of the Chinese difference tends often to be made on supposedly intrinsic literary grounds. Beginning with a set of binary oppositions, in which the Western literary tradition is understood to be metaphorical, figurative, thematically concerned with transcendence, and referring to a realm that is beyond this world, they tend to conclude that the Chinese literary tradition is metonymic, literal, immanentist, and self-referential (with literary signs referring not to an otherworldly realm above but, instead, to the cosmic order of which the literary universe is part). The effort to valorize and promote China, in other words, is made through an a priori surrender to, rather than problematization of, Western perspectives and categories.[30] Accordingly, if mimesis is the chief characteristic of Western writing since time immemorial, then nonmimesis, the sinologists claim, is the principle of Chinese writing.[31]

In the insistent invocation of a Chinese tradition—and, with it, Chinese readers with Chinese habits, sensibilities, perspectives, points of view, and so forth—seldom, if ever, has the question been asked, what exactly is meant by "Chinese"? Why should it be necessary at all to reiterate what is Chinese in Chinese poetry by way of so-called Western attributes of poetic writing? What does it mean to supply this particular copula—to graft a term that is, strictly speaking, one of ethnicity, onto discourses about literary matters such as allegory? If the erudite and authoritative accounts of the sinologists have succeeded in explaining the formal details of texts (by expounding on literary and historical commentaries that deal with the various uses of poetic conventions, for instance), little, if anything, has been done about the nonliterary term "Chinese" even as it is repeatedly affixed to such studies. The (rhetorical) status of the term remains external to the formal issues involved, and the question of cultural difference, which such discussions of literary matters are supposedly addressing, simply refuses to disappear because it has, in fact, not yet been dealt with.

What happens as a result of latching the investigation of literary specificities to this unproblematized, because assumed, notion of Chineseness is that an entire theory of ethnicity—what we might call *the first-world hailing of the third-world difference*—becomes embedded (without ever being articulated as such) in the putative claims about Chinese poetics and literary studies. For instance, when it is assumed that poets, literati, commentators, and readers engage in literary practices in the Chinese way, the discourse of literary criticism, regardless of the intentions of the individual critic, tacitly takes on a cross-disciplinary significance to resemble that of classical anthropology. And, once classical anthropology is brought in, it becomes possible to see that the practitioners of Chinese writing—or the Chinese practitioners of writing—are, in effect, read as ethnics, or natives, who are endowed with a certain primitive logic. As the paradigm of anthropological information retrieval would have it, such treasures of primitive thought, however incomprehensible to the contemporary mind they may be (and precisely because they are so incomprehensible), must be rescued. The Western sinologist (who may or may not be ethnically Chinese) thus joins the ranks of enlightened progressives engaged in the task of salvaging the remains of great ancient civilizations. Since it is no longer possible to interview the natives of ancient China—the writers of classical Chinese narratives and poems and their contemporary readers—the texts left behind by them will need to be upheld as evidence of their essential ethnic difference.

But what is this essential ethnic difference? Paradoxically, it is, according to these sinologists, nonmimeticism, a way of writing and reading that is said to be natural, spontaneous, immanentist—and, most important, lacking in (the bad Western characteristics of) allegorical, metaphorical, and fictive transformation. While ostensibly discussing literary matters, then, these sinologists have, de facto, been engaged in the (retroactive) construction of a certain ethnic identity. The Chinese that is being constructed is, accordingly, a nonmimetic, literal-minded, and therefore virtuous primitive—a noble savage.

As readers will notice, I hope, the implications of this particular literary-ethnic scenario go considerably beyond the study of an esoteric literary tradition. Despite the humanitarian operational premise of these scholars, with their cry of "Let us give this other culture due recognition for its differences from ours!" the characterization of an entire group of people (the Chinese of ancient China) in such cognitive, psychological, or behavioral terms as a disposition toward nonmimetic literalness is, I contend, racist.[32] Such racism is, to use the words of Ien Ang, "reinforced precisely by pinning down people to their ethnic identity, by marking them as ethnic."[33] To use the words of Etienne Balibar, this is a racism "whose dominant theme is not biological heredity but the insurmountability of cultural differences." Culture, here, functions as "a way of locking individuals and groups a priori into a genealogy, into a determination that is immutable and intangible in origin."[34]

As is consistent with the Western study of non-Western cultures in modernity (in what is another major divergence between Jameson and the sinologists), it follows that antiquity remains privileged as the site of the essence of Chineseness, which appears to be more bona fide when it is found among the dead, when it is apprehended as part of an irretrievable past. Within the field of Chinese, then, the dead and the living are separated by what amounts to an entangled class and race boundary mediated by the implicit requirements of coercive mimeticism: high culture, that which is presumed to be original, authentic, and ethnically pure, belongs with the inscrutable and inimitable dead; low culture, that which is left over from the contaminating contacts with the foreign, belongs with those who happen to be alive and who can still speak and write. Yet, in the eyes of the specialists, those who are alive and who can still speak and write are never quite Chinese enough; they are, at best, poor imitations of the real thing.

The ideological contradictions inherent in the study of premodern Chinese writing are not exactly resolved in modern Chinese studies, but, because of the conscious efforts to politicize historical issues in modernity, scholars of modern Chinese literature are much more sensitized to the inextricable relation between formal literary issues and nonliterary ones such as ethnicity. In modernity, the equivalence between Chinese literature and Chineseness enjoys none of the comfortable security of the dead that it has in classical sinology. Instead, it takes on the import of an irreducibly charged relation, wherein the historicity of ethnicity haunts even the most neutral, objective discussions of *style*, resulting in various forms of mandated reflectionism.[35]

In his book *Rewriting Chinese*, Edward Gunn demonstrates how, in modern Chinese writing, literary style—a presumably formal matter involving rhetorical conventions that may be rationally explained through numerical analysis—has never been able to separate itself from tensions over regional diversities.[36] Since the early twentieth century, every attempt to stake new ground in Chinese literature through the recourse to more universal or global linguistic principles has, in turn, been weighed down and derailed by a corresponding set of demands about addressing specificities of native, local, rural, disenfranchised, and downtrodden voices, which, according to their defenders, have been left out and need to be given their place on the new stylistic ground. I think, for instance, of the May Fourth Movement of the late 1910s to the 1930s, with its advocacy for adopting Western linguistic styles in Chinese writing; the urbane Modernist Movement in the 1950s and 1960s in Taiwan, initiated by the Chinese elites who had left the mainland; the renewed attempts at modernizing Chinese fiction and poetry in the People's Republic in the 1970s and 1980s, after the climax of the Cultural Revolution. In retrospect, it is possible to say that the politics of style is as much an index to the organization of ethnicity inherent to nation building as more overt bureaucratic measures and that even the People's Republic's official strategies to stylize Chinese writing—to the extent of sacrificing "the aesthetic value of the unpredictable"—for the purpose of political cohesion must be seen as symptomatic of a postcolonial global modernity marked, as always, by massive ethnic inequalities.[37]

Interestingly, if we read such political strategies (to stylize and stabilize language) from a literary or representational perspective, we would have to conclude that, in the global scene of writing (understood as what defines and establishes national identity), third-world nations such as China have, in the modern era, been compelled into accepting—and thus incorporating within the national consciousness—a kind of collective linguistic/stylistic mandate under which writing has to be reflectionist, has to be an authentic copy of the nation's reality. From the standpoint of the Chinese state, it was as if Chineseness had, in the twentieth century, become the burden of an ethnicity that was marginalized to the point of unintelligibility—and the only way to be intelligible, to regain recognition in a world perpetually ignorant of and indifferent to Chinese history, is by going realist and mimetic: to institute, officially, that writing correspond faithfully to life of the Chinese nation as an ethnic unit.

In other words, the administering of writing in modernity, whether at the level of native intellectuals' advocacy for large-scale formal changes or at the level of explicit intervention by the revolutionary state, is always, ultimately, a regimenting or disciplining of ethnicity as a potentially disruptive collective problem. To this, we may add the work of cultural critics and area specialists (outside China) who are determined to argue for the Chinese difference.[38] It is in this light—the light of the politics of Chinese writing in *modernity*—that we may finally appreciate the full implications of sinological arguments about *ancient* Chinese writing. Like the Chinese political state, the sinology that specializes in classical Chinese poetics/narratology, insofar as it attempts to ground Chineseness in specific modes of writing, can also be seen as a kind of ethnicity-management apparatus. Once this becomes clear—that is, once the attempt to ground Chineseness is understood to be, in fact, a managerial operation dictated by extraliterary circumstances—the idealistic assertion of a nonmimetic, nonallegorical tradition that distinguishes Chinese writing, that makes Chinese literature *Chinese* literature, can only crumble in its own theoretical foundations. For isn't equating a definitive classification (the nonmimetic) with what is Chinese precisely a coercively mimeticist act—an act that, even as it claims to resist mimesis, squarely

reinscribes literary writing within the confines of a special kind of reflectionism—the reflectionism anchored in the referent "Chineseness"?

Mimeticism here is no longer simply a literary convention, however.
Rather, it is a type of representational copula-tion forged at the juncture
between literature and ethnicity, a duplication that, explicitly or implicitly, establishes equivalence between a cultural practice and an ethnic label—in the form of "Hey, this kind of poetic/narrative convention *is* Chinese!" In this equation, this act to validate a particular kind of writing
as ethnic difference per se, mimeticism, chastised though it may be, at the
formal level, as an evil Western tradition, returns with a vengeance as *the*
stereotyped way to control and police the reception of literary writing.
In the hands of the sinologists, even ancient poems and narratives are, it
turns out, documentaries—of what is Chinese, that radical third-world
difference. If Jameson's argument about third-world literature as national allegories has been ritualistically demonized for its theoretical imperialism, it is ironic that the same kind of criticism has not been laid at the
door of area specialists such as the sinologists, who have gone much further in nailing the third-world difference to the wall but have managed
to disguise their own theoretical imperialism (that is, their own reliance
on cultural stereotyping) by displacing it onto others. As I have been trying to indicate, the latter's institutional practices, while ostensibly engaged in the humanistic dissemination of knowledge about a non-Western culture, in fact also constitute an ideological apparatus that actively
interpellates the ethnic subject with rewards, the most important of
which is that of a compulsory self-ownership, a legitimate, but always
subordinate, social and cultural existence.

The Ethnic Body Without the Ethnic Language

In the study of an ethnic culture that is still considered "over there"
in another continent (such as China), the authority of knowledge is derived less from the embodiment of ethnic difference by persons of color
(such as Chinese Americans living in the United States) than from the ab-
sorption and cultivation of knowledge about that ethnic group by the so-
called specialists. In this regard, the ownership of ethnicity through the

ownership of the ethnic language remains a thorny issue. Since the ethnics that happen to be alive tend to be considered imperfect, because contaminated, copies of their culture, the language at their disposal and the manner in which they use it are also suspect. Hence a common criticism of modern and contemporary Chinese writers (poets, for instance) by Western sinologists is that they are too "Westernized"—specifically, that their use of the Chinese language is no longer sufficiently or authentically Chinese.[39] As I already mentioned, the same type of moral judgment simply does not apply in the case of the white Westerner fantasizing about, toying with, or seriously studying the Chinese language: these split Western subjects are, instead, lauded for their noble enthusiasm for a culture other than their own, while never having to worry about the indictment that they have become less authentic in their ethnic identity or that their English, French, German, or Dutch is no longer genuinely theirs.

What does the language issue tell us about the kind of *value* that is implicitly attached to a marginalized ethnicity in cross-ethnic representation? First, it is assumed that such ethnicity is something that can be lost in the contact with foreigners and needs to be protected. Second, although contact with others is inevitable, such ethnicity is often treated as if it were an essence beyond exchange and circulation. Third, those ethnics who are dead, it follows, are more safe in their ethnicity than those who are alive—and the more distant in time they are, the more authentic they are considered to be. Fourth, unlike the white man, who does not have to worry about impairing his identity even when he is touched by a foreign culture, the ethnic must work hard to keep hers; yet the harder she works at being bona fide, the more of an inferior representation she will appear to be. Fifth, and most disturbing of all, precisely because it occupies such an ideologically overdetermined position in modernity, such ethnicity can be used as a means of attacking others, of shaming, belittling, and reducing them to the condition of inauthenticity, disloyalty, and deceit, despite the fact that this historically charged, alienating situation is a collectively experienced one. Such attacks are, moreover, frequently issued by ethnics themselves against fellow ethnics, that is, the people who are closest to, who are most *like* them ethnically in this fraught trajectory of coercive mimeticism. (I will return to this last point in greater detail in the postscript.)

The issue of language-cum-ethnicity as embedded in the entire fabric of cross-ethnic representation must also be discerned in the context of ethnic studies in North America, where, in many cases, the investigation of ethnicity is no longer entirely or at all grounded in language pedagogy. To give the most obvious example, Asian American studies is conducted by and large in English, the medium in which Asian American authors compose their primary texts. Unlike the case of Asian studies, in which epistemic authority is still by and large disembodied in the sense that it is based on the academic, disciplinary incorporation, by specialists who may not themselves be Asian, of the languages and cultures of peoples who are "over there" on the other side of the world, in Asian American studies, epistemic authority is frequently and implicitly located in the bodies of the ethnics themselves. Hence the *imagistic, self-referential turn* and the *confessional mode of representation* are, arguably, deemed much more essential practices in the latter field. As Tomo Hattori has observed: "Asian American literature is still understood, for the most part, as literature written by Asian Americans."[40] Because many of them no longer have the claim to ethnic authority through the possession of ethnic languages, Asian Americans are perhaps the paradigmatic case of a coercive mimeticism that physically keeps them in their place—that keeps them, in Balibar's terms, in their *genealogy* and, I would add, in their *genre* of speaking/writing as nothing but *generic* Asian Americans. The visible, *genetic* signs of "ethnic difference" on their bodies—an accident of birth—become, in this light, the referential limits embedded in their otherwise proliferating discourse. (The *generative* logic of Foucault's repressive hypothesis, as discussed in the introduction, is fully at work here.) Without the authentication (however unsatisfactory) of the ethnic language, these bodies bearing the signs of otherness are adrift in a society that will only recognize their existence through the strategy of continual, systematic marginalization, through "the interpretive will to insert the qualities of the author's physical, racial body into the corpus of his textual output" (218).

Thus, although Asian American texts are overwhelmingly written and read in English, the national language of the United States and Canada, Asian American studies tends, to this day, to be programmatically segregated from the historical canon of American literature, even by those who welcome it into the melting pot of multiculturalism. More often than not, Asian American studies is grouped together with ethnic studies rather than with English studies, even though English studies should, properly speaking, long have been renamed Western European studies or British American studies—indeed, made a subspecialty of ethnic studies itself. This situation is what has led Hattori to call for "the gradual phasing out of the Ethnic Studies paradigm as we know it," the paradigm that is designed to keep "them" in their place:

> Rather than use race and ethnicity for the purpose of delineating the boundaries and specificities of cultures, voices, and essences (foundational concepts in the project of ethnic literary criticism), an anti-racist project aligned with the elimination of social oppressions and inequalities calls for the gradual phasing out of the Ethnic Studies paradigm as we know it. The retirement of the well-intentioned culturalist segregation under ethnicity would be accompanied by the abandonment of the models of impermeable individual identity, ethnic singularity, and cultural accommodation under nationalism that have been the foundations of Ethnic Studies discourse in the three decades that it has been in existence in the United States.[41]   (217)

The point of this chapter has been to demonstrate that any consideration of cross-ethnic representation would need to take into account the multiple, overlapping layers of projection, automatization, and self-ethnicization involved in the articulation of the ethnic subject and ethnic culture as such. The Western critic's earnest attempt at tracking down ethnic difference—of which Jameson's reading of third world national allegories is but one convenient example—is simply the first step in a complicated process in which incessant, ubiquitous interpellations and internalizations, accompanied by so many forms of confession, self-display, and conscious mimicry of ethnicity-as-object inform the politics of representation. Such politics may, as I have been arguing, be designated by the phrase "coercive mimeticism," a general cross-ethnic mechanism that provides the connection among otherwise disjointed events such as the pedagogical cultivation and circulation of arcane cultural knowledge; the activist clamor for institutional space for underrepresented disciplines (demonstrated, for instance, by students going on hunger strikes on campuses); and the ever-renewable government efforts to fabricate and stabilize the kind of genealogy mentioned by Balibar, in which ethnics can be securely contained (through surveys, statistics, scientific studies, intelligence networks, and police and immigration records). While they demand and reward the reiterations of self-mimicry in Western societies by Asian, Asian American, African American, Latino, and other such demographic groups, the forces of coercive mimeticism are ultimately what engender the profound sense of self-hatred and impotence among ethnics, because, however conscientiously they attempt to authenticate themselves—and especially when they attempt conscientiously—they will continue to come across as inferior imitations, copies that are permanently out of focus.

In the following chapter, I will discuss how compulsive self-referentiality in the case of ethnic narratives, far from being the royal road to existential freedom, often painfully unveils the abject reality of a thwarted collective narcissism.

CHAPTER 4

The Secrets of Ethnic Abjection

We were mongrels, confused children whose parents came from different worlds, which in our cases meant Asia and Europe. We were what was left after the collision; we were the things they had dropped on the floor. . . .

. . . We live on the poison we secrete, and spend our nights character-izing ourselves in derogatory terms. It is the only defense we know.

—John Yau, "A Little Memento from the Boys"

The Difference Revolution

An indispensable and indisputable accomplishment of poststruc-turalist theory in the past several decades has been the permanent unsettling of the stability of referential meaning, what had been pre-sumed to be anchored in the perfect fit between the signifier and sig-nified. We might say that what poststructuralist theory ushered in was the era of difference—to be further amplified as both the acts of differing and deferring—which would take the place of sameness as the condition for signification. As Ferdinand de Saussure's sum-mary statements indicate: "In language there are only differences. Even more important: a difference generally implies positive terms between which the difference is set up; but in language there are only differences *without positive terms*." "*Language is a form and not a substance.*"[1] With this difference revolution, it is no longer possible to speak casually about an anchorage for meaning: if the very ground of intelligibility itself is now understood as the temporal movement of differencing, a permanent process of delay and differentiation, then the old-fashioned presumption about epistemological groundedness cannot hold. In its stead, the conception of linguistic identity becomes structurally defined, with linguistic elements mutually dependent on one another for the generation of meaning.

Such a revision of the fundamental assumptions about signification (or what some would still prefer to call human communication) has major ramifications for many fields of study in the humanities and the social sciences, including those that seem at first to have only a distant relation with semiotics. It is not difficult to see that the most basic tenets of structuralist linguistics and semiotics—difference, identity, value, arbitrariness, convention, systematicity—carry within them connotations that have resonances well beyond the terrain of a narrow sense of language. Not surprisingly, therefore, one of the most productive uses of what I am calling the difference revolution is to be found in an area where existential identity itself is most at stake—the area of multiculturalism, postcoloniality, and ethnicity that is the focus of this book.

A theorist and critic such as Stuart Hall, for instance, astutely makes use of the poststructuralist dislocation of the sign to articulate a radically different manner of conceptualizing identity in the postimperialist, postcolonial age. In his well-known essay "Cultural Identity and Diaspora," Hall argues that there are at least two different ways of thinking about cultural identity. The first way reminds us of the prepoststructuralist sign, dedicated as it is to the production of a unified oneness anchored in specific locations and histories; the second way takes as its point of departure the ineluctable presence of difference:

> The first position defines "cultural identity" in terms of one, shared culture, a sort of collective "one true self," hiding inside the many other, more superficial or artificially imposed "selves," which people with a shared history and ancestry hold in common; . . . [the] second position recognizes that, as well as the many points of similarity, there are also critical points of deep and significant *difference* which

constitute "what we really are." . . . Cultural identity, in this second sense, is a matter of "becoming" as well as of "being." It belongs to the future as much as to the past.[2]

Hall's use of poststructuralism for an antiessentialist identity politics is especially germane for the histories of diasporic populations, who are, as a rule, caught among their original, native homelands, the lands of their colonizers, and (possibly also) the lands of their eventual settlement. Referring to the case of Caribbean identity, he points out that its construction moves through Africa and Europe, finally to arrive in the "Third, 'New World' presence"—"the juncture-point where the many cultural tributaries meet, . . . where strangers from every other part of the globe collided" (400). Hall goes on to describe the " 'New World' presence" as "itself the beginning of diaspora, of diversity, of hybridity and difference" (401). What defines diasporic realities, paradoxically, is what cannot be unified—"precisely the mixes of colour, pigmentation, physiognomic type; . . . 'blends' of tastes . . . the aesthetics of the 'cross-overs,' of 'cut-and-mix' " (402). For Hall, this new, hybrid space, which was derived from former cultural spaces but can no longer be reduced to them, is the paradigmatic space of diasporic identity—a type of identity that, much like the poststructural sign, is permanently in flux.

For an undoing of entrenched ways of approaching identity and cultural tradition, as Hall demonstrates, the relevance of the difference revolution cannot be emphasized enough. In retrospect, it is precisely the broad-minded work of theorists such as him that has made it possible for others working in similar areas to reconceptualize the existential issues accompanying cultural dislocation in the aftermath of Western imperialism and colonialism.[3] At the same time, it is important to remember that the flip side of the difference revolution is its refusal of reference, a refusal whose consequences are no less problematic for those engaged in postcolonial cultural and ethnic studies. In an essay published several years ago, for instance, Pheng Cheah challenges this notable encounter between poststructuralist theory and identity politics, which I just outlined by referring to the work of Hall, by questioning the philosophical bases that inform it.[4] Rather than using the term "difference," Cheah focuses on a special variety of difference—hybridity and hybridity theory—

as his primary concern. The drift of his critique, however, is commensurable with what I have been discussing as the legacy of poststructuralist theory, which Cheah examines in close relation to the concept of culture.

Cheah argues that, in their tendency to place an eminently positive value on tropes having to do with flux, activity, mobility, displacement, contingency, the indeterminacy of the sign, and so forth,[5] contemporary hybridity theorists—his primary examples being Homi Bhabha and James Clifford—are working largely within the framework, characteristic of philosophical modernity, in which culture—and, with it, the human acts of signification and symbolization—is assigned the status of *freedom from the given* ("given" in the sense of a predetermined condition, such as nature, for instance). "Contemporary postcolonial studies," Cheah writes, "has modulated from antiuniversalist/anticosmopolitan discourses of cultural diversity to discourses of cultural hybridity that criticize the neo-organicist presuppositions of the former" (160). What is significant in this modulation is that culture itself has taken on an emancipatory function as opposed to various forms of oppression. In terms of topography, then, what is given (that is, what is oppressive) tends to be imagined in terms of the stagnant, immobile, firmly-in-place, and unchanging, whereas the opposite tends to be viewed (by hybridity theorists) as inherently liberating. In the "translational understanding of transnationalism" often proposed these days, Cheah continues, "globalization . . . is reduced to cultural hybridization in transnational mobility" (167). As a result, "hybridity theorists are especially attracted to historical cases of migration and diasporic mobility because they see such cases as empirical instances of the flux they regard as the ontological essence of culture" (168), while "those postcolonials for whom postnationalism through mobility is not an alternative" (172) more or less fall outside the purview of such emancipationist, hybridist thinking. Because of this, hybridity theory is, Cheah concludes, a kind of "closet idealism" (172). What makes it idealist, I would add, is precisely the euphoric valorization of difference or, to be more accurate still, the hasty, optimistic replication of the difference revolution (together with its implied modes of mobility) as found in poststructuralist linguistics in the sociocultural and geopolitical realms.

Just how is the insufficiency of hybridity and the difference revolution to be grasped? In what kinds of situations does it become clear that a simple affirmation of hybridity, difference, and mobility and a refusal of reference fall short of being viable formulations? I believe Cheah's critique can also be understood in a somewhat less philosophical light. There is a way in which, in North America, at least, the current euphoria about hybridity must be recognized as part of a politically progressivist climate that celebrates cultural diversity in the name of multiculturalism, which, as a Western phenomenon, needs to be understood, as Barnor Hesse writes, "as discursively organised around the various discrepancies that circulate within the cultural afterlife of modern Europe's imperialisms."[6] In this context, the criticism voiced is often not so much an objection directed at multicultural hybridity itself as an attempt to call attention to what is effaced by its ostensible celebration.[7] Speaking of Canada's Multiculturalism Act, for instance, Smaro Kamboureli refers to such a state of affairs as a "sedative politics":

When the Canadian government introduced multiculturalism as an official policy in 1971, entrenched it in the Charter of Rights in 1982, and tabled the Canadian Multiculturalism Act in 1988, it made substantial proclamations of responsibility concerning ethnic diversity. The Multiculturalism Act (also known as Bill C-93) recognizes the cultural diversity that constitutes Canada, but it does so by practising a sedative politics, a politics that attempts to recognize ethnic differences, but only in a contained fashion, in order to manage them. It pays tribute to diversity and suggests ways of celebrating it, thus responding to the clarion call of ethnic communities for recognition. Yet it does so without disturbing the conventional articulation of the Canadian dominant society. The Act sets out to perform the impossible act of balancing differences, in the process allowing the state to become self-congratulatory, if not complacent, about its handling of ethnicity.[8]

What Kamboureli's passage clarifies is that the difference revolution, far from being simply the accomplishment of high theory, has, in fact, also taken place at the level of the official articulation of the political state—that it is none other than ethnic "difference" and "diversity" that the policy makers of Canada try rhetorically to encompass within the nation's raison d'être. Yet this awareness of difference, an awareness that, at the level of government policy, becomes an attempt to be inclusive and celebratory, serves, in the end, to mask and perpetuate the persistent problems of social inequality.[9]

M. Nourbese Philip, in a piece entitled "Why Multiculturalism Can't End Racism," puts it in a similar and more succinct manner: "The mechanism of multiculturalism is . . . based on a presumption of equality, a presumption which is not necessarily borne out in reality."[10] If, as Cheah writes, culture is imagined, in an a priori manner, as a kind of freedom from the given, then the presumption of equality to which Philip alludes can be translated as multiculturalism = freedom x multiple cultural times. For Philip, however, it is precisely this positive endorsement of culturalism (rather than a negative use of it as a way to point up the differences suppressed from normative reality) that is symptomatic of a certain blindness toward those inequalities that remain in the midst of multicultural enlightenment.[11] Chief of such inequalities is racism. Also addressing the situation of Canada, Philip writes:

> In short, multiculturalism, as we know it, has no answers for the problems of racism, or white supremacy—unless it is combined with a clearly articulated policy of anti-racism, directed at rooting out the effects of racist and white supremacist thinking.   (185)

> However, unless it is steeped in a clearly articulated policy of anti-racism, multiculturalism will, at best, merely continue as a mechanism whereby immigrants indulge their nostalgic love for their mother countries.

> At worst, it will, as it sometimes does, unwittingly perpetuate racism by muddying waters between anti-racism and multiculturalism. It is not uncommon to read material from various government departments that use these words interchangeably so as to suggest that multiculturalism is synonymous with anti-racism. It is not. It never will be.   (186)

In a different but comparable argument to Kamboureli's and Philip's, Philip Deloria has proposed, through his work on Native American culture, that multiculturalism, by assuming that identity is by choice and consent, is simply fraudulent.[12] As ethnic identities become part of a commodified global culture—a phenomenon Deloria demonstrates with the many forms of "playing Indian" in American and world history— there also remains an entrenched hostility toward those ethnics—often dispossessed, dislocated migrants—who are poverty-stricken.[13]

Let me sum up the points I have made so far in this brief opening discussion. First, poststructuralist theory has made a crucial contribution toward undoing the deadlock in signification by loosening the presumed fixed correspondence between signifier and signified. In terms of signification, difference rather than sameness now becomes the key to a radicalized way of thinking about identity. Second, one of the consequences of theory defined this way is the replication of the dislocated sign in the sociocultural frame of identity formation, so that (the experience of) dislocation per se, as it were, often becomes valorized or even idealized—as what is different, mobile, contingent, indeterminable, and so on. Third, as Pheng Cheah points out, these poststructuralist arguments about identity are, philosophically speaking, traceable to the same tradition in which culture itself is considered definitively as a form of emancipation from the tyranny of the given. Culture, in other words, occupies something of the status of difference, which is associated with fluidity and movement and thus with freedom. Obviously, this is not an entirely accurate view of culture, since, far from being essentially emancipatory, culture often also partakes of the constraints, oppressions, and inequalities of the given. Fourth, from this we may understand why culture in the plural—as multiple forms of differences, as cultural diversity, as multiculturalism—is fraught with unresolved tensions such as those of racism (inequality between different racial and/or ethnic groups) and class discrimination (inequality between groups of the same racial/ethnic background as well as between groups of different racial/ethnic backgrounds). In other words, once transposed into sociocultural and/or geopolitical terrains, the poststructuralist specialization in difference, a revolution on its own terms, appears quite inadequate in accounting for how the purportedly liberating movements of difference and hybridity can and do become hierarchically organized as signs of minoritization and inferiority in various contemporary world situations.

Ethnicity, Temporality, and Writing

What the foregoing indicates is that there is a certain rift between the laudable theorizations of difference, on the one hand, and the numerous sociocultural and/or geopolitical situations in which difference has led not so much to emancipation as to oppression, on the other. This rift—this incommensurability between what are, to my mind, equally compelling arguments about difference—is the key problem for any ethically responsible discussion of the politics of ethnicity today, and one ought not to think that a solution can be had simply by choosing one over the other. It would be more instructive to let the rift stand as a reminder of the ineluctable, overdetermined complexities at hand.

While I do agree with Cheah, Kamboureli, Philip, and Deloria in their persuasive critiques of the contemporary theoretical and/or institutional espousals of liberated culturalisms, I propose that something more must be at stake because of the strong, impassioned sense of discomfort they express toward such espousals. This something more needs, ultimately, to be grasped in terms of the politics of *writing*—and in particular the politics of writing about ethnic and multicultural identities in our post–civil rights age. To put it in a different manner, one of the issues that have surfaced prominently in the relevant debates is not cultural difference or ethnic diversity per se but rather a distinctive affective dissonance between theoretical writing, on the one hand, and fictional and autobiographical writing, on the other. It is, I believe, to this affective dissonance, which marks many plaintive responses to the euphoria about hybridity and multiculturalism theory, that we should be devoting more attention. For this reason, it is not sufficient simply to criticize theorists for ignoring the realities of cultural difference; it is more important, perhaps, to recognize that theoretical discourse itself, however attuned it may be to such realities, is always subject to its own discursive limit of rationalism and abstraction—a limit that translates into a necessary distance from the experiences being alluded to—in such a manner as to neutralize precisely the very emotional effects of injustice that persist as the remnants of lived experience. When critics protest against (poststructuralist) theory's inadequacy, they are implicitly alluding to these remnants of lived experience; consequently, it is also to the rift, the incommensurability, between theoretical and nontheoretical writing as such that they are unwittingly pointing.

Such affective dissonance may be further defined in terms of the difference between a conceptual, declarative mode of speech and an experiential, suggestive one. While the former, by its very operation, tends to be forward-looking—since the declarative enunciates by projecting ahead—the latter tends instead to double back on experiences that are felt to be not quite finished, whose effects are still with us, haunting us, and waiting for some kind of articulation, however inchoate such articulation might be. The difference between these two modes of speaking, expressed in this manner, is also a temporal disjunction, but this is not so much a disjunction simply among the future, the present, and the past as it is a matter of producing different—perhaps irreconcilable—values through varied relations to time, wherein time may be in the form of anticipation, of looking ahead, or in the form of memory, of revisiting in yet another way what has become past. With the foregrounding of time and value in writing, Cheah's point that hybridity theorists tend to associate hybridity with freedom can now be restated in this manner: freedom, as implied in the difference revolution and in hybridity theories, is the futurist, anticipatory mode of speech. Creative writers, on the other hand, tend to go in a different temporal direction because their mode of speech is derived from looking backward even as they are propelled forward in time: it is life remembered yet explored in language as though it were lived and grasped for the first time that constitutes the libidinal force of such writing. When the subject matter involved is of the nature of injustice—such as the controversial issues of ethnicity, cultural diversity, and racism—these fundamental discursive incommensurabilities in time (and its value production) simply become critical.

Such incommensurabilities at the level of writing regarding a similar set of social situations cannot exactly be characterized as a new problem. The closest parallel to our current concern is the well-known discussion in Marxist theory about literary writing and aesthetic representation—indeed, about the entire issue of reflection itself.[14] Albeit theoretically forward-looking, Marx and Engels, it should be remembered, were careful to advise writers who solicited their opinions not to turn literature into socialist propaganda in which fictional characters simply become mouthpieces for revolutionary doctrines. "The solution of the problem," writes Engels, "must become manifest from the situation and the action themselves without being expressly pointed out and . . . the author is not obliged to serve the reader on a platter the future historical resolution of the social conflicts which he describes."[15] Embedded in these discussions is an astute sense that theoretical and literary discourses are distinguished by an essential articulatory difference and that literary discourse, which specializes in indirection, can only become dull and mediocre should one turn it into a platform for direct proletarian pronouncements. Even where the subject matter cries out for justice to be done, literary writing tends to accomplish its task more effectively when it does not explicitly solicit the reader's sympathy. In literature, in other words, the modus operandi is not to speak about things expressly—even when one feels one must—in a way quite opposite to the clarity and forthrightness of theoretical argumentation. "The more the opinions of the author remain hidden, the better for the work of art"[16]: a very different kind of power for producing change, in other words, is in play. As David Craig puts it in a nutshell: "Surely, if literature affects action or changes someone's life, it is not by handing out a recipe for the applying but rather by disturbing us emotionally, mentally, because it *finds* us . . . , so that, after a series of such experiences and along with others that work in with it, we feel an urge to 'do something' or at least to ask ourselves the question (the great question put by Chernyshevsky, Lenin, and Silone): 'What is to be done?' "[17]

These are, of course, old and well-debated issues having to do with the politics of representation. My point in introducing them is not really to repeat arguments that many others have made before about the literary and nonliterary as such but rather to bring the gist of such arguments to bear on the politics of writing-in-ethnicity. For, as I have been suggesting throughout this book, the problem of ethnicity, much like that of the working class in nineteenth-century Europe, is precisely the problem of social liminality; it is, furthermore, a problem that finds itself both in the forefront of highly politicized and theorized debates and in the forefront of new ideas about literary writing. Yet, because of the limits set by each type of writing, this encounter—and collision—between theory and literature is always a difficult one. Today, with theory occupying a more or less hegemonic, managerial position in the humanities, it is not surprising that discourses about ethnicity constitute one of the places at which criticisms of theory's *oversight* are the strongest and most vociferous.

The incommensurabilities occasioned by hybridity are perhaps best seen in actual cases of authors who have been writing as cultural hybrids. I will turn next to a collection of personal essays edited by Garrett Hongo, *Under Western Eyes*, which offers excellent instances for furthering the discussion of the issues at hand.

Ethnicity, Autobiography, and Narcissism

If hybridity is, as Hall argues, the core of immigrant experience in the New World, and if immigrant writing, as Azade Seyhan points out, "is almost exclusively autobiographical in nature,"[18] what is the relation between hybridity and autobiography? How is it that a mode of experience that allows theorists an occasion to speak generally and abstractly about difference, hybridity, and freedom is, by contrast, always handled by nontheoretical writers in the autobiographical mode, in what seems to be a retreat into the personal, a withdrawal that is, in terms of temporality, a retrospective search, a looking back through the fragments of history? This discrepancy may be understood in part by way of the phenomenon of coercive mimeticism, which, as I suggested in the previous chapter, interpellates ethnic subjects into acts of confessions about themselves, in what may be called self-mimicry. But how does such self-mimicry feel for those performing it? I believe this question is best addressed by turning to what is perhaps the most banal, yet unshakable, issue of writing—the problematic of self-formation, around which ethnic hybridity produces important consequences. Hongo's collection, for instance, features a variety of autobiographical, personal voices, all of which acknowledge—indeed, take as their points of departure—the hybridized historical contexts in which they are speaking. Instead of a valorization of hybridity itself, however, what we discover is more often ambivalence, anger, pain, melancholy, shame, and abjection on the part of these authors. How might we elaborate this very different way of inscribing difference and hybridity?

When I taught Hongo's book, at least once I taught it in the context of an undergraduate course on narcissism. My point was to ask my students to see ethnicity and its representation in relation to a set of theoretical issues that were relevant to but seldom juxtaposed with them in this pedagogical manner. The vicissitudes of sexuality defined in the broad psychoanalytic sense provided a framework in which my students became able to read the personal essays in terms of the symptoms of a kind of narcissism that was, arguably, central to cultural self-formation in much of North American ethnic and immigrant writing. Again, it is important to emphasize that my intended focus, in that course as much as in the present chapter, is on writing: what kind of writing is possible under the conditions of cultural migration, of ethnicity hailed and refracted narcissistically through verbal language?

Contrary to the conventional associations of narcissism as an excessive selfishness, Freud, we recall, defines narcissism as an essential concomitant of life. Rather than a misplaced perversion, narcissism is, he argues, simply the basic instinctual mechanism of self-sustenance—"the libidinal complement to the egoism of the instinct of self-preservation, a measure of which may justifiably be attributed to every living creature."[19] And, yet, as in the case of human sexuality in general, things are never that simple. Among Freud's extended comments, the most thought-provoking is that narcissism is something we have to give up at an early point in our lives. He thus sets up a scenario for the unfolding of an inevitable psychological disorder: though essential to the human organism, narcissism is something that tends to be blocked—and out of reach. Narcissism, in other words, is constructed by Freud as a lost object, a part of the self that is, somehow, destined to becoming missing. This is the reason, he writes, that we tend to be attracted to those who appear narcissistic—who appear somehow not to have been obliged to surrender that precious, intimate relation with the self that we ourselves have been obliged to surrender. As we look with adoration on such still-narcissistic people, we are unconsciously reliving the part of ourselves that has been sacrificed. Freud's passage goes as follows:

It seems very evident that one person's narcissism has a great attraction for those others who have renounced part of their own narcissism and are seeking after object-love; the charm of a child lies to a great extent in his narcissism, his self-sufficiency and inaccessibility, just as does the charm of certain animals which seem not to concern themselves about us, such as cats and the large beasts of prey. In literature, indeed, even the great criminal and the humorist compel our interest by the narcissistic self-importance with which they manage to keep at arm's length everything which would diminish the importance of their ego. It is as if we envied them their power of retaining a blissful state of mind—an unassailable libido-position which we ourselves have since abandoned. (113)

If narcissism is, libidinally speaking, about self-preservation, why is it also something we have to give up? What are the factors that extirpate it, and what is the cost of this to those who can no longer be healthily narcissistic? Approached in these terms, Freud's conceptualization of narcissism does not simply teach it as a love of the self but rather paves the way for a cultural theory to be formulated as to how even something as fundamental as self-preservation is always mediated and *assailed* by social forces. Because of the likelihood of a conflictual encounter between self and society, narcissism is capable of becoming a disorder. The rest of his essay goes on to argue how "self-regard"—in the visual as well as social senses of the term—is the complicated result of the self's negotiations with the observing collective conscience ("The institution of conscience was at bottom an embodiment, first of parental criticism, and subsequently of that of society" [118]): how we look at ourselves and how much we value ourselves, that is, depends a great deal on our sense of being watched, approved of, and loved by others.

Contemporary ethnic and immigrant writings provide illuminations for these psychoanalytic questions while at the same time showing up their limitations. An affective complaint that surfaces time and again among Asian American writers, for instance, is that there is no corresponding image or reflection—what may be redefined as "regard"—in the culture at large of the truth of Asian American experience: Asian Americans, it is often pointed out, are simply omitted from mainstream representations. To this extent, the phrase "under Western eyes" in the title of Hongo's collection is meant to underscore the preemptive indifference to and vigilant assailing of the ethnic subject by mainstream society at large even as that society, in so many varieties of coercive mimeticism, calls on her to perform herself. Whereas a legalistic response to such a complaint might involve increasing the number of Asian American representations in the media and providing larger quotas for various ethnic groups in major professions, the affective implications of the complaint can only be grasped by way of another type of question: what does this complaint mean in terms of narcissism? What is known as marginalization—the lack of proper societal representation, the absence of societal approval—can now be redefined in terms of a narcissistic relation that cannot be developed or, as Freud puts it, has to be forsworn early on. Because of this need (imposed by mainstream society) to abandon one's narcissism, because the love of oneself, a love that is vital, is thus thwarted, every interaction with the social order at large by necessity turns into a painful reminder of this process of suppression and wounding.

At the same time, the Asian American instance goes significantly beyond the parameters set by Freud. As in the case of many of his other works, Freud's analysis here remains confined to a binary opposition between self and society, an opposition that does not apply without problems in the case of the Asian American because the narcissism that is thwarted is not necessarily individualistic in nature. Indeed, precisely because the label "Asian American" (and its equivalents in American society, such as "African American" and "Native American") is construed as relating to a minority culture or minority community that mediates between the single individual and society at large, its status is that of an extra category—one that is neither strictly a private, personal self nor strictly a public society that includes everybody. The self-versus-society opposition is no longer sufficient for the purpose of analysis.

If and when the notion of a lost or wounded narcissism—a narcissism that is not allowed to take its course, that has become inaccessible—is felt by an entire group of people, narcissism becomes, arguably, a transindividual issue of attachment and belonging. Would it be possible, therefore, to say that in the complaints about marginalization from Asian American writers, what we witness is the symptom of a perceived narcissistic damage, an aggression that is felt to be directed by American society at large against the self that is the "Asian American"? But what is the "Asian American"? Would it not be necessary to locate the loss and wounding of narcissism more specifically at the transindividual level of ethnicity, so as to clarify that what the "Asian American" feels she cannot love is not just any part of her but precisely her "Asian Americanness"—a mark that is not reducible to a single individualized self (because the identity it designates is collective by definition) yet meanwhile is a fluid, historical sign of difference, something that cannot be positivistically pinned down and categorized once and for all (as a statistical reality, for instance) without being turned into the most objectionable kind of cultural stereotype?[20]

At this juncture, representation such as writing becomes an intricate matter. How is the experience of an inaccessible narcissism to be represented? How can something that has not, as it were, been allowed to develop, and is therefore not empirically available, be written about? It is at this limit of what is representable—of the need to write about something whose existence has nonetheless been placed out of reach—that the tendency to be autobiographical among immigrant writers takes on special significance. For, seen in this light, autobiographical writing is perhaps not simply a straightforward account about oneself but more a symptomatic attempt (born of coercive mimeticism and social interpellation, to be sure) to create access to a transindividual narcissism—to grope for a "self-regard" that does not yet exist. If this is, indeed, the case, then to be autobiographical could be seen as the narcissistic act par excellence because it is the act through which it becomes apparently possible, perhaps for the first time, to connect and *compose* oneself and thus to attain a modicum of the "self-regard" that seems to be absent all along. Moreover, might not access to such self-regard, however remote in the present, promise, in the end, to vindicate the group's identity—the elusive yet undeniable something called "Asian Americanness"? Pursued along these lines, ethnic writing returns us to the question of freedom: does such writing, autobiographical in the sense of a cultivation of the ethnically hailed self, finally make narcissism available, albeit in a belated fashion? If so, does such belated narcissism lead to freedom, and for whom? What is the relation among ethnic writing, narcissism, and freedom?

Hongo's "Introduction: Culture Wars in Asian America" cogently articulates the ambivalence toward these questions. From the premise of the injustice faced by Asian Americans, Hongo focuses on the issue of what it means to attempt to speak about/against such injustice. It is immediately clear that autobiographical speaking and writing are not simply and straightforwardly therapeutic or liberating activities. Instead, the writer faces a dilemma. On the one hand, "it is nearly impossible to ignore issues of representation, white privilege, and freedom of expression when we examine the images of peoples of color authorized by our culture. African Americans, Native Americans, Hispanics, and Asian Americans have long been subject to the power of the stereotype regarding their portrayals in the cultural mainstream."[21] On the other hand, "to speak *about* a trauma or social prohibition, to speak against silencing, can initiate further acts of trauma, silencing, and prohibition of the speaker" (8; emphasis in the original). What this means, in the terms of this discussion, is that the pattern of a thwarted narcissism may, in fact, be perpetrated precisely through the act of writing, in such a manner as to turn one's relation to the self into self-hatred—into just another round of internalization of the exclusion it experiences from society at large. Hongo uses the traumatic example of the internment of Japanese Americans in the United States during the Second World War to make his point about the vicious circle of entrapment involved in the attempt to be autobiographical:

When you have to be silent about something as cataclysmic and monumental as the relocation camps were, it tends to govern your willingness to live in *any* emotion at all. You feel your exclusion quite acutely. You feel your *difference*, your perception as an outcast *Other* in your society that is hostile to you. And you begin to internalize this hostility as self-hate—the inability to cherish your own inner life, your own social history, your own status as an individual and member of a community. At the level of the unconscious, you begin to perform an internalized silencing of your own perceptions and to rewrite your story according to patterns other than those of your own life. You uphold what is *not you* and live as if your own experiences were of little value. It's kind of a censorship or handicap—an illness.

(10; emphases in the original)

This "illness" can then become contagious within the ethnic community, turning one member against another through the repeated acts of mutual silencing, internalized oppression, discrediting of others' authenticity, and so forth.

Paradoxically, it is in this fraught context of the difficulties of speaking about trauma and injustice under Western eyes—what in the terms of this discussion is already an autobiographical act, an effort to gain access to the self and to ethnic narcissism—that Hongo locates the relevance of the "personal essay" as the appropriate genre for what he calls "internal questing" (25). In its relation to ethnicity, thus, should not the personal essay really be thought of as a second-order autobiography, an autobiography that writes about the failure of a narcissism (itself a kind of autobiography) that was, culturally speaking, always already blocked and silenced?

Because the narcissism in question is, as I have been arguing, one that exceeds the boundaries of the individual self, the autobiographical tendency in immigrant writing, more often than not, takes as its point of reflection the history of the entire group rather than any single individual's life. Indeed, one of the prominent features that link the diverse essays in the collection—by men and women authors of Indian, Filipino, Chinese, Japanese, Okinawan, and Vietnamese descent—is the question of heritage, of what is being handed from one generation to the next among immigrants. In his own essay on his grandfather, "Kubota," for instance, Hongo recalls how the old man, having lived through the injustice of the Japanese internment during the Second World War, would, unlike other people, insist on not forgetting that experience but passing it on to his grandson:

> Japanese Americans were busy trying to forget it ever happened and were having a hard enough time building their new lives after "camp." It was as if we had no history for four years and the relocation was something unspeakable.
>
> But Kubota would not let it go. In session after session, for months it seemed, he pounded away at his story. . . . I was not made yet and he was determined that his stories be part of my making. . . . He gave his testimony to me and I held it at first cautiously in my conscience

like it was an heirloom too delicate to expose to strangers and anyone outside of the world Kubota made with his words.   (118)

While other Japanese Americans choose to silence themselves, for Hongo, ethnicity is a kind of defiled history that demands articulation: "It
was out of this sense of shame and a fear of stigma, I was only beginning
to understand, that the Nisei had silenced themselves. And for their children, among whom I grew up, they wanted no heritage, no culture, no
contact with a defiled history. I recall the silence very well. The Japanese
American children around me were burdened in a way I was not. Their
injunction was silence. Mine was to speak" (120).

Other essays in Hongo's collection are similarly written from a sense of
ethnic tenacity, an attempt to hold on to something from the transindividual past that is not quite finished. In almost all of them, hence, the point
of representation lies in the act of remembering. The loose or casual structure of each piece notwithstanding, these essays typically begin with a
memorable incident or series of incidents, which then leads to the larger
question of family, ancestry, and heritage, a question that is often introduced through some object (Lillian Ho Wan), practice (Peter Bacho,
Jeanne Wakatsuki Houston, David Low), use of language (Amy Tan,
Chang-rae Lee), or personal figures from the past (Chitra Banerjee Diva-
karuni, Geraldine Kudaka, Li-Young Lee). In those pieces in which there
is a visit to the native home, real or imaginary, the idea of home usually
becomes the occasion for irresolvable ambivalence (Debra Kang Dean,
Geeta Kothari, Nguyen Qúi-Duc). The authors, long displaced from and
often never having set foot in these homelands, are self-conscious of their
appearances, attitudes, habits, and uses of language, all of which mark
them as neither of the "original" place nor of their current home—North
America. Permeating their writings is a strong sense of ontological liminality, of existing between cultures, and of being stigmatized themselves or
being witnesses to others' stigmatization for precisely that reason.

In the more extreme case depicted by David Mura in his piece "The
Internment of Desire," the sense of alienation from mainstream society
since childhood becomes a determinant in his sexual formation. Looking
at the pornographic images from *Playboy* and fantasizing about white
girls dominate his fantasy life. In this way, he becomes obsessed with mas-

turbation, an ultimate narcissistic act, here situated in a context in which it is part of a confused adolescence in a "foreign" land where he feels powerless and ashamed of being who he is. Interestingly, Mura compares the shame he feels about being trapped in his pornographic desires—a private and individual affair—to the collective experience of internment undergone by the Japanese Americans during the Second World War (289–91). Shame about the former, he writes, is like the racism that has been internalized by the victimized groups (281). The fluidity and mutuality perceived between the self and the minority group, across history, makes this intense personal essay especially fascinating to read.

Yet despite the permeability of boundaries between the current self and the distant collective past, that past is not always readily available. Mura compares the fragmented nature of ethnic writing to briocolage: "Like a bricoleur, I must make do with the tools at hand—a few anecdotes from my aunts, some stray remarks from my parents, history books, a few works of literature by Japanese Americans, and my own guesses and intuitions" (292–93). Putting this in a different way, he writes: "A Japanese American writer I know says that those of us who come from marginalized cultures are often bequeathed fragments, brief bits of the past, and nothing more. There are no unbroken threads, no fully developed tales or histories. There are too many secrets and occlusions, there are too many reasons to forget the past. And there are forces which do not want us to remember, do not want us to take those fragments and complete them, to restore them to some fuller life" (193).

Contrary to the poststructuralist theorists of hybridity, the writers of these personal essays, all of which are about the experience of actually living as cultural hybrids, offer pictures that are anything but freedom from the given. Instead, hybridity itself, as the cultural given, becomes for these ethnically marked writers a form of existential entrapment; some, as in the case of Mura, would go so far as to compare it to internment, an oppressive condition that does not automatically improve with its representation and confession in writing. The act of writing autobiographically in these pieces is much more than being selfish; it is simultaneously writing collectively about the inherited, *shared* condition of social stigmatization and abjection.

The Secrets of Ethnic Abjection

In the final piece to the volume, entitled "A Little Memento from the Boys" (321–32), John Yau brings this sense of stigmatization and abjection to the crux by narrating the "secret" three ethnically hybrid men deposit on the walls of a woman, Lila, who has hired them to renovate her apartment. From the beginning, the essay is marked by a plenitude of references to bodily elimination—decay, discharge, things being dropped. John and his friends first meet in a crummy, dilapidated bar— suggestively named Mike's Last Dive—and their friendship literally develops, in an ambience filled with smells of urine and disinfectant, when they are on their way to the bathroom:

> Mike's Last Dive was a decaying, turn-of-the-century bar with sawdust on the floor. It had one pool table in the center of its square, high-ceilinged room, like a brightly lit, grass-covered traffic island at night, meandering lines of cars rushing by. There was a long, narrow bathroom that smelled as if grizzled whalers used to line up and piss there. A sweet, sickly smell of disinfectant, urine, cigarettes, and stale beer had soaked into the bathroom's tile walls, tin ceiling, and wooden floor. I always felt like I was pissing in a cold cave or a decrepit refrigerator. . . .
>
> Late one night, Johnny, Virgo, and I kept crossing each other's paths on the way to the toilet or, while standing and watching some of the regulars playing pool, we'd look up and see a face looking back, curious. We began checking each other out, circling each other, slowly, like animals in heat.
>
> Why did we begin talking? Well, the obvious reason is that we immediately recognized that we were mongrels, confused children whose parents came from different worlds, which in our cases meant Asia and Europe. *We were what was left after the collision; we were the things they had dropped on the floor.*   (323–24; my emphasis)

It is possible to think of the psychological landscape constructed by Yau in terms of what Julia Kristeva calls the abject—the often culturally tabooed condition of an excessive, rejected being that nonetheless remains a challenge to the body that expels it. Kristeva writes:

> What is *abject*, . . . the jettisoned object, is radically excluded and draws me toward the place where meaning collapses. . . . And yet, from its place of banishment, the abject does not cease challenging its master. . . .
> . . . Abject. It is something rejected from which one does not part, from which one does not protect oneself as from an object. Imaginary uncanniness and real threat, it beckons to us and ends up engulfing us.
> It is thus not lack of cleanliness or health that causes abjection but what disturbs identity, system, order. What does not respect borders, positions, rules. The in-between, the ambiguous, the composite.[22]

Examples of the abject, as Elizabeth Grosz comments, would be substances such as "tears, saliva, faeces, urine, vomit, mucus," which are "neither simply part of the body nor separate from it." Although "the subject must expel these abjects to establish the 'clean and proper' body of oedipalization," they can "never be expelled, for they remain the preconditions of corporeal, material existence."[23]

In Yau's essay, there is a powerful suggestion that ethnic hybridity itself is a form of abjection. The essay's conscious comparison of the lives of these men to things people "had dropped on the floor" resonates with the feelings of neglect, dismissal, and humiliation that we often come across in autobiographical accounts of peoples of color living in North American society. Though the perfect embodiments of hybridity—the three men are Japanese, German, English, Chinese, Dutch, and Spanish by heritage—they certainly do not feel their mongrelized status is an advantage. Quite the contrary. The question that arises with their very first descriptions is: what kind of self-representation is being produced? If these men are what was "dropped on the floor" by their parents after their collision, they are neither objects nor subjects of their environment; rather, they exist as abjects, along the fluid line of demarcation, undecidedly both inside and outside, precariously inerasable yet vulnerable. What kind of an autobiography is possible with abjects?

As the men spend their days and nights telling one another their life stories, the narrator comments: "We live on the poison we secrete, and spend our nights characterizing ourselves in derogatory terms. It is the only defense we know" (325). How is self-derogation a defense? To defend something is to set up a safe boundary around it, so that it is less likely to be attacked by others. Here, however, that boundary is set up paradoxically through self-attack. In this conscious play on the notions of defense and boundary, the slippage of meaning Yau introduces between "secret" and "secrete" is highly evocative.

As we all know, there is nothing intrinsically enigmatic or valuable about secrets. Although a secret may occupy the status of a precious hidden treasure, it may also simply exist as something about which one knows or cares. In this sense, a secret is not unlike what I have been describing as narcissism, a condition whose reality lies both inside and outside in that it is liminally between the need for self-preservation and the need for others' attention, recognition, and respect. Insofar as the details about these men's existences are unknown and ignored by most people, they are secrets; at the same time, because no one cares, their secrets take on the status of precisely that thwarted narcissism which is deprived of self-regard. In this manner, narcissism, the secret of the self, turns poisonous: the only defense (self-preservation) of which the men are capable is "characterizing [themselves] in derogatory terms." The inaccessibility of narcissism stands here both as a secret, a hidden inner wound, and as a kind of foul secretion or discharge outward. In this secretive/secreting state, the hybrid ethnic men become abjection in human form.

So, what do the three men do in Lila's apartment? Out of sheer mischief, they have been looking through the woman's belongings while moving furniture around during their work and have found a gigantic vibrator under her pillow. They also turn up her diary, which is filled with fantasy confessions of fantasy sex experiences with various men. Stimulated by the exposure of their employer's hidden secrets, John and his friends decide to play a practical joke on her. First, they use the remaining film in her camera to take pictures of each of them posing with the vibrator and ejaculating into the remaining can of paint (the camera with the film in it is afterward left behind in the apartment); then they use the paint, now mixed with their semen, to finish their job on her walls.

Understandably, some readers will find the ejaculators offensive and exploitative of the space belonging to a woman. Leaving their semen on Lila's walls in the manner John, Virgo, and Johnny did can be seen as a metaphor for gang rape, as if the woman whose sexual privacy has been intruded upon must also be subjected to their collective mockery, defilement, and defacement. This, of course, is another reason the story is disturbing: the victims of social marginalization, the very recipients of social dismissal, we are made to realize, tend to become themselves perpetrators of cruelty against a more or less innocent person. By juxtaposing their own penises against the enormous vibrator, the three men not only deflate Lila's fantasy object but also forcibly make her self-pleasure practice part of their own narcissistic "self-abuse" and part of their own abjection.[24] What remains crucial is the fact that, when the victimized insist willfully on being recognized, such insistence almost by necessity takes the form of an aggression. It is as though the bodies that are abject—and whose secrets are considered mere excrement—must implode from within a society's boundary between what it wants and what it does not want, with a secretive secretion that is, literally, "in your face" (walls being, after all, faces).

By playing on the affinities between the secret (as what is unknown and unrecognized and therefore confined within) and secretion (as what is discharged outside into the public realm), Yau has crafted a provocative statement on the peculiar nature of the violence involved in ethnic Americans' negotiations with their historical situations. Ostensibly, this violence is the violence of boundaries breaking, as evidenced in the three men's transgressive ejaculation and writing on the wall; but it is, on closer reflection, also the violence of boundaries making—the violence that is built into the division, categorization, and class-ification of peoples by way of race and ethnic differences, the violence that is responsible for these men's exclusion in the first place. It is the latter, that is, the enforcement of a certain kind of secretive inside—as society proper (a space unreachable for those without permission)—an enforcement that simultaneously requires the elimination of "improper" others who end up oozing around society's edges like an offensive kind of pus, that is the focus of Yau's implied critique.

In the woman's apartment, then, these men stumble on an opportunity to make their secrets/secretions part of a permanent display, part of the new (sur)face of her walls. Much as this collective act itself once again turns into another secret—the secretion permanently frozen on the wall, staring at the woman in a way unbeknownst to her until, perhaps, she develops the film they leave behind—it has also acquired the status of writing, both in the sense of the semen being a kind of writing on the wall and in the sense of the personal account that will eventually be read by Yau's readers. The protestant ethnics have sufficiently performed themselves here—but what remains startling is the utter destitution of their collective narcissistic act. In that act, Yau brings together the multiple forms of brutality that constitute ethnic negotiations of identity in a society not yet capable of understanding racial and/or ethnic otherness except by rendering such otherness in terms of class. And class is reinforced precisely through the images of waste matter, of secret-ions to which no one cares to pay attention. The dried-up sperm, deprived of its reproductive function, is now simply detritus, the seedy underside of another's habitat. Contrary to the fashionable sentimentalism attached to racial and ethnic otherness as some kind of exotic difference, Yau gives us a stark portrayal of such otherness as something lethal—and the first ones to become poisoned, his tale tells us, are the bearers themselves.

Does the writing on the wall, the permanent inscription of the secrets of ethnic abjection in someone else's space, accomplish anything for the men apart from being a wicked joke at another's expense? Does the expression with semen amount to any kind of freedom through representation? Yau's ending does not so much give an affirmative answer as it repeats the plaint of ethnic voices wanting to be heard. The wish for recognition, that social response that makes narcissism available to the self, persists because it is not yet fulfilled:

Hey, Lila, there's three mongrels out there, somewhere in America, who have drifted into different orbits. But they still have one thing in common, their sperm mixed in the paint covering your walls.

Hey, Lila, it's okay if you went out and hired someone to paint them over. It's even okay if your walls are now blue or pink or gray, because the sperm is still there, beneath whatever you have done. . . .

. . . Wishing a person or a thing was never born, that's why Johnny, Virgo, and I did what we did. We wanted a different kind of diary, one that was written permanently on a wall where everybody could read it. It's why we took the pictures. We wanted someone to know who and what we had been. (332)

In this desperate cry for a self-regard that seems forever out of reach, the autobiographical act remains haunted by and trapped within the given of abject hybridity—of hybridity as abjection. This sense of haunting and entrapment is probably the protestant ethnic's ultimate answer to the poststructuralist euphoria about difference, mobility, and freedom mentioned at the beginning of this chapter. The answer poses discomfiting questions about the real function of autobiographical writing by those whose very acts and utterances are considered in an a priori manner autobiographical or representative of their group. What precisely is the status of authors writing about themselves-always-deemed-to-be-writing-about-themselves anyway? How would poststructuralist theory respond to *this* border—between transindividual narcissistic attachment and persistent social dismissal—along which the ethnic is destined to pick up the scraps of her psychic economy? However migratory, hybridized, and in flux it might be, is not ethnicity in this context finally assigned the value of a referent that confines and immobilizes? Despite being full-bodied personifications of difference, global migranthood, multiculturalism, nomadism, and related trendy theoretical paradigms, the ethnics in Yau's story are affectively stuck in their secretive condition. The self-mimicry encouraged by their society ("Confess yourself!" "Perform yourself!") turns out to be a vicious circle in which the reward of social recognition, if and when it comes, is likely to bring about further humiliation and self-loathing. "We wanted someone to know who and what we had been": as the bearers of the secrets of ethnic abjection, these self-mimicking figures are far from having set themselves free.

CHAPTER 5

When Whiteness Feminizes . . . : Some Consequences of a Supplementary Logic

The actual practice of autobiographic ethnic writing, as discussed in the last chapter, serves as a compelling reminder of the schism that persists between difference as a theoretical paradigm and difference as a sociological effect and psychic economy. Although poststructuralist theory remains unparalleled in the ways it has radicalized thinking about difference and related questions of identity, the difference revolution itself is increasingly challenged as the fields of academic inquiry to which poststructuralist theory has contributed major conceptual possibilities move on, as they should and must, to other questions, in particular, questions as to how specific kinds of differences are produced, legitimized, made visible, and sustained—while other kinds of differences tend to remain unheeded or eclipsed. In this chapter, I would like to approach this problematic of difference from yet another perspective—that of feminism and its ways of conceptualizing "woman" in the past few decades.

Insofar as it began as a movement to eradicate the historical discrimination against women and bring about an egalitarian society based on a respect for sexual difference, feminism in the West may, I believe, be seen as a fellow traveler to liberalism. As I have indicated at various points in the foregoing discussions, what is troubling about liberalism is its often hierarchical relation to the minority others it seeks to affirm and make equal, so that, as these others receive benevolent support for their undertakings, they must at the same time remain subordinate to their (often white) sponsors. The liberalist modus operandi, which is as self-contradictory as it is successful, is endemic to the institutionalization of ethnic studies as we know it to date and continues to characterize many scholarly pursuits of ethnicity as an academic subject. In a similar fashion, the logic of feminism tends to be most tested when what it has to confront is no longer its own claim to victimized otherness but rather its textual, theoretical, and political self-positioning in relation to the others who happen not to be white middle-class men and women. If the term "woman" first became visible in the capacity of a minority identity striving for recognition—in ways that may be comparable to the protestant ethnic—how has that identity been elaborated and substantiated over time, in fictional as well as theoretical representations? Has that identity developed and transformed beyond itself? How might we read representations of "woman" *cross-culturally* by foregrounding the issue of ethnicity, including the ethnicity that is whiteness?

Is "Woman" a Woman, a Man, or What? The Unstable Status of Woman in Contemporary Cultural Criticism

Since the introduction of poststructuralist theory into the English-speaking academic world, a point of tension between feminists sympathetic toward poststructuralism and feminists hostile toward it has been the controversy over none other than the status of "woman" in representational politics. Whereas, for Anglo-American feminist critics, the individual woman, woman author, or woman critic continues to be understood in terms of the agency derived from the philosophical foundation of individualism, of the gendered person as an ultimate reality, the pivot

of French poststructuralism has been precisely to put such foundational-
ist thinking into question through theories of language, text, signification,
and subject, so that what is hitherto considered as an irrefutable certain-
ty, including the individual self, now becomes known more often as a referent, a point in signification that is always *en procès*—that is, constantly disrupted, deferred, dislocated, postponed, if not altogether dissolved.
This bifurcation between "Anglo-American" and "French" forms the basis of Toril Moi's 1985 bestseller *Sexual/Textual Politics*.[1] Moi, whose
critical sympathies lie with the French, presents Anglo-American feminist
critical practice in terms of an unconscious adherence to a Lukácsian realism and humanism that remain securely inscribed within patriarchal
ideology (4–7). Her conclusion about American feminist literary critics
such as Elaine Showalter, Kate Millet, Myra Jehlen, Susan Gubar, Sandra
Gilbert, Annette Kolodny, and others is devastating. To be sure, Moi argues, these critics are politicizing texts through readings of sexuality—but
theirs is a naive politics that leaves patriarchal aesthetics entirely intact
(69). In other words, while she gives Anglo-American feminist criticism
ample credit for its overt political stance, Moi charges that this sexual
politics is far from being political enough:

> The radically new impact of feminist criticism is to be found not at
> the level of theory or methodology, but at the level of politics. Femi-
> nists have *politicized* existing critical methods and approaches. If
> feminist criticism has subverted established critical judgements it is
> because of its radically new emphasis on *sexual politics*. . . .
>   . . .The central paradox of Anglo-American feminist criticism is
> thus that despite its often strong, explicit political engagement, it is *in
> the end* not quite political enough; not in the sense that it fails to go
> *far* enough along the political spectrum, but in the sense that its rad-
> ical analysis of sexual politics still remains entangled with depoliti-
> cizing theoretical paradigms.   (87–88; emphases in the original)

For these reasons, Moi has inserted the word "textual" in her book title
in order to emphasize the importance of deconstructing linguistic structures alongside a sexual politics. Reading her analyses, one has the im-
pression that textual politics is the more radically political because that

is where essentialism, including the essentialism of the term "woman," can be properly confronted and undone. In particular, Moi is taken with the manner in which Julia Kristeva brings attention to the materiality of textual production. From Kristeva, Moi tells us, we learn that the subject position (it is no longer radical enough to talk of the self or the individual) is what indicates revolutionary potential (12).

In retrospect, Moi's discussion is interesting not least because it is an early example, within the realm of contemporary feminist studies, of an attempt to take note of ethnicity as cultural difference ("Anglo-American," "French," "Norwegian")—indeed, to foreground culture itself as having an undismissable bearing on critical practices. Yet this astute awareness of cultural difference—which in her readings translates into a critique of essentialism and an endorsement of poststructuralist textual politics—does not necessarily save Moi herself from falling into certain kinds of essentialist pitfalls. In this regard, it is necessary to recognize the rhetorical strategies she adopts.

Chief of these strategies is Moi's attempt to dichotomize politics and textuality. As I will go on to demonstrate in the rest of this chapter, such a dichotomy is a fallacious one. Among other things, it tends to ignore completely the implications of race and ethnicity—in particular, of whiteness as social power—in discourses about sexuality and femininity. In Moi's text, however, this dichotomy serves important tactical purposes. It enables her to give acknowledgment to the accomplishments of Anglo-American feminist critics exclusively in terms of their politics and to argue, by the same gesture, that these critics have not dealt at all with the textuality of their texts. Quickly, then, what looks at first like a straightforward differentiation turns into a specific value judgment. Accordingly, politics, which is what makes Anglo-American feminist critics "Anglo-American," is simple-minded and unsophisticated—*even though it is all they are capable of.* As Deborah E. McDowell points out, this category of "Anglo-American" also includes black and lesbian women: "Lesbian and/or black feminist criticism have presented exactly the same *methodological* and *theoretical* problems as the rest of Anglo-American feminist criticism." "This is not to say that black and lesbian criticism have no . . . importance"; rather, that importance, like that of the rest of Anglo-American feminist criticism, is to be found "not at the level of theory or methodology, but at the level of politics."[2] By contrast, the French theorists are much more supple in the way they deal with texts. But instead of confining them to the "text" half of her divided world (a division she herself proposes), Moi suggests that what they are doing is radically "political" as well, so that the French—and Frenchness—are, strictly speaking, inhabiting both sides of the divided world as women who not only know how to read texts but also how to do politics. As an account not simply of varied feminist practices but also of cultural difference, Moi's discussion presents Anglo-American feminists as heavy-footed country bumpkins who are trapped in their parochial women's worlds (who just want to find and proclaim "woman" everywhere) and the French as suave and nimble cosmopolitans because they know how to read. In terms of their respective performances, the Anglo-Americans are only second-rate even when they do their best; the French, on the other hand, are already doing revolutionary politics without necessarily even trying (as they are just paying attention to the marginality and dissidence of texts).

By bifurcating the question of women critics' relationship to texts in this manner, Moi inadvertently introduces a larger problem—what might be called the feminization of culture. Taken in the broadest sense, this phrase may simply refer to a cultural process in which femininity, together with the figure of woman, becomes visible and active as an agent and producer of knowledge, yet this is exactly where the controversy begins. Indeed, the debate that revolves around Ann Douglas's book of 1977, *The Feminization of American Culture*, takes this issue of the relationship between women and culture as its central focus.[3] Douglas associates feminization with the rise of mass culture and with the conspicuous consumption habits of American society since the early nineteenth century. For her, feminization means emasculation; a culture feminized is thus a culture in demise, weakened in comparison with its previous tough—that is, manly—state. The claims made by the second-wave feminism in the United States in the 1970s and the 1980s (the feminism whose proponents include many of the authors that Moi criticizes in her book)[4] were thus explicitly or implicitly aimed at Douglas's unsympathetic view of women and mass culture.[5] Rather than the demise of culture, the tenet of second-wave feminism adamantly affirmed an independent women's tradition and genealogy, demonstrating that despite the discrimination they experienced historically in Western societies, women were creative, imaginative, and as capable of authorship as men. The feminization of culture, thus, became a feminist revision of culture, specializing in bringing women from the margins of history to the center of academic attention. Ironically, it is the overtly tough stance taken by feminists during this period, a stance that was aimed at asserting women's difference from, as well as equality with, men, that becomes in Moi's reading a sign that these second-wave feminists are political naïfs mired in patriarchal aesthetics. We thus arrive at a paradox: by focusing on "woman," Anglo-American feminists are, by the criteria of one account (Douglas), furthering the emasculation of culture; yet, by those of another (Moi), they are becoming too much like men.

The paradox does not end here. In an essay called "Mass Culture as Woman," Andreas Huyssen gives this topic yet another twist by arguing that the very equation of femininity with lowbrow culture, mediocrity, and leisurely consumption—in other words, precisely what Douglas has called the feminization of culture—is characteristic of high modernism with its interest in promoting "high art."[6] What Douglas characterizes, by way of the twosome man-woman, as the feminization of culture, is hence recast by Huyssen as a socioaesthetic move, in which the debasement of "woman" is part and parcel of a constructed relation between high art and mass culture that is aimed at preserving the interests of high modernism, which nonetheless is dependent on mass culture as its hidden subtext. Moreover, once the use of "woman" is historicized in this manner, Huyssen is able to reveal how high modernist art often derives its authority not so much from radical hedonism (as it would like us to believe) as from a kind of puritanism, one that can be said to be based on the reality principle rather than the pleasure principle:

> The autonomy of the modernist art work, after all, is always the result of a resistance, an abstention, and a suppression—resistance to the seductive lure of mass culture, abstention from the pleasure of trying to please a larger audience, suppression of everything that might be threatening to the rigorous demands of being modern and at the edge of time. There seem to be fairly obvious homologies between

this modernist insistence on purity and autonomy in art, Freud's privileging of the ego over the id and his insistence on stable, if flexible,
ego boundaries, and Marx's privileging of production over consumption. The lure of mass culture, after all, has traditionally been described as the threat of losing oneself in dreams and delusions and of
merely consuming rather than producing. Thus, despite its undeniable adversary stance toward bourgeois society, the modernist aesthetic and its rigorous work ethic as described here seem in some fundamental way to be located also on the side of that society's reality
principle, rather than on that of the pleasure principle. It is to this fact
that we owe some of the greatest works of modernism, but the great-
ness of these works cannot be separated from the often one-dimen-
sional gender inscriptions inherent in their very constitution as autonomous masterworks of modernity.   (55)

In an uncanny manner, Huyssen's reading of man-woman through
high modernism–mass culture and vice versa also returns us to Moi's account of the *cultural difference* within feminist criticism of the 1970s and
1980s. Whereas Moi endorses the textual politics of the French poststructuralists with the assumption that it is a more radical and rigorous
politics, Huyssen's account shows us that it is precisely this kind of assumption of itself as more modern, more ahead than others, and more at
the edge of time that is characteristic of the continual workings of high
modernism. By implication of Huyssen's terms, we may say that the
reading practices of Anglo-American feminist critics have, in fact, been
implicitly equated in Moi's reading with deluded, simple-minded mass
culture (woman), while French poststructuralist *écriture féminine* has
been equated with the rigor of autonomous high art (man).

This brief account of the divergent, often incompatible or self-contra-
dicting, views of femininity and the feminization of culture is testimony
to what I would call the supplementary logic of "woman" in the contemporary West. If the singularity of the name "man" is what is being
questioned and challenged by the addition of "woman" as a (minority)
category, then, by the same logic, "woman" itself can hardly be expected
to remain a stable, unchanging frame of reference. Even in an account
that is so apparently unsympathetic toward women as Douglas's, it seems

to me that the term "feminization" is much less an attempt to define the essence of woman as such than it is a manner of articulating the historical—that is, mutating—relationships among various parts of culture as they have been socially institutionalized. In the counter move, on the part of the second-wave feminists, to elevate women's status to a respectable separateness from men's, the economic and cultural resonances of Douglas's original argument seem to have been bypassed. What remains takes on the semblance of a project aimed single-mindedly at legitimizing the idea of woman, which then easily lends itself to the pertinent charge of essentialism when poststructuralists such as Moi come along.[7]

Were we, however, to recognize in the epistemologically unstabilizable status of "woman" the supplementary logic of the supplement, a different type of question could be raised. No longer would it be sufficient to think of "woman" simply in relation to "man" (since that addition has already been accomplished); nor would it be sufficient simply to pluralize, to talk of multiple "women" while the assumption of something called "woman" remains intact. Rather, it would be imperative to see how, precisely at the moment "woman" is added to "man," the world can no longer be thought of in terms of the "man-woman" relation alone. This is because "woman" brings with it not only an essential content that can be added on or subtracted at will but also a function of reconceptualizing the status quo itself as fiction, a function whose most radical aspect is its irreversibility and unstoppability. By the time "woman" arrives at man's side, as it were, the coupling of "man-woman" is already obsolete, not so much because its twosomeness is heterosexist as because such a twosomeness itself will have to be recognized as part of something else, something whose configuration—as class or race, for instance—becomes graspable exactly at the moment of the supplement's materialization. This, in part, is the reason it is much more difficult to stabilize "woman" than "man." As we have seen, both the attempts to demote and promote "woman" remain ever unsatisfactory; it is as if, once the term is invoked—once "woman" is made analytically viable—we are already, in spite of our ostensible efforts, moving in and into another realm of cultural relations that can no longer be confined to gender.[8]

To explore this supplementary logic of "woman" further, I will next turn to two fictional narrative models that give us two significant moments of the feminization of Western culture in modern times. Since one model is Anglo-American and the other French, their juxtaposition will also offer an opportunity to rethink certain differences that some have insisted on between these two ethnic classifications. As I will try to argue, there is, on the contrary, a discernible genealogical continuity, at least, between the narrative models.

The "Realist" Model: The Rich Man's Loyal Second Wife

The first narrative model is the familiar story of Charlotte Brontë's *Jane Eyre*, in which Jane, the apparently orphaned girl who suffers wrongs and abuse at various stages of her life, eventually becomes the wife of her beloved Mr. Rochester.[9] For those interested in Brontë's classic, the presence of the other woman, the creole Bertha Mason, Rochester's first wife whom he brought back from the West Indies and locked up in the attic, has always served as a kind of narrative puzzle to be solved. For feminist critics, in particular, it is clear that Bertha somehow provides the clue to the meaning of the entire novel and, for that matter, to the project of feminist revision itself. This is the reason Sandra Gilbert and Susan Gubar titled their notable feminist rewriting of the history of English literature *The Madwoman in the Attic*.[10] Their project, like those of their feminist critic contemporaries, may be described in terms of what Cora Kaplan calls the "Subject of Feminism"—"a figure of speech who represents not a person, an author, or a character, or even an established discourse, but rather a developing stance, a set of ideas in process which question the logic of women's subordination in culture and nature."[11] Intent as their contemporaries were on consolidating the status of "woman," Gilbert and Gubar interpret Bertha as a double of Jane. The racial and/or ethnic difference between the two women characters is thus elided in favor of what was, in the 1970s, a political act of unifying womanhood.[12] In the course of time, this very political act would come to be recognized by many as an act of essentialism.

As it became necessary to rethink the singularity of "woman" according to the logic of the supplement, various critics have since the 1970s alerted us to the imperialist cultural underpinnings of Brontë's book. Written in a historical period during which British society took a substantial interest in ethnographic and ethnological discourses, Brontë's novel was, as Kaplan writes, symptomatic of "the protofeminist writing that initially emphasized the female child's likeness to and/or identifications with racial, hybrid, or deformed others en route to presenting her adult self as the ethical model of national subjectivity" (181). Jane's empowerment of herself through language and writing[13] is at the expense of Bertha's ever having access to human personhood and subjectivity in the post-Enlightenment sense.[14] In a text that is considered one of the first major examples of a woman overcoming patriarchal and class domination in modern times, then, we have an uncanny reminder and remainder of the non-Western other—the savage madwoman in the attic—who, as part of the same process, must be defeated, imprisoned, and driven to destruction and suicide. The presence of Bertha compels us to think anew of Brontë's work as a story about what happens when a woman attains social status and credibility in British culture. This process of feminization, accordingly, cannot simply be considered as a matter of the ascendancy of "woman" as such but must rather be seen as the emergence of a discursive network in which forces of class and race as well as gender become imbricated with one another.

Whereas Cora Kaplan, Nancy Armstrong and Leonard Tennenhouse, Gayatri Spivak, and others have drawn attention to the historical racial makings of the *Jane Eyre* story,[15] I would like, as a complementary gesture, to foreground its fictional, narrative elements. By isolating these elements structurally in a kind of morphology—"a description of the tale according to its component parts and the relationship of these components to each other and to the whole"[16]—my point is to show them as constituents of a fairy tale that become convertible and transportable from one culture to another.

1. *The lonely orphan girl who becomes a loyal wife.* An orphaned child, who must fend for herself, Jane provides the paradigmatic example of someone who moves from complete material lack and social inferiority to the condition of self-possession, a condition in which she becomes her own master. In Victorian England, this self-possession of necessity includes knowing how to handle the demands placed on female sexuality.

Jane's success in this regard can be seen in her using her intelligence (rather than her body) to attain the status of being a married woman who can reproduce biologically.

2. *The sensitive rich man with a mysterious past.* The orphan girl meets the experienced rich man, who has a dark secret that haunts him but somehow he cannot articulate. Many eligible ladies of his prestigious class background desire him, but he singles out the orphan girl because he senses in her a capacity for sympathetic understanding. Importantly, even though the man is wealthy and often has dark moods, he is presented, like the orphan girl, as a kind of victim who has been wronged and oppressed.

3. *The spectral other woman, the first wife.* In order for the story to proceed, there has to be an obstacle or an enemy, a threat to the well-being of the main characters. In *Jane Eyre*, this obstacle is provided by Bertha Mason, the foreign, beastly woman-object who stands in the way of the harmony of the present society. With the presence of Bertha, the representation of "woman" is split in two. Femininity is polarized into love, understanding, and a capacity to listen to the powerful man who perceives himself as a victim, on the one hand, and uncontrolled sexuality, madness, and a refusal to cooperate with the (white) patriarchal order, on the other.

4. *The confession.* The rich man tries to evade the past but is forced, in the end, to confess to Jane the nature of his relationship with Bertha. The revelation of the truth—namely, that Bertha is the legal wife and Jane the potential mistress—leads to Jane's temporary departure, but it also bonds her to Rochester forever.

5. *The setting of the enormous, stately mansion.* Thornfield Hall in *Jane Eyre* is a symbol of wealth and worldly power; at the same time, metaphorically speaking, it is also an isolated, haunted interior, like the heart of the rich man. It is haunted because there is a madwoman in it somewhere. Now that it houses another woman, what will happen?

6. *The catastrophe.* In terms of plot structure, the fire removes the impediment, the mad woman. But she is also the one who sets it: literally, therefore, the mad woman has to remove herself in order to liberate herself—in suicide. While the destruction of his manor leaves the rich man in a state of ruin, it also makes way for a new beginning (in the sense of an almost religious cleansing, a baptism by fire).

7. *The ending: social acceptance and reproduction.* Jane and Rochester are finally able to become a married couple and produce a son. The lonely orphan girl with no one to protect her becomes, in the end, a powerful agent carrying on the reproductive imperative that lies at the heart of social progress.

This intentionally reductionist and formalistic summary of Brontë's fairy tale enables certain crucial issues to emerge with clarity. In terms of the politics of gender, the most important legacy of the *Jane Eyre* plot is, as critics have already noted, the structural division of "woman" into the good, passionate, but innocent new girl and the evil, dangerous first wife. The point that needs to be emphasized, though, is that this splitting of woman means that it is the man who remains at the narrative center. This point tends to be eclipsed because Jane has been constructed by Brontë as the narrator of her own tale. The medium of writing, assumed by a mature Jane who has attained social power, wealth, status, and motherhood, conveys her character as that of a knowledgeable woman whose claim to moral integrity comes with a retrospective mastery of the past. At the same time, her ability for verbal self-representation also considerably complicates—and makes less credible—the very innocence and goodness that are supposedly the qualities of this independent and headstrong female.[17] It is, therefore, when the *Jane Eyre* story is translated into the medium of film—not so much in the film versions of Brontë's novel as in Alfred Hitchcock's 1940 classic *Rebecca* (the first film he made in Hollywood), itself adapted from Daphne du Maurier's novel of the same title—that this discrepancy between the innocent, girlish protagonist and the knowing, cerebral woman writer is effectively removed.[18] In Hitchcock's film, which is similarly the story of a young woman's initiation into a mysterious rich man's haunted world through a discovery of the unmentionable past (also concerning a first wife, the beautiful and unconventional Rebecca), the nameless girlish character (played by Joan Fontaine) is diagetically stripped of her authority as the narrator of the tale except during the beginning few minutes, after which Hitchcock simply drops her voice-over. This little technical change positions the young woman much more convincingly as the helpless, unknowing one who is caught between her suffering husband and the evil females at the Manderlay household—the dead Rebecca (described posthumously by her doctor as "tall" and "dark") and her diabolic representative, Mrs. Danvers—with their apparent sinful knowledge and their capacities to do harm.

By doing away with the authoritative narrative voice of the second wife, Hitchcock enables the sexual politics embedded in the narrative positionings of the characters to be seen much more unambiguously as male-dominant. In other words, Hitchcock makes us realize that although a woman may act as the narrator, it is still a man's story that serves as the hinge of the entire narrative. In the film *Rebecca*, as in *Jane Eyre*, the man makes a confession that constitutes the critical narrative turn. By his own account, Maxim de Winter (played by Laurence Olivier) did not actually kill Rebecca but had put her in a boat, which he let sink in the sea, after she had accidentally killed herself during their quarrel. This confession, made at the climactic point of the film when Rebecca's body is found again after she has supposedly long been buried, positions the unknowing young wife as the confidante and in the process turns her in no uncertain terms into the rich man's accomplice.[19] It is one of the remarkable features of Hitchcock's narrative that, while the resurfacing of Rebecca's body prompts a new series of investigations jointly by the police, the law, and medicine, precisely the discovery made by these social institutions ends up concealing forever the truth of her death. The real function served by the revelation of this truth in its entirety (to the young wife and to the audience), therefore, is the production of the socially approved married couple (Max and the young wife). By finally confiding in his young wife, Max has, as has Rochester in *Jane Eyre*, found himself a new partnership, a female community in which his secret will be safe, while he is emancipated to be a new man.

As in the case of *Jane Eyre*, the structural division of woman into good and evil is resolved in *Rebecca* through a catastrophe with symbolic significance. A fire set by Mrs. Danvers destroys the stately mansion at Manderlay. From the perspective of the evil woman, the fire is, as I already mentioned, a suicide (putting an end to Rebecca and her legacy). From the perspective of the rich man, it is a destruction of what has been haunting him and thus a brand-new beginning. From the perspective of the innocent young wife, the significance of the fire can be seen, as Tania Modleski writes, as a final severance of her maternal ties—that is, she is finally leaving behind her connections with the other, older women in order to comply with the patriarchal requirements of a heterosexual marriage.[20] Remembering the imperialist underpinnings of *Jane Eyre*, I would add that these maternal ties are not simply about "woman" or even the man-woman relation alone.[21]

If feminization is, as I mentioned, taken broadly to mean a cultural process in which "woman" becomes an active, observable agent and producer of knowledge, then the elements of the *Jane Eyre* narrative model may be said to constitute the generic actions of a prevalent plot of the feminization of culture in modern times. This plot follows a *protoliberalist* rationale and attributes power to woman sentimentally—on account of her original lack, her exclusion from social power unless and until she is allied properly with a man. As becomes clear in *Rebecca*, this is an alliance in which the second wife has to play the subordinate role of the selfless recipient of knowledge and consenting accomplice. This subordination of "woman" as the minority figure—through her union with the man, in which he rather than she remains the center of her narrative—is what makes it possible for the successful elimination of the other woman.[22] To invoke the terms of Anglo-American criticism that continue to be in use, the "agency" allowed the woman as "self," as someone coming into her own "personhood," depends on a concrete moral choice: to live by letting the other woman live also (as a person, or as a haunting memory) or to live as a social subordinate to men. The feminization process offered by the *Jane Eyre* model has the young woman choose the latter.[23] To this fundamental, morally self-righteous aggression against the other woman, critics such as Kaplan, Armstrong and Tennenhouse, and Spivak have added the gloss of race; they have taught us that this "woman's picture" is, historically speaking, white.

The "Avant-Garde" Model:
Promiscuous and Cosmopolitan, and Still Giving Herself

In some respects, the *Jane Eyre* legacy may be described in the same manner that Moi has described Anglo-American feminist criticism, in terms of "the radical contradiction it presents between feminist politics and patriarchal aesthetics."[24] In the case of the fictional narrative, feminist politics is primarily a matter of an interest in the rise of the domestic woman, the wife, who must nonetheless conform with the patriarchal moral-aesthetic requirement that she be sexually virginal and loyal only to the man and his values (however passionate and cerebral she herself may be). Eventually, this Victorian definition of female power would have to come to terms with another kind of femininity, this time of the woman who no longer stays put as the faithful little wife but who has become sexually liberated. Again, by extending the implications of Moi's terms, it is possible to articulate a special discursive affinity between sexual and textual politics: if female sexual chastity (in Jane Eyre and her Victorian sisters) can be seen as a kind of stable referent, which, in turn, accounts for the production of certain "realist" ("Anglo-American") feminist practices, then female promiscuity should, by extension, result in something quite different, in terms of both sexual mores and textual politics.

It is in this light that Marguerite Duras's *Hiroshima mon amour* (1959, directed by French New Wave director Alain Resnais) may be seen as a "French" response and complement to the Anglo-American fairy tale.[25] First, a brief summary of the film, which one critic has described as "what may well be the most remarkable motion picture landmark of the century":[26] Fourteen years after the end of the Second World War, a French actress comes with a film crew to Japan to make a film about Hiroshima. During her stay, she meets a Japanese architect, with whom she has a brief affair. The encounter with the Japanese man triggers in the woman memories that have long remained inarticulate. These are memories of her traumatic personal experience during the war in Europe. A young girl then, she had fallen in love with a German soldier, and the two were planning to elope to Bavaria to get married. On the eve of their elopement, he was killed by partisans. She was then ostracized as a national traitor and had her hair shorn as part of her punishment. She sank into madness for months, and her family kept her in the cellar. When she recovered, the war had come to an end, and she was sent to Paris. On the day she arrived in Paris, there was news all over the place about the atomic bomb that had been dropped on Hiroshima. Fourteen years later, as a happily married woman, she has come to Japan and met a man who reminds her of her German lover. She recalls the story of her past to the Japanese architect, who urges her to stay longer with him. Caught between the past and the present, between the pain of memory and the intensity of the current romance, the woman seems not to know what will or should happen next. The film ends in this ambiguous, open-ended condition.

Stylistically, *Hiroshima mon amour* is obviously in sharp contrast to Hollywood dramas such as *Rebecca*. To mention just one instance, whereas, in *Rebecca*, the plot is important because its progress is essential to the revelation of the truth, in *Hiroshima mon amour*, the point is rather to experiment with nonlinear narrative, in which memory takes the place of external events to constitute the main action. Instead of a well-plotted story, then, we are looking at psychodrama, the woman's involuntary and unexpected remembrance of her past. By juxtaposing such psychodrama with the documentary or documentarylike images of what happened to the people in Hiroshima because of the atomic bomb, the film problematizes the limits of representation in a self-conscious manner that is characteristic of high modernist and avant-garde works. These obvious stylistic divergences notwithstanding, I think it is more interesting to note the affinities here with the narrative elements of the *Jane Eyre* story. To that extent, it is helpful to borrow loosely from Vladimir Propp's work on Russian fairy tales the notion of "function," which can be understood as "an act of a character, defined from the point of view of its significance for the course of the action." For Propp, such functions are "independent of how and by whom they are fulfilled"; they "constitute the fundamental components of a tale" and tend to remain constant from tale to tale.[27]

I contend that the functions of the *Jane Eyre* paradigm are most strikingly recognizable, paradoxically, when Duras introduces variations—modern-day conversions—in her film text:

1. The figure of the virginal orphan girl is changed into *the sexually experienced and knowledgeable woman*. Importantly, it is she, rather than the man, who now occupies the central position in the narrative as the one with the mysterious past.
2. As in the case of the rich man with a past in the *Jane Eyre* and *Rebecca* stories, in the French woman's past is *the other sexual partner*.

But, whereas in the earlier stories the other woman exists as a threat that needs to be removed, in *Hiroshima mon amour*, the German soldier is recalled with emotional intensity. Rather than trying to get rid of him, the French woman feels guilty that she may be betraying and losing him simply by telling their story.

3. In the present diagesis there is *the new sexual partner*, the Japanese architect. As Jane and the young wife in *Rebecca* listen to their men, the Japanese man listens to the French woman. In other words, the presence of the current partner, again, enables the revelation of what actually happened in the past.

4. Similarly, there is *an act of confession* (of recalling the past), with the difference that it now comes from the woman. As in the Victorian stories, this confession bonds the new lovers. The Japanese man is happy to hear the French woman say that even her husband has not heard her story.

Whereas in *Jane Eyre* and *Rebecca* it is still the man's inner world around which the plot revolves, in *Hiroshima mon amour*, the woman's inner world has come fully to the fore. Whereas in the Anglo-American stories "woman" remains objectified and metaphorically divided into the good girl and the femme fatale, in the French story, it is man who is divided into a past and a present, with no attempt at demonization involved in the woman's own mind (even though the German soldier was a national enemy). As in the case of *Jane Eyre* and *Rebecca*, moreover, the partner in the present is put in the position of someone who has to discover what took place in the past. In *Rebecca*, the innocent wife at first thinks she should become more and more like Rebecca, only to find out that her husband loves her rather for her difference from the dead, older woman. In *Hiroshima mon amour*, the Japanese architect reminds the French woman of her former lover, so much so that she addresses him as "you" when she is talking about the German soldier. In their conversation, the Japanese man willingly plays the role of the other man. In each case, albeit in very different ways, the gendered roles involve questions of identification and disidentification—of the new lover becoming like or unlike the old one—that are critical to the progress of the narrative.

There are also the remaining elements:

5. In contrast to the stately mansion in the Victorian stories, *the setting* in *Hiroshima mon amour* is rather public—a hotel room, the street, a train station, a teahouse, and so forth. But, as in the case of the Victorian stories, these external spaces are meant to foreground the haunted interior of the protagonist, in this case, the French woman.
6. There is also *a catastrophe*. The point of *Hiroshima mon amour* is, however, to raise questions about what the real catastrophe is. Is it Hiroshima? Is it the murder of the woman's German lover in Nevers?
7. While it remains ambiguous and open, *the ending* nonetheless poses a similar question of social reproduction and continuance. After this confrontation between her and him, Nevers and Hiroshima, what?

Here, the most interesting point of contrast with the *Jane Eyre* and *Rebecca* stories is that *Hiroshima mon amour* begins with a public catastrophe (the site at which the atomic bomb was dropped), about which there is no secret. Nevertheless, as in the case of *Jane Eyre* and *Rebecca*, it is an internal journey to the past that takes us to that other, more traumatic catastrophe—with the difference that it is the woman who now assumes center stage as the confessing subject. If Hiroshima is the site of a ruin, Duras's text says, it must now share the focus with the French woman's private life, the interior of her mind, which, too, has experienced destruction and desolation.

Indeed, this division of the past (and its catastrophes) into the public and the private is perhaps *Hiroshima mon amour*'s most significant point of departure from the "realism" of the nineteen-century English woman's novel and the plot-driven drama of Hollywood. In what amounts to a competition introduced at the discursive level between the massive destruction of the population in Hiroshima, on the one hand, and a woman's memory of her love affair, the murder of her lover, her descent into madness, and her recovery, on the other, Duras takes the feminization of Western culture to a new stage of spectacularity, with the powerful suggestion that what happened in a woman's love life, unbeknownst to most, ultimately deserves as much attention as an unprecedented historical disaster that erased an entire city. As Leslie Hill writes, "love and the nuclear holocaust, Japan and France, remembering and forgetting—all the agents of subversion Duras enumerates exist in a relationship of reciprocal equivalence."[28] The boldness of Duras's conception is clearly indicated in the title of the film, which epitomizes in a scandalous fashion the tension between the two ways of remembering the past and naturally provokes the question: "Is this analogy between a personal trauma and an historical one justified? . . . Is historiography akin to the operation of individual memory?"[29] But this seeming scandal is precisely the point of what I would call Duras's avant-garde moralism— namely, that, yes, a banal, commonplace love affair can indeed dominate Hiroshima because in it lies (for Duras) the possibility of *elevating the significance of Hiroshima above the mere documentary level*:[30]

A banal tale, one that happens thousands of times every day. The Japanese is married, has children. So is the French woman, who also has two children. Theirs is a one-night affair.

But where? At Hiroshima.

Their embrace—so banal, so commonplace—takes place in the one city of the world where it is hardest to imagine it: Hiroshima. Nothing is "given" at Hiroshima. Every gesture, every word, takes on an aura of meaning that transcends its literal meaning. And this is one of the principal goals of the film: to have done with the description of horror by horror, for that has been done by the Japanese themselves, but make this horror rise again from its ashes by incorporating it in a love that will necessarily be special and "wonderful," one that will be more credible than if it had occurred anywhere else in the world, a place that death had not *preserved*. . . .

Their personal story, however brief that may be, always dominates Hiroshima.

If this premise were not adhered to, this would be just one more made-to-order picture [*film de commande*], of no more interest than any fictionalized documentary [*documentaire romancé*]. If it is adhered to, we'll end up with a sort of false documentary that will probe the lesson of Hiroshima more deeply than any made-to-order documentary [*documentaire de commande*].

(9–10; emphasis in the original)[31]

There is little doubt as to Duras's authorial intention in these remarks. For my purposes, what matters is not whether her text corresponds exactly to her intention but the manner in which she goes about realizing it. To make a story that is not "just one more made-to-order picture," Duras, like Brontë and Hitchcock before her, makes use of sexuality as it is attached to womanhood. Not being Victorian, she does not require her heroine to be sexually chaste. Instead, she gives us an attractive and experienced married woman, to whom occasional sexual infidelity is not a moral concern. Moreover, it is this openness to sex with multiple partners, we might say, that allows the woman a unique means of access to the meaning of her existence, her postcatastrophic survival. By making her protagonist a promiscuous woman, Duras has therefore moved the narrative constituents of the *Jane Eyre* fairy tale to a fresh level of sophistication: not only is the "loose" sexual behavior of woman no longer an issue; it is, on the contrary, such looseness, such rejection of bygone sexual constraints, that becomes the key to an intense emotional experience, transgressing and subverting the boundaries of what is conventionally (socially and nationally as well as morally) acceptable. Sex and love are, we are compelled to think, not so banal after all: like Hiroshima, sex and love, when attached to a liberated woman, are equally, if not more, violent and earthshaking events.

Significantly, sexuality is no longer only situated on the woman's body but primarily in her mind, her "subjectivity." This otherwise invisible, interior depth is what is being displayed on the screen as the woman recalls the past. Instead of the body surface, then, it is sexuality as remembered in the cavities of the woman's mind that have been brought to light and laid bare in her act of confession. Like the Japanese architect, the film's viewers become voyeurs who are privileged to enter this sexuality and engage with its unique revelations. For Duras, the French woman's act of confessing is the equivalent of a gift of the most sacred kind:

To give oneself, body and soul, that's it.

That is the equivalent not only of amorous possession, but of a *marriage*.

She gives this Japanese—*at Hiroshima*—her most precious possession: herself as she now is [*son expression actuelle même*], her *survival* after the death of her love *at Nevers*.

(112; emphases in the original)

Whereas the man's confession about his past in *Jane Eyre* and *Rebecca* is what makes the young second wife give her body and soul to him, here, the promiscuous woman's confession about her past is the equivalent of her giving body and soul to the new man. Despite the apparent contrasts in technique between the Anglo-American and French stories of feminization, in both cases, confession is ultimately linked to the *giving of herself* by the woman, which is, in turn, sanctified as "marriage." Albeit operating with a different set of sexual mores, the French woman arrives at this remarkable resemblance to Jane Eyre and the nameless second wife in *Rebecca* because Duras's presentation of her, in the final analysis, is that she is a victim, vulnerable and helpless before the weight of a repressed memory. Like her Anglo-American sisters, Duras tells us, the French woman is a survivor, who has now, through her act of giving herself, successfully captured a man of her desire.

In the hands of Duras, Western female subjectivity has become fully vindicated, beyond the mere physical body, as a kind of dissident, delirious, poetic text—a text that is at "play" between absence and presence and amply "resistant" to "recuperation" by public history (I am citing from the repertoire of terms that are commonly invoked to describe the revolutionary pleasures of the avant-garde text). To go one step further, I would argue that Duras's rewriting of female sexuality is homologous to the poststructuralist rewriting of textuality. Like the poststructuralist text, female sexuality is now treated as an unstable, mobile signifier, no longer to be confined to a realist referent, and *that*, so the logic goes, is what makes "woman" interesting. But precisely at the place at which the woman is, as Duras believes, at her most vulnerable and helpless (because she is exposing herself to her new lover and thus to the audience's gaze), feminization in its avant-garde form becomes racial power. If, in the *Jane Eyre* narrative, the ascendance of the rural, orphaned woman to second-wifehood means the elimination of the other woman, in Duras, the ascendance of the cosmopolitan woman as text—in the form of her open sexuality, her memory, her subjectivity—goes hand in hand with a minimization, if not disappearance, of the other man. This is not the white man, the German lover who continues to be a cherished part of the woman's memory, but the second partner, the Japanese architect, whose presence, much like that of the nameless little wife in *Rebecca*, is mainly for the purpose of serving as a screen on which the woman can recall and project her past.

Apart from its genealogical linkages with the Anglo-American fairy tales in terms of narrative functions, therefore, the status of the French woman's story should also be understood in contrast to the absence of a story from the Japanese architect, who is in the main presented as a male pursuing a female in the classic romantic manner. In a story that is otherwise astutely attentive to issues of memory, suffering, and survival, the Japanese architect, who is also a survivor of the war, strangely does not enjoy the same kind of psychological and textual exploration that is given the French woman. This point, I would like to stress, is not as simple as it may sound, because it is not a matter of faulting Duras for not writing an equally profound story about the Japanese. Rather, it is a questioning of the distribution of narrative investments on the very terms that Duras herself proposes to distinguish her avant-garde project.

To begin to see this, we need to remember that the explicit or implicit target of much of high modernist and avant-garde literature and film is, as Moi's reading of Anglo-American feminist criticism pointedly suggests, realism—the hardcore referentiality that, for modernists and avant-garde writers, is a kind of representational ideology of a bygone era, something that is quite beneath notice. This rather condescending tone toward the realist and the referential is the one in which Moi couches her assessment of the Anglo-American feminists, who are, she implies, not as theoretically advanced as the French women theorists because they are somehow (alas, still) stuck in the primitive (Victorian) modes of representation (hence they are *merely* political). Duras's work, insofar as it consciously sets itself apart from what she calls "made-to-order" documentaries, insofar as it firmly rejects a realist and public historical approach to Hiroshima, must be understood also in terms of this representational dialectic between so-called referentiality and its avant-garde dislocation. It is in the context of these progressivist theoretical arguments about representation that the absence of a story about the Japanese takes on significance. For, in *Hiroshima mon amour*, the "primitive" modes of representation have not exactly disappeared; they are simply displaced.

In a text whose avowed aesthetic aim is to resist the superficiality of documentary realism, exactly the documentary approach, it appears, is adopted in relation to the racial other—Hiroshima, the Japanese people, the architect and his family. There are, for instance, the realist newsreel images of massive destruction and bodily remains that accompany the camera tour of the Hiroshima War Museum and hospital at the beginning of the film. Captured in a series of fast-moving tracking shots that assemble disparate fragments of visual information into a narrative of facts, the racial other appears here in the form of a public history and record for all to see. The point of the nominal, cursory recognition of this history and record, which remains a spectacle we scan rapidly from the outside, is in order to show that it will pale—become meaningless, perhaps—in due course, in comparison with the unseen, psychological, private history and record we are about to discover, through a more slowly paced and reflective narrative, lying deep inside the woman. The Japanese man's voice, repeatedly refuting the woman's account of the knowledge about Hiroshima culled from the public images, comes across as a sign of the so-called limit of Western knowledge that the Western avant-garde habitually attributes to the non-Western other—in such a manner, however, as to leave that other in an essentialized, almost mechanical condition (the Japanese man is making the same noise over and over again: "Tu n'a rien vu à Hiroshima"). Even as this other insists that the French woman has "seen nothing," then, his status does not go beyond that of a personification—an acoustic as well as visual objectification in human form—of the "impossibility," the "impasse" of Western thought. Western thought, now feminized, remains the central drama. (I am reminded of Derrida's invocation of Chinese writing as a way to deconstruct, to show the limit of, Western logocentrism.)

Remembering Huyssen's point about high modernist art—that it is, despite its adversary stance toward bourgeois society, epistemologically bound to the reality principle rather than the pleasure principle of that society—we can begin to see the evaluative hierarchy that structures Duras's conception of her story. Realism and referentiality, being scorned mimetic orders, are no longer good enough for a progressive, avant-garde representation of the French woman, who embodies a profound, psychologically individuated reality. But realism and referentiality, she seems meanwhile to say, remain adequate and appropriate for the representation of yellow people, whose reality, being less profound, can continue to be treated as a group event (in a manner similar to what I have been referring to as coercive mimeticism). On the one hand, then, the Japanese architect is presented as a member of a collective, and his victimization, like the victimization of Japan, has this public (accessible) meaning only, in contrast to that of his lover. When he asks what kind of film she is making in Hiroshima, for instance, the French woman says: "A film about Peace. What else do you expect them to make in Hiroshima except a picture about Peace?" (34). Cultural difference, in other words, is organized on the representational plane in terms of an opposition between the refinement of sexual and textual play and the elementariness of a crude and old-fashioned factographicity (of that which is already understood and can bring no surprise, as the woman's words imply: what else do you expect?). On the other hand, cultural difference, even though found throughout the text and already organized in this representationally hierarchical manner, is simultaneously disavowed by authorial direction. Duras insists:

> It is preferable to minimize the difference between the two protagonists. If the audience never forgets that this is the story of a Japanese man and a French woman, the profound implications of the film are lost. If the audience does forget it, these profound implications become apparent.
>
> Monsieur Butterfly is outmoded. So is Mademoiselle de Paris. We should count upon the egalitarian function of the modern world. . . . This Franco-Japanese film should *never* seem *Franco-Japanese*, but *anti-Franco-Japanese*. That would be a victory.
>
> His profile might almost seem French. A high forehead. A large mouth. Full, but hard lips. Nothing affected or fragile about his face. No angle from which his features might seem vague (indecisive).
>
> *In short, he is an "international" type* [*En somme, il est d'un type "international"*]. . . .

. . . He is a modern man, wise in the ways of the world. He would
not feel out of place in any country in the world.

> (109–10; first three emphases in the original, last emphasis mine)

What, we might ask, is an " 'international' type" if not precisely a "made-
to-order" documentary representation?

All in all, whether hierarchically organized (in which case, it is disparaged as mere realism and referentiality) or disavowed (in which case,
it should be forgotten in favor of a modern, internationalist humanism),
cultural difference—"Japan"—is there simply in order for the subjectivity—the existential survival, the attainment of individual being—of the
French woman to be performed. As Sharon Willis puts it, "In refusing
the capitalizing gesture, along with the totalizing gesture of the mastery
of history, *Hiroshima mon amour* risks denying its own particular investments, the specific effects of history, and the inescapability of the referent which as much conditions the textual enterprise as does that referent's very inaccessibility."[32] As in the dialectic between high modernism
and mass culture that Huyssen dissects, Duras's avant-garde text fully
depends on mass culture—the "made-to-order" documentary that it consciously disdains—in order to be what it is. Only thus does her avant-
garde text achieve its puritanist revolutionariness.

By the standards set by Moi, a text such as Duras's, on account of its
textual radicalness, should be deemed more political than a naive political protest against the horrors of Hiroshima. In my brief comparison of
Duras's text to the *Jane Eyre* model, I hope I have demonstrated—
against the common belief that Anglo-American and French feminisms
are drastically different phenomena—some of the structural and imaginary continuities between two major instances of feminization that bear
these ethnic labels.

To clarify this further, let me reiterate that it is, of course, pertinent
to recognize the different moral-aesthetic premises on which each of
these fairy tales operates. In the Anglo-American model, representation
still functions on the basis of a classic opposition between an inside and
an outside, so that in the course of the second wife's progress, she gradually moves from being a powerless outsider, rejected by her society, to
being an insider firmly rooted in the patriarchal order, its angel of the

house. Her power as woman, notably, is achieved through the removal and exclusion of others, especially other women, from her arena. Instead of her, it is these other women who must now remain forever on the outside. The plot of feminization at this juncture has simply confirmed and perpetuated the logic of a well-worn masculinist moral aesthetic. In the French model, moral-aesthetic issues are articulated differently because representation itself, as is often the case in high modernist and avant-garde texts, is no longer assumed to be a transparent process. Whereas, in *Jane Eyre* and *Rebecca*, it is still possible to concentrate on the story, in *Hiroshima mon amour*, the story is about the process of storytelling, the act of representation (hence Duras's many remarks as to what she wants her film text to be and how it should be received, etc.). It is in this sense that the text has taken on a material, opaque status, removing the moral-aesthetic distinctions that used to divide inside and outside, reality and fiction, or history and memory and rendering these oppositions as different points on the same representational plane.[33] Despite this highly self-conscious understanding of representation, however, despite the magisterial manner in which she has done away with the moralism of an earlier era and lifted the status of fiction and memory to a level as solemn as "reality" and "history," my point is that Duras's avant-garde film text introduces a new kind of moralist opposition—this time, in a progressivist manner—between the mimetic realism of "made-to-order" documentaries and the avant-gardism of her own aesthetics, into which she respectively inserts nonwhite people (as a mass) and her white heroine (as an individual).

Duras's example demonstrates that the maneuver of textualizing politics, while oftentimes a necessary and instructive complement to the simple practice of politicizing texts, is not itself ideology-free, although ideology has now taken the form of theoretical advancement—by way of a subtle redivision of narrative/representational investments. If the most radical aspect of the textualization of politics—of the move to dislocate even a weighty historical referent such as Hiroshima—turns out to be dependent, for its own avant-garde battles, on a recuperation of referentiality and mimeticism as the semiotic ghetto in which to banish the nonwhite other, then "French," we might argue, is not so distinguishable from "Anglo-American" after all. Duras's text, which I have, for my own purposes, used as a referent for the fraught politics around feminization and representation, simply goes to show how sophisticated textualist politics does not necessarily preclude cultural imperialism, which is most successful when victimhood can continue to be used to expound particular subjectivities at the expense of other historical victims, when the difference between their respective representational statuses is, a priori, raced and/or ethnicized.[34]

If I am suggesting an alternative way of politicizing the text in order to counter the poststructuralist euphoria of textualizing politics, it is not simply by way of a return to Lukácsian realism. Rather, it is a practice of reading that, even as it must become sensitive to textual nuance and experimentation, would also be on the alert to detect precisely the avant-garde, textualist, and theoretical complicity with the perpetuation of any racialist hold on victimhood itself as cultural capital.[35]

What Ails White Feminism?

Whether the text concerned is Victorian, modernist, or avant-garde, then, the tendency to monopolize and capitalize on victimhood is, to parody the title of Susan Gubar's 1998 article, what ails white feminism, which, since the second-wave feminism of the 1970s and 1980s, has been reluctant to dislodge white women from their preferred status as the representatives of alterity throughout Western history. As Sherene H. Razack puts it: "Confronted with white racial superiority, white women can deny their dominance by retreating to a position of subordination—that is, since we are oppressed as women, we cannot be oppressors of women of colour." Razack argues that only an "interlocking analysis" can remind us "of the ease with which we slip into positions of subordination . . . without seeing how this very subordinate location simultaneously reflects and upholds race and class privilege" (14).

This racialist reluctance to give up the hold on victimhood is what Nancy Armstrong in her work on Anglo-American fiction refers to as the lingering power of the notion of captivity, a notion that, as I argued in chapter 1, is firmly inscribed in Lukács's influential theory of class consciousness and the many subsequent versions of minority identity struggles (including prevalent forms of feminism) that have wittingly or unwittingly modeled themselves after it. Armstrong argues a very different politics of captivity from Lukács's in her reading of the captivity narratives that were produced during British colonial days in America, circulated back to the mother country, and remade into sentimental novels.[36] Whereas, in Lukács's work, captivity is transformed through (the proletarian's) resistance to capital into class consciousness and thus emancipation, for Armstrong, captivity is inseparable from a form of power that is distinguished by its twin capacity for sustaining victimhood (as a way to legitimize social protest) and for transforming victimhood into the very means of cultural domination. Armstrong's argument is thus much closer to Max Weber's about the Protestant work ethic in that the transformation of victimhood (or lowly social status) is accomplishable precisely through hard work, which is then duly rewarded in worldly terms. In the context of *Jane Eyre*, accordingly, Armstrong shows that it is Jane, rather than Bertha, who personifies the power of captivity. In her tortuous personal development as a heroine, Jane becomes both a critic of the sexism of the dominant order and an agent of English imperialism. Jane's "claim that 'this social order is bad, because it excludes me,' " Armstrong writes, "is perfectly compatible . . . with the claim that 'this social order is good insofar as it includes me.' " This is because captivity, exclusion, and subordination—negative experiences that justify Jane's anger and protest as a social outcast—are, in the course of the narrative, converted by her diligence, honesty, courage, and endurance into the means of her empowerment, her final acceptance by the social order. This process of empowerment also entails her control and expulsion of others. "Where the first claim launches a critique," Armstrong adds, "the second claim limits that critique to a demand that never threatens but, indeed, updates the status quo and imbues it with a sense of adequacy" (390).

Once the lingering power of captivity is understood in tandem with the Weberian economic-spiritual framework of labor and its cumulative rewards, the complaints we hear from time to time from second-wave feminist critics about the current theoretical climate in the academy can be seen as part and parcel of an endeavor to keep the cultural capital of victimhood on the side of white feminism. This is the light in which I, for one, read Susan Gubar's text "What Ails Feminist Criticism?"[37] This title provides the key to the Victorian mode in which Gubar conceives of her narrative. Accordingly, it is feminist criticism itself that now occupies the position of the wronged and abused heroine. This remarkable "woman," so the logic of this tale goes, was filled with healthy rage at an unjust social order and made her rightful protests. But, despite the battles she had to fight and despite the accomplishments she has made for herself and others, she is once again maligned, besieged, held captive—this time by "a number of developments in the eighties and nineties," which pose "a hazard to the vitality of feminist literary studies" (880). These developments include, on the one hand, "racialized identity politics," which "made the word *women* slim down to stand only for a very particularized kind of woman" and, on the other, poststructuralist theory, which "obliged the term to disappear altogether" (901; emphasis in the original). Gubar's account is filled with the vocabulary of dis-ease such as "maladies," "infirmities," "sickbed," "ailment," and the like. For scholars like her, who, to borrow the words of Razack, "have been arguing from a point of subordination, a position of innocence and non-implication in systems of oppression," "it is white women who are really disparaged . . . and it is they who are the outsiders in the academy today."[38]

Despite having become dominant, in other words, white feminism as voiced by Gubar continues to position itself as a culture on the defense. What must be defended is precisely the realm of spiritual as well as material power stockpiled through hard work, through the elaboration and belaboring of "woman" as captive. Armstrong's words about the larger historical implications of the lure of captivity offer a sobering account of the vested interests at stake:

Even after the culture held captive has become the dominant culture, the captivity narrative represents that culture as a culture on the defense. Compelled by its own logic to expand the domain of capital, this culture defines its distinctive values in precisely other than economic terms and imagines those values as perpetually in danger. For this culture imagines itself in a feminine position under conditions of cultural warfare, in which the purity of its women, the safety of its children, and the sanctity of its basic unit, the household, are up for grabs. This is no less true for England and the United States under conditions of globalization, instantaneous communication, and hi-tech warfare, than it was during the epochs of Richardson, Austen, and Brontë."[39]   (395)

As Robyn Wiegman points out, what Gubar fails or refuses to see is that perhaps it is precisely the new, interdisciplinary developments of intellectual inquiry, demonized by her as "debilitating" her heroine, which are keeping feminist criticism alive and healthy today.[40] But whereas Wiegman sees the tensions and conflicts brought by these other developments as opportunities for feminist criticism to rethink its tasks—indeed, to reassess the conditions of its own continued existence in relation to others—Gubar chooses instead to hold on to the sentimental language of captivity, injury, defense, and healing. The history of feminist criticism she writes remains articulated from the "celebratory vantage point of a gender privileged approach" (370), for which the emergence of "woman" is the originary, Edenic event, while any attempt to challenge it, however historically reasoned such an attempt may be, will have to be construed as a rude assault on the identity of an innocent victim.

So, when whiteness feminizes . . . the myth is that the world would from then on be fairly redistributed on the new basis of a man-woman relation. As white feminists soon discover, things have not quite stabilized in the way they expect. Because she is figured as supplementary to man, "woman," by necessity, comes with two possible types of epistemological consequences. One of these would always involve attempts to strip the supplement of its supplementary force and recontain it within a single entity; the other would follow the supplement's logic to make way for other supplements to the supplement that is woman. In the morphology of fictional elements I have discussed (Gubar's narrative about feminist criticism being one of their latest variations), it would appear that what often surfaces in classic white feminine/feminist texts is precisely a restriction and containment of the supplement. Even so, the supplements to "woman" will undoubtedly persist. In the form of demons and specters, or else in the form of made-to-order documentaries, these other supplements—the other kinds of women, the non-Western men as well as women—will continue to remind us of the fundamentally open, indeed unfinishable, story of the emergence of "woman" in the midst of unequal multiethnic representational practices.[41]

Beyond Ethnic *Ressentiment*?

In his well-known work *Black Skin, White Masks*, Frantz Fanon has given us some of the most memorable arguments about how the culture of colonialism leaves indelible psychic damage on the colonized. One of the inescapable traumatizing experiences of being black in the French colony, Fanon points out, is that of being objectified, stigmatized, and thus humiliated *into* consciousness. While his account remains to this day an indispensable resource of insights into the ideological legacy of political and cultural domination and of racial discrimination, it is in his controversial discussion of the sexual practices of women of color that we discover perhaps the most profound affective disorders afflicting the colonized subject, including the anticolonialist critic himself. Fanon's indictment of women of color stems from his observation that they tend to desire sexual relations with white men as a means of upward social mobility. In his impassioned criticism of their behavior, he seems to have resorted precisely to the mechanisms of stigmatizing, objectification, and discrimination that he otherwise associates with the white colonizer. A passage from his text offers a glimpse into his acrimonious, self-conflictual mode of relating to the female members of his ethnic group:

> For, in a word, the race must be whitened; every woman in Martinique knows this, says it, repeats it. Whiten the race, save the race, but not in the sense that one might think: not "preserve the uniqueness of that part of the world in which they grew up," but make sure that it will be white. Every time I have made up my mind to analyze certain kinds of behavior, I have been unable to avoid the consideration of certain nauseating phenomena. The number of sayings, proverbs, petty rules of conduct that govern the choice of a lover in the Antilles is astounding. It is always essential to avoid falling back into the pit of niggerhood, and every woman in the Antilles, whether in a casual flirtation or in a serious affair, is determined to select the least black of the men. Sometimes, in order to justify a bad investment, she is compelled to resort to such arguments as this: "X is black, but misery is blacker." I know a great number of girls from Martinique, students in France, who admitted to me with complete candor—completely white candor—that they would find it impossible to marry black men.[1]

I have elsewhere provided a substantive critique of Fanon's predicament in terms of the difficulties facing the male critic who is attempting, in the postcolonial aftermath, to articulate a vision of a future community.[2] Rather than simply faulting Fanon for being a classic male chauvinist, I suggested, as I would still do, that Fanon's apparently misogynist statements should be understood in their full psychic complexity, in which people who are ethnically akin to him are converted into dangerous enemies aggressing against his community from the outside. Ironically, by their licentious sexual behavior, the women of color come rather close to putting into reality Fanon's own political aspirations—aspirations toward the possibility of a kind of community that is based not so much on biological determinants of race, blood, and skin color as on the freedom to cross and move beyond such boundaries. In using their sexuality to bring about the material effects of miscegenation, these women of color embody the potential eventually to transform a society that is rigidly polarized between black and white. In their supposedly deplorable tendency toward what Fanon calls lactification, then, lie the threat and the promise of a new epistemological horizon—a racially mixed world with a new kind of human being who is not pure but thoroughly hybrid—to which the righteous, anticolonialist ruminations of Fanon, in fact, also point. In other words, although it may appear that these women are being disparaged on account of their lasciviousness and greediness for power, in the end it is perhaps their proximity to, and hence rivalry with, the male critic's own theoretical vision (and the enormous political consequences it entails) that explains his indignant reaction, his need to differentiate himself from them. This reaction is triggered by the intuition that the new epistemological horizon of which he has been dreaming can, alas, be engendered and represented independently of him—not through the community of black males, as he wishes, but instead (if only inadvertently) through the sexual force and reproductive labor of black women.

In thus literally marking the women as whores and converting them into traitors to their own community, could Fanon be seen as being caught in a familiar condition, the condition of *ressentiment*?

According to Max Scheler, who bases his analysis of *ressentiment* on the work of Nietzsche,[3] two characteristics are essential to the occurrence of *ressentiment*, which can be loosely defined as a repeated negative response, a persistent emotional movement of hostility, that nonetheless cannot be overtly expressed and must remain repressed. First, Scheler writes, *ressentiment* tends to accumulate in those social situations in which there is, on the one hand, a general assumption of equality among all human beings and, on the other, persistent inequities and discriminatory practices. By this formulation, a caste society in which the hierarchical differentiations among people are clearly acknowledged is much less charged with the potential buildup of *ressentiment* than one in which there is a contradiction between the official story that all men are equal regardless of their class, gender, race, and age and people's actual lived experiences. Second, *ressentiment*, which, as mentioned, is normally a repressed structure of feeling, tends to become externalizable when a particular target (a person or group) can be identified as the cause for our privation, for our impotence in altering the situation in which we feel injured (32–33).

In the colonial situation, the target at which *ressentiment* is usually directed is, for obvious reasons, the colonizer (the party who, as is historically the case, rhetorically advocates universal human rights even while it oppresses and exploits those who are colonized). But, from the perspective of the colonized, there is an additional dimension to the trajectory of *ressentiment* in the aftermath of colonialism, at the time when the old, rigid polarization of social identities based on racial difference has supposedly given way to a new situation in which those who were colonized have now gained the right to self-determination. Exactly at this juncture of a seeming liberalization from colonial domination (territorial and ideological), when those who were previously subjugated begin to enjoy a modicum of democratized access to the representation of their own historical existence, *ressentiment* tends, I would contend, to assume its hold fiercely on the postcolonized ethnic community. In Fanon's case, we see the resurgence of this emotion in the name of nationalist or ethnic group solidarity for the future but directed in no uncertain terms against the women of the black community, who are at once pathologized for their *sexual* lewdness and repudiated for having sold out to *white* supremacy.[4]

This psychic structure of a reaction to the injustice created by the coercive and unequal encounter with the white world, a reaction that, in the course of postcoloniality, ends up directing rancor toward certain members of the one's own ethnic group—that ends up, as it were, ethnically profiling, shaming, and scapegoating these members—can also be demonstrated by more contemporary incidents. Let me mention a fairly recent example.

In 1999 the Chinese novelist Ha Jin's novel *Waiting* won the National Book Award in the United States. In the summer of the following year, the Beijing Publishing Group, which had made a verbal agreement with Ha Jin's American publisher, Pantheon Books, to publish a Chinese translation of the novel, dropped its plans after the book had been attacked in the Chinese media as "a tool used by the American media to slander China." A Beijing University professor, Liu Yiqing, was quoted as accusing

Ha Jin of "selling out his country in order to win the National Book Award." The book's success, Liu reportedly wrote in a book review, was "part of a plot by the American media to demonize China by showing China's backwardness and the stupidity of the Chinese people."[5]

Importantly, Ha Jin's "crime" is defined in the following manner: not only has he sold out his own culture by depicting its backwardness; more depravedly, he has done it in order to gain approval from Westerners, the Americans. Just why does such accusation of treachery and betrayal tend to occur precisely at the moment of an ethnic author's achievement of international success, when he has received a kind of recognition that, to all appearances, should bring pride and jubilation to his own ethnic/national community?

The colonized, writes Fanon, are those "in whose soul an inferiority complex has been created by the death and burial of [their] local cultural originality."[6] To "death and burial," which are final, we should add "degradation" and "demotion," ongoing processes the effects of which last considerably into postcoloniality. To repeat the point that I have made in different ways throughout this book, what is at stake here is the superimposition of a ruthlessly hierarchized class structure on ethnic and racial differences, predestining those who, by the accident of birth, belong to the colonized ethnic group to that "inferiority complex" Fanon mentions, whenever they are faced with the image, the language, and the culture of those who are, by this historical divide, deemed superior. But the most long-lasting symptom of this inferiority complex is perhaps not so much the negative emotion directed against those who are deemed superior as a profound self-hatred, a negative emotion that is, in turn, directed against those who ethnically most resemble oneself. (This resemblance, this similarity, would, of course, not have been significant were it not for the fact that, in the postcolonized situation, it is typically imagined as the basis for anticolonial group solidarity. Consequently, it is also such group solidarity that tends to be assumed as the moral high ground by those who attack the "traitors.")

In Ha Jin's case, we witness a good instance of the familiar cycle of ambivalent feelings toward the West that had resulted from China's history of humiliating contact with Western countries since the mid-nineteenth century. This is a history in which the West has been alternately desired and feared, admired and hated. The predominant legacy of this history is that the Western gaze has come to stand as the determinant of Chinese identitarian and cultural value. "They don't see us!" "How can we make them see us?" "Look at how they look at us!" "Why do they look at us this way?" "How can we change the ways they look at us?" "Forget it—they will never see us right!" The intense investment in—and cathexis to—the Western gaze arises from the belief that this gaze carries with it a kind of power that matters. For the same reason, we almost never hear complaints about how Africans, Indians, Palestinians, or Native Americans see or stereotype Chinese people; it is as though, in modernity, the Western gaze, and the Western gaze alone, counts as what can give China and Chinese people their needed self-esteem.

This historical emotional structure typically finds its moment of impassioned, and often antagonistic, externalization when a fellow ethnic Chinese achieves non-Chinese, especially Western, recognition. Much like the renowned film director Zhang Yimou, whose early films depicting the decrepitude of feudal China won him international recognition, only then to meet with repeated censorship in the People's Republic and moral disdain from Chinese scholars and critics,[7] or the conceptual artist Cai Guoqiang, whose re-creation of a propaganda work of the Cultural Revolution period won him high honors at the Venice Biennale but stirred outrage among academic critics back in China,[8] an author/intellectual, such as Ha Jin, who has received a major award in the West, is commonly subjected to suspicion and condemnation as pandering to the tastes of foreign devils. Fully implicated in the politics of ethnicity in postcolonial modernity, such suspicion and condemnation are but the flip side of an equally characteristic situation in which, for instance, the Nobel Prize in Literature has been coveted yearly among contemporary Chinese writers;[9] long lines of applicants wait daily outside the U.S. embassy in Beijing, Shanghai, and other Chinese cities to obtain visas to go to America; and dreams of being able to *chuguo*, to "leave the country" or "go abroad" and obtain degrees from institutions such as Yale, Princeton, and Harvard, continue to preoccupy many who are obligated to stay at home. This is a situation in which, even as the West is rhetorically denounced for being imperialist and orientalist, knowledge of the West, access to the West, and recognition by the West remain the very criteria by which ethnics judge one another's existential value and social success in the postcolonial world.

In this process, the initial anger at and hatred of the West, and the culturally inferior status to which the ethnic culture has been reduced by Western contact, are subsequently directed against those members of the ethnic group who happen to have "made it"—who happen to have attained the knowledge of, access to, and validation by the West that are, in fact, consciously and unconsciously longed for by the postcolonial ethnic community as a whole. Once attained, however, *their* success tends to be disparaged because, so goes the logic of *ressentiment*, it is what deprives *us*—those who are stuck at home and who are more authentic (by virtue of the fact that we have not been recognized by Westerners in the same way)—of our agency in representing ourselves. Under the burden of the Western gaze, what understandably begins as envy for a fellow ethnic's success thus reworks itself into contempt for that success, so as to veil the gnawing sense of one's own inadequacy or failure in the guise of a vigilant superego, a moral conscience proclaimed in the name of the collective. In light of the analysis in the chapter "Keeping Them in Their Place," this attempt at establishing critical distance by devaluing a fellow ethnic is, of course, not entirely without its justification: the recognition of non-Western works and authors by the West is, more often than not, itself problematic. As Aijaz Ahmad puts it, "the retribution visited upon the head of an Asian, an African, an Arab intellectual who is of any consequence and who writes in English is that he/she is immediately elevated to the lonely splendour of a 'representative'—of a race, a continent, a civilization, even the 'third world.'" [10] To extend Ahmad's argument, I would add that this "retribution" includes the scorn of the ethnic community as well. In this manner, ethnic *ressentiment* and coercive mimeticism fatefully complement each other, and the wheel of postcolonial cross-ethnic representational politics comes full circle.

At the same time, what accompanies the ethnic habit to spurn those who have "made it" is a deep-rooted anxiety and defensiveness about what the ethnic culture amounts to and how it ought to be represented to the world at large. The fact that someone—indeed, one of the same ethnicity—can be attacked for not representing it "correctly" (for whatever reason) is probably the best evidence for the awareness, however repressed and disavowed, that there is no unanimity, no absolute consensus on this issue; that conflict is actually a locus of reproduction and regeneration; and that even the most long-held and cherished assumptions about the ethnic culture are contestable and potentially dismantleable. Hence the criticism of treachery and betrayal, however justified it may be in some cases, paradoxically always lends credence to the very thing it is trying to condemn—namely, that the representation of the ethnic culture is a historical, discursive event, one, moreover, that is up for grabs and can never be made the exclusive and permanent propriety of any single party, not even a totalitarian regime. For exactly this reason, perhaps, such criticism must strike with that well-tried and seemingly invincible game plan, the deployment of stereotypes. We therefore encounter time and again, as we do in the cases of Fanon's denunciation of the black whores, Professor Liu Yiqing's denunciation of Ha Jin, ethnic Chinese audiences' dismissal of Zhang Yimou, mainland Chinese academic critics' denunciation of Cai Guoqiang and belittlement of Gao Xingjian, and so forth, the well-honed stereotype of the successful ethnic who has sold out and who is thus "inauthentic." As Garrett Hongo writes in regard to the comparable politics of Asian American literary production: "If a writer was adjudged successful in the larger culture, either by bestseller popularity or by virtue of certain awards, then this very success invalidated that writer as an *authentic* Asian American one. This judgment often licensed out-and-out rudeness toward some Asian American writers when they visited college and university campuses. Others could be excluded for 'inauthenticity' or boycotted by the faithful if their visits arose from an invitation by an English Department rather than from Ethnic Studies."[11]

This gesture of stereotyping *another* as treacherous, a move always made altruistically on behalf of the entire ethnic community from within, becomes finally the violent ostracizing of that ethnic who has, as it were, already gained recognition beyond the community. In some instances (often those pertaining to women authors, artists, or intellectuals), the implicit charges of treachery and betrayal are accompanied by an effort to pathologize—to turn the works of the "suspects" into psychobiographies of their inner disturbance and imbalance. By thus chastising the successful ethnic as a turncoat, a comprador, a collaborationist, or simply a mental patient with some psychically transgressive disorder—in brief, by making him or her a flawed copy of the real thing—the ethnic community wishfully discredits his or her (contentious) representation of the ethnic culture in question and reinforces the status quo—and the fantasy—of the proper that it seeks to maintain.

But Ha Jin's work already exists in English and will soon in many other languages. What does it mean to halt its translation into Chinese?[12] Behind the anxious claim to national and ethnic propriety is an even more desperate, indeed futile, endeavor to block the traffic, into the ethnic language, of information about China that already has currency in the world outside China. Much like the attempts made by the Chinese government to control the flow of information on the Internet, this attempt at impeding translation, too, was an attempt to prohibit not only the production but also the exchange of information—ironically, when China had been greatly eager to become a member of the World Trade Organization for precisely the benefits of commercial exchange. The exchanges that China does not want, however, are the kinds that would finally redefine what constitutes China, the Chinese people, the Chinese language, and Chinese culture itself—representational exchanges that materialize through signs, images, and discourses; weightless things that cannot exactly be policed, deterred, and intercepted at borders.

The unbearable lightness of postcolonial, postmodern ethnicity! This little book has attempted to describe, in a series of theoretical readings, some of the critical junctures in its productive but tortuous trajectory. While callings to the protestant ethnic will no doubt continue to be generated everywhere, in the spirit of capitalism, with sumptuous worldly and otherworldly rewards, one can only hope that the readings here will provide an incentive, however minimal and preliminary, to interrupt such ethnicity's self-loathing emotional structure—and help put an end to its entrenched discriminatory logic.

Notes

Introduction: From Biopower to Ethnic Difference

1. Michel Foucault, *The Order of Things: An Archaeology of the Human Sciences* (London: Tavistock, 1970).

2. Michel Foucault, *The History of Sexuality*, vol. 1, *An Introduction*, trans. Robert Hurley (New York: Vintage, 1980), 135–59. Foucault's remark about "the fundamental" part of the book is found in Michel Foucault, *Power/Knowledge: Selected Interviews and Other Writings, 1972–1977*, ed. Colin Gordon, trans. Colin Gordon, Leo Marshall, John Mepham, and Kate Soper (New York: Pantheon, 1977), 222.

3. Some authors have argued that biopower is characteristic of the passage, within capitalism, from the older forms of European imperialism to the new global (often U.S.) form of sovereignty. "In the postmodernization of the global economy, the creation of wealth tends ever more toward what we will call biopolitical production, the production of social life itself, in which the econom-

ic, the political, and the cultural increasingly overlap and invest one another" (Michael Hardt and Antonio Negri, *Empire* [Cambridge: Harvard
University Press, 2000], xiii; see also pp. 22–41 for a more detailed engagement with Foucault's notion).

4. See Ann Laura Stoler, *Race and the Education of Desire: Foucault's* History of Sexuality *and the Colonial Order of Things* (Durham, N.C., and
London: Duke University Press, 1995).

5. The abbreviation TM refers to the last of Foucault's 1976 Collège de
France lectures, published posthumously as "Faire vivre et laisser mourir:
La naissance du racisme," *Les Temps Modernes* 46, no. 535 (February
1991): 37–61. Toward the end of her book, Stoler comments on the historicity of Foucault's concern with racism in this manner: "A French
post–world war II episteme defined his understanding of racism in some
predictable ways. His central reference for racism was still that of the
holocaust and the Nazi state, not the discourses and dislocations of de-
colonization that, in the last two decades, have transfigured the face of
Europe, the United States, and those who speak through and against
racist politics within them" (196–97).

6. Foucault's analysis of racist genocide is echoed in this comment on globalized biopolitics: "Although the practice of Empire is continually bathed
in blood, the concept of Empire is always dedicated to peace—a perpetu-
al and universal peace outside of history" (Hardt and Negri, *Empire*, xv).

7. Albert Memmi, *The Colonizer and the Colonized* (1967), expanded ed.,
trans. Howard Greenfeld, intro. Jean-Paul Sartre, afterword by Susan
Gilson Miller (Boston: Beacon, 1991), 74. In Hong Kong, there have all
along been other ethnic groups in addition to the Han Chinese—a fact that
I have been obliged to understand from an early age because I happen to
come from a Moslem family. Under the circumstances of British hegemony, the non-Chinese ethnic minorities (many of whom had migrated from
the Indian subcontinent and Southeast Asia), too, typically identified—and
identified with—English- rather than Chinese-using channels as their means
of social success. Obviously, the complex histories of these minorities deserve a much more nuanced examination than I can provide here. However, because those who consider themselves Chinese (including Chinese
Moslems such as the members of my family) make up over 97 percent of
Hong Kong's population to this day, I don't think it is entirely erroneous,
for the purposes of this brief discussion, to refer to the implications of
knowing Chinese as my primary example of colonial subordination.

8. Robyn Wiegman, "Whiteness Studies and the Paradox of Particularity," *boundary 2* 26, no. 3 (fall 1999): 119.

9. Wiegman also extends her analysis to include a problematization of the split, antiracist white subject, who must take on a kind of prewhite ethnicity in order to be antiracist: "The desire [among current thinkers] to combat white privilege seems unable to generate a political project against racism articulated from the site of whiteness itself. . . . In other words, only in becoming 'nonwhite,' only in retrieving a prewhite ethnicity, can the antiracist subject be invented, and this is the case in much of the productions of both the popular and academic realms" (139).

10. Etienne Balibar, "Is There a 'Neo-Racism'?" trans. Chris Turner, in Etienne Balibar and Immanuel Wallerstein, *Race, Nation, Class: Ambiguous Identities* (New York: Verso, 1991), 21–22; emphasis in the original. I will be referring to Balibar's arguments again in chapters 1 and 3.

11. Stoler, *Race and the Education of Desire*, 90.

12. Foucault, *The History of Sexuality*, 1:145.

13. Stoler, *Race and the Education of Desire*, 69.

14. Among other works, I have found the essays collected in part 2 ("Disciplining Knowledge") of *Contemporary Postcolonial Theory: A Reader*, ed. Padmini Mongia (London: Edward Arnold, 1996), to be useful for my thinking about the relation between postcolonial studies and cultural legitimation. In particular, I have learned from the arguments by Biodun Jeyifo, Dipesh Chakrabarty, and Paul Gilroy.

1. The Protestant Ethnic and the Spirit of Capitalism

1. The incident is reported as follows: "Before the Clintons (including Hillary, her mother and Chelsea) even left Washington, China refused visas to three journalists from Radio Free Asia, the US-financed station that beams independent news into China. Then Beijing riled the 250 reporters who did make the trip by barring a handful of Chinese dissidents from meeting with them. (After the rebuff, ABC's Sam Donaldson vowed 'to do the human-rights story every day.')" (Steven Strasser, "Skirmish in Beijing," *Newsweek*, July 6, 1998, 28).

2. In the fall of 1998, another prominent dissident, Liu Nianchun, was released and allowed to go to the United States. During the same period, dissidents Xu Wenli, Wang Youcai, and Qin Yongmin were given sen-

tences of eleven to fourteen years for subversion of state power, while a large number of others were reported to have been arrested. In February 1999, two weeks before the visit of U.S. secretary of state Madeline Albright, Chinese authorities released Gao Yu, a prominent journalist who since 1993 had been serving a six-year sentence for revealing state secrets. In 2001 the saga of arrest and imprisonment continued with the highly visible cases of Li Shaomin and Gao Zhan, social science scholars who were charged with espionage, tried, and subsequently expelled or released on medical grounds.

3. For an interesting and well-informed discussion of the trade in body organs involving China and other countries, see John Frow, *Time and Commodity Culture: Essays in Cultural Theory and Postmodernity* (Oxford: Oxford University Press, 1997), 162–79. Frow's discussion is part of a detailed and complex analysis of commodity exchange pertaining to the tradition of gift giving, law, ethics, property, personhood, and other related issues of social relations in the modern (post-Lockean) world.

4. Michel Foucault, *The History of Sexuality*, vol. 1, *An Introduction*, trans. Robert Hurley (New York: Vintage, 1980).

5. Etienne Balibar and Immanuel Wallerstein, *Race, Nation, Class: Ambiguous Identities*, Balibar trans. Chris Turner (New York: Verso, 1991).

6. See "Part I: Etymology," in *Theories of Ethnicity: A Classical Reader*, ed. Werner Sollors (New York: New York University Press, 1996), 2–14. See also Sollors, "Foreword: Theories of American Ethnicity," in *Theories of Ethnicity*, x–xliv, for a summary of major works on ethnicity (especially in relation to the United States) as well as a history of the uses of the word. Generally speaking, however, Sollors's reader tends to privilege the paradigm of white immigrant experiences as a model for understanding ethnicity in the United States. His earlier work *Beyond Ethnicity: Consent and Descent in American Culture* (New York: Oxford University Press, 1986) also contains vast reservoirs of interesting information on the topic; see, in particular, the first chapter, "Beyond Ethnicity," for a discussion of the controversial debates concerning who is and who is not ethnic.

7. Max Weber, "What Is an Ethnic Group?" in *The Ethnicity Reader: Nationalism, Multiculturalism and Migration*, ed. Montserrat Guibernau and John Rex (Oxford: Polity, 1997), 15–26. Weber's essay is reprinted from chapter 5 of Max Weber, *Economics and Society*, ed. and trans. Guenther Roth and Claus Wittich (Los Angeles: University of California Press, 1978). The essay was originally published in 1922 but written be-

fore 1914; it is also reprinted under a slightly different title, "Ethnic Groups (1922)," in *Theories of Ethnicity*, 52–66. The notion that ethnicity is conceptually vague is echoed by other scholars. Nathan Glazer, for instance, writes: "Ethnicity shares with class . . . a vagueness of boundaries and limits and uncertainty as to the degree to which any person is associated with any grouping. . . . The voluntary character of ethnicity is what makes it so distinctive in the American setting" ("The Emergence of an American Ethnic Pattern," in *From Different Shores: Perspectives on Race and Ethnicity in America*, ed. Ronald Takaki [New York: Oxford University Press, 1987], 23). Glazer's essay is reprinted from his book *Affirmative Discrimination: Ethnic Inequality and Public Policy* (New York: Basic, 1975). Werner Sollors also describes ethnicity in terms of "a quality which cumulatively achieves the status of a somewhat mystical, ahistorical, and even quasi-eternal essence" ("Ethnicity," in *Critical Terms for Literary Study*, ed. Frank Lentricchia and Thomas McLaughlin, 2d ed. [Chicago: University of Chicago Press, 1995], 290). For other sociological accounts of ethnicity, see John Rex, *Race and Ethnicity* (Milton Keynes: Oxford University Press, 1986); and *Theories of Race and Ethnic Relations*, ed. John Rex and David Mason (Cambridge: Cambridge University Press, 1986).

8. Anthropologist Fredrik Barth is a notable exception of a theorist who holds that ethnicity is about boundaries rather than about the cultural contents enclosed within those boundaries. See his *Ethnic Groups and Boundaries: The Social Organization of Culture Difference* (Bergen, Norway: Universitetsforlog; and Boston: Little, Brown, 1969). In Sollors's words, Barth "states his different assumptions in plain antithesis to many American discussions about ethnicity," and his "focus on boundaries may appear scandalously heretical to some" ("Foreword," xxii).

9. "Liberal theoretical claims typically tend to be transhistorical, transcultural, and most certainly transracial. The declared and ostensible referent of liberal principles is quite literally a constituency with no delimiting boundary, namely, that of all humankind. The political rights it articulates and defends and the institutions such as laws, representation, and contract all have their justification in a characterization of human beings that eschews names, social status, ethnic background, gender, and race" (Uday S. Mehta, "Liberal Strategies of Exclusion," in *Tensions of Empire: Colonial Cultures in a Bourgeois World*, ed. Frederick Cooper and Ann Laura Stoler [Berkeley: University of California Press, 1997], 63). Mehta's essay is a

critique of the tensions, characteristically exhibited in British philosophers such as John Locke and John Stuart Mill, between liberalist, universalist intentions and authoritarian, procolonialist attitudes toward nonwhite cultures such as India.

10. Thomas Hylland Eriksen, "Ethnicity, Race and Nation," in *The Ethnicity Reader*, 37.

11. See, for instance, the last section, "Is Ethnicity Obsolete?" in *The Invention of Ethnicity*, ed. Werner Sollors (New York: Oxford University Press, 1989), 226–35. The authors who respond—Ishmael Reed, Shawn Wong, Bob Callahan, and Andrew Hope—are all skeptical about the idea that ethnicity is obsolete.

12. Ulf Hannerz, "Some Comments on the Anthropology of Ethnicity in the United States (1976)," in *Theories of Ethnicity*, 417. Hannerz's essay is reprinted from *Ethnicity in the Americas*, ed. Frances Henry (The Hague and Paris: Mouton, 1976), 429–38. An example of what Hannerz means can be found in a statement such as the following: "Although all Americans, save the Indians, came here as immigrants and are thus in one sense ethnics, people who arrived in the seventeenth and eighteenth centuries, and before the mid-nineteenth-century old immigration, are, except in some rural enclaves, no longer ethnics even if they know where their emigrant ancestors came from" (Herbert J. Gans, "Symbolic Ethnicity: The Future of Ethnic Groups and Cultures in America [1979]," in *Theories of Ethnicity*, 449). Gans's essay is a reprint of chapter 9 in *On the Making of Americans: Essays in Honor of David Riesman*, ed. Herbert Gans et al. (Philadelphia: University of Pennsylvania Press, 1979), 193–220.

13. Eriksen, "Ethnicity, Race and Nation," 40–41.

14. Sollors, "Foreword," x–xi; emphasis in the original.

15. Jon Stratton and Ien Ang, "Multicultural Imagined Communities: Cultural Difference and National Identity in Australia and the USA," *Critical Multiculturalism*, ed. Tom O'Regan, *Continuum: The Australian Journal of Media and Culture* 8, no. 2 (1994): 138, 135–36; emphases in the original.

16. Or else, it simply remains a voluntary option of identification at one's disposal. Such an understanding of ethnicity is, of course, really from the perspective of white Americans, the descendants of European immigrants. As Mary Waters writes, for members of such groups, being ethnic is indeed "the best of all worlds: they can claim to be unique and special while simultaneously finding the community and conformity with others that

they also crave" (*Ethnic Options: Choosing Identities in America* [Berkeley: University of California Press, 1990], 151). Waters's book goes on to show how being ethnic in America means very different things for peoples of non-European origins. My discussion here also dovetails well with Wallerstein's analysis in "The Construction of Peoplehood: Racism, Nationalism, Ethnicity": "Ethnicization . . . resolves one of the basic contradictions of historical capitalism—its simultaneous thrust for theoretical equality and practical inequality" (Balibar and Wallerstein, *Race, Nation, Class*, 84).

17. Again, examples abound in U.S. history. Referring to the recruitment of Chinese laborers into the United States in the nineteenth century, Ronald Takaki writes: "The inclusion of the Chinese in the economic structure was accompanied by their political exclusion. Not 'white,' they were ineligible for naturalized citizenship. They were, in effect, migrant laborers, forced to be foreigners forever. . . . They were a part of America's production process but not her body politic" ("Reflections on Racial Patterns in America," in *From Different Shores*, 28). This essay was excerpted from Ronald Takaki, "Reflections on Racial Patterns in America: An Historical Perspective," *Ethnicity and Public Policy* 1 (1982): 1–23. For examples in contemporary Britain, see some of the essays in *New Ethnicities, Old Racisms?* ed. Phil A. Cohen (London and New York: Zed, 1999).

18. Fredrik Barth, "Ethnic Groups and Boundaries (1969)," in *Theories of Ethnicity*, 296. This essay is reprinted from the introduction to Barth, *Ethnic Groups and Boundaries*, 9–38.

19. See, for instance, Werner Sollors, "Introduction: The Invention of Ethnicity," in *The Invention of Ethnicity*, ix–xx.

20. For an account of some of the problems inherent in dominant theories of ethnicity, see Michael Omi and Howard Winant, *Racial Formation in the United States: From the 1960s to the 1980s* (New York: Routledge, 1986), in particular, part 1, chapter 1, "The Dominant Paradigm: Ethnicity-Based Theory," 14–24. See also the critiques of ethnicity (as the term is used in the United States) offered by E. San Juan Jr., *Racial Formations/Critical Transformations: Articulations of Power in Ethnic and Racial Studies in the United States* (London: Humanities, 1992), in particular, the introduction, chapter 1, and chapter 2. For an account that sees ethnicity as categorically subordinate to race, see Wallerstein's distinction between race (which he defines in terms of labor in transnation-

al capitalism) and ethnicity (which he defines in terms of cultural representations and household structures within nations) in the chapter "The Construction of Peoplehood," in Balibar and Wallerstein, *Race, Nation, Class*, 71–85.

21. For discussions of the relationship between ethnicity and migrant labor in the context of the United States, see Ronald Takaki, "Reflections on Racial Patterns in America"; see also the essays in the sections on class and gender in *From Different Shores*.

22. In this regard, contemporary theory has too hastily focused on migration and immigrants as hot topics. For a critique of this trend and related issues, see Pheng Cheah, "Given Culture: Rethinking Cosmopolitical Freedom in Transnationalism," *boundary 2* 24, no. 2 (summer 1997): 157–97. Meaghan Morris has depicted academics' fondness for dramatizing themselves as heroes and heroines of mobility in the following manner: "As practitioners of a seriously sedentary mode of action (traveling theorists *sit* on planes, as they sit at desks), we dramatize our engagement with a wider world by projecting ourselves discursively as heroes and heroines of mobility: the intellectual as nomad, detective, tourist, pedestrian, social-climbing gorilla" (*Too Soon, Too Late: History in Popular Culture* [Bloomington: Indiana University Press, 1998], 228–29; emphasis in the original).

23. Wallerstein, "The Ideological Tensions of Capitalism: Universalism Versus Racism and Sexism," in Balibar and Wallerstein, *Race, Nation, Class*, 29–36. See also Balibar's discussion of the institutionalization of manual labor (in the form of mechanized physical work) in "Class Racism," in ibid., 210–12.

24. Wallerstein, "The Construction of Peoplehood," in Balibar and Wallerstein, *Race, Nation, Class*, 84.

25. Wallerstein, "The Ideological Tensions of Capitalism," in Balibar and Wallerstein, *Race, Nation, Class*, 34.

26. San Juan Jr., for instance, urges "the need to formulate a conception of U.S. racism (not a sociology of race relations) as part of a complex historical totality—that is, the United States as a racially ordered capitalist system—where the hegemony of the bourgeoisie has been constructed through the articulation of race, through the production of subjects inscribed in racist discursive/institutional practices" (*Racial Formations/Critical Transformations*, 57).

27. Georg Lukács, *History and Class Consciousness: Studies in Marxist Dialectics*, trans. Rodney Livingstone (Cambridge, Mass.: MIT Press, 1971).

Hereafter this work will be referred to as HCC, with citations provided in parentheses in the text. See also the recent publication of Lukács's response to his critics (written in German in the mid-1920s but rediscovered in Moscow only during the last years of the Soviet Empire), in idem, *A Defence of History and Class Consciousness: Tailism and the Dialectic*, trans. Esther Leslie, intro. John Rees, postface by Slavoj Žižek (London: Verso, 2000).

28. Terry Eagleton writes that "there are really two discrepant theories of ideology at work in *History and Class Consciousness*—the one deriving from commodity fetishism, the other from a historicist view of ideology as the world-view of a class subject" ("Ideology and its Vicissitudes in Western Marxism," in *Mapping Ideology*, ed. Slavoj Žižek [London: Verso, 1994], 188). Eagleton's essay is an excerpt taken from his book *Ideology* (London: Verso, 1991), chapters 4 and 5.

29. Georg Lukács, *Labour*, trans. David Fernbach (London: Merlin, 1980), 46, 136, 42.

30. Leonard Tennenhouse, "The Case of the Resistant Captive," *The South Atlantic Quarterly* 95, no. 4 (fall 1996): 919–46. For related interest, see also the extended arguments about British and American literature in Nancy Armstrong and Leonard Tennenhouse, *The Imaginary Puritan: Literature, Intellectual Labor, and the Origins of Personal Life* (Berkeley: University of California Press, 1992). In certain respects, Tennenhouse's theory about the resistant captive may be seen as a sympathetic response to Foucault's critique of the "repressive hypothesis" in *The History of Sexuality*, vol. 1. However, whereas Foucault concentrates on the manner in which repression has been popularized in discussions of sexuality, Tennenhouse has extended the implications of the repressive hypothesis to historiography itself, especially to the writing of modernity in the West. Importantly, Foucault himself, despite his insights, has, in fact, been complicit in the modernist historiographic habit of imagining the past in terms of a spectacular (but uncomplex) barbarism, as he demonstrates, perhaps most notably, at the beginning of *Discipline and Punish: The Birth of the Prison*, trans. Alan Sheridan (New York: Vintage, 1979). See Tennenhouse's comments on this point on page 922 of his essay.

31. See Frow, *Time and Commodity Culture*, 140–43, for a succinct critique of the Marxist conceptualization of the commodity form that underlies Lukács's analysis. Frow traces this conceptualization to Schillerian Romanticism and post-Romanticism:

Lukács's rhetoric, which flows through to the writings of the Frankfurt School and its successors, has the nostalgic structure of all of the great post-Romantic binarisms that oppose a state of immediacy to a state of mediation (the authentic to the inauthentic, the organic to the mechanical, non-reflexive experience to abstract rationality . . .). The commodification process . . . replaces "natural" and "personal" relations . . . with relations that are "more complex and less direct." . . . Complex and highly mediated systems are taken to be inherently incompatible with human value. . . . More broadly: *despite the force of its historical and relational conception of the commodity form, its conceptual ground is a myth of presence* which leads it to understand this form on the one hand as the alienation of the integrity of the person, on the other as the replacement of the simplicity, transparency, and immediacy of use value with a complex system of representations. (142–43; my emphasis)

32. Max Weber, *The Protestant Ethic and the Spirit of Capitalism* (first published in German in 1905–1906), trans. Talcott Parsons, intro. Anthony Giddens (New York: Scribner's, 1958, 1976). See also the chapters "The Social Psychology of World Religions" and "The Protestant Sects and the Spirit of Capitalism," in *From Max Weber: Essays in Sociology*, ed. and intro. by H. H. Gerth and C. Wright Mills, new pref. Bryan S. Turner (London: Routledge, 1991), 267–301, 302–22. These essays can be treated as companion pieces to Weber's famous work. For an account of some of the debates over this work among sociologists, historians, and theologians, see Alastair Hamilton, "Max Weber's *Protestant Ethic and the Spirit of Capitalism*," in *The Cambridge Companion to Weber*, ed. Stephen Turner (New York: Cambridge University Press, 2000), 151–71.

33. Bryan S. Turner, "Preface to the New Edition," in *From Max Weber*, xix.

34. Weber, "The Protestant Sects and the Spirit of Capitalism," in *From Max Weber*, 321; emphases in the original.

35. Turner, "Preface to the New Edition," xxii.

36. See Frederic Jameson, "The Vanishing Mediator; or, Max Weber as Storyteller," in *The Ideologies of Theory: Essays, 1971–1986*, vol. 2, *The Syntax of History* (Minneapolis: University of Minnesota Press, 1988), 25. (This essay was originally published in *New German Critique* 1 [winter 1973]: 52–89.) Jameson writes that "Weber's anti-Marxism has frequently been misconceived" and that "much of the material generally supposed

to amount to a repudiation of Marxism as a whole (for example, *The Protestant Ethic*) is in fact explicitly directed against vulgar Marxism and against that economism of the Second International to which Engels had himself objected" (4).

37. One could conceivably invoke Louis Althusser's notion of interpellation, which was itself derived from religious models, as a comparison. (See his "Ideology and Ideological State Apparatuses [Notes Towards an Investigation]," in *Lenin and Philosophy and Other Essays*, trans. Ben Brewster [New York: Monthly Review, 1971], 127–86.) But whereas Althusser's emphasis tends to be on the repressive nature of interpellation, Weber's model zeroes in on the economically productive dimension of calling and is thus more effective in demonstrating how capitalism works by providing material-cum-spiritual rewards. See also Balibar's "The Nation Form: History and Ideology" (in Balibar and Wallerstein, *Race, Nation, Class*, 102–3) for a reading of Althusser's account as a way to explain not only the reproduction of labor power but also what Balibar calls fictive ethnicity. I will return to Althusser's notion of interpellation in chapter 3.

38. Harvey S. Goldman, "Weber's Ascetic Practices of the Self," in *Weber's Protestant Ethic: Origins, Evidence, Contexts*, ed. Hartmut Lehmann and Guenther Roth (Cambridge: Cambridge University Press, 1987, 1993), 168; emphases in the original.

39. In a slightly different context, Fredric Jameson calls this process of commodification "the properly postmodern transformation of ethnicity into neoethnicity, as the isolation and oppression of groups is lifted up (in a properly Hegelian *Aufhebung*, which preserves and cancels that at one and the same time) into media acknowledgment and the new reunification by the image" ("On Cultural Studies," in *The Identity in Question*, ed. John Rajchman [New York: Routledge, 1995], 282). (This essay was originally published in *Social Text* 34 [1993].)

40. A decade or so after the bloody massacre at Tiananmen Square, a number of the leading Chinese dissidents who played major roles in the democracy movement back home and who are in exile in North America have become church-going Protestant Christians and/or successful capitalist entrepreneurs embracing America as a land of opportunities. For these remarkably Weberian developments, see two reports by Ian Buruma: "The Pilgrimage from Tiananmen Square," *New York Times Magazine*, April 11, 1999, 62–65; "Tiananmen, Inc.," *New Yorker*, May 31, 1999, 45–52.

2. Brushes with the-Other-as-Face:
Stereotyping and Cross-Ethnic Representation

1. Walter Lippmann, *Public Opinion* (New York: Free, 1922), 65, 3–20. For an informative discussion of stereotyping that includes substantive comments on Lippmann as well as multiple other authors, see Michael Pickering, *Stereotyping: The Politics of Representation* (New York: Palgrave, 2001). Unfortunately, I came across Pickering's book only when my own was already in production, but I would like at least to note its significance.

2. A parallel situation occurred with the usage of the word "cliché." Lois Parkinson Zamora, for instance, provides this account: the word "cliché"

> initially described a ready-made unit of type, a metal plate from which issued unending, standardized reproductions of print or design. The word was derived from the onomatopoeic French verb *clicher*, a variant of *cliquer* (to click) and mimicked the sound of typesetting machines. Now, of course, it has come to figure fragmented, ready-made units of (primarily) spoken speech. In English and Spanish, the word "stereotype" (*estereotipo*) denotes the same device, and the Spanish locution "frase acunada" (a "coined" or "minted" phrase), also refers to a process of repeated metallic imprinting, with its presumed accompanying din. The French term, however, carries the greatest opprobrium, for French writers of the mid- to late-nineteenth century saw the mechanization of print as pressing literary language into common currency, making it too readily available to undiscriminating bourgeois (mass) consumption. In contemporary literary culture as well, most audiences will deprecate clichés as such.
>
> (*The Usable Past: The Imagination of History in Recent Fiction of the Americas* [Cambridge: Cambridge University Press, 1997, 179])

See also Mireille Rosello, *Declining the Stereotype: Ethnicity and Representation in French Cultures* (Hanover, N.H.: Dartmouth College, University Press of New England, 1998), 21–40, for an informative discussion of the ironic relationships between the literal and figurative, or mechanical and ideological, meanings of the word "stereotype." An interesting thematic intertext in this instance is Marshall McLuhan, *The Gutenberg Galaxy: The Making of Typographic Man* (Toronto: University of Toronto Press, 1962). McLuhan argues that print technology in the West, with its key characteristic of repetition, has pushed to the extreme the phenomenon of detribalization and decollectivization (of human beings) that began with the phonetic alphabet, leading to a homogenization of experience through the reduction of everything to a visual mode of sequence, which is, in turn, interiorized by what he calls the "mass man."

3. See Lippmann, *Public Opinion*, 59–60, 63–64.

4. See, for instance, the discussions in *Stereotyping and Prejudice: Changing Conceptions*, ed. Daniel Bar-Tal, Carl F. Graumann, Arie W. Kruglanski, and Wolfgang Stroebe (New York: Springer, 1989); and in *In the Eye of the Beholder: Contemporary Issues in Stereotyping*, ed. Arthur G. Miller (New York: Praeger, 1982). The approaches adopted in these publications and multiple others on stereotypes are usually those of cognitive psychology, which have not been very useful for the kinds of issues I would like to foreground.

5. See *Images that Injure: Pictorial Stereotypes in the Media*, ed. Paul Martin Lester (Westport, Conn.: Praeger, 1996); and William Brennan, *Dehumanizing the Vulnerable: When Word Games Take Lives* (Chicago: Loyola University Press, 1995).

6. For an example of a study of sexual and racial stereotypes in modern European culture, see Sander L. Gilman, *Difference and Pathology: Stereotypes of Sexuality, Race, and Madness* (Ithaca, N.Y.: Cornell University Press, 1985).

7. Gilman, for instance, writes: "Stereotypes are a crude set of mental representations of the world," in *Difference and Pathology*, 17. Like many others, Gilman uses popular psychology to explain what he considers to be the functional necessity of stereotypes: "Stereotypes arise when self-integration is threatened. They are therefore part of our way of dealing with the instabilities of our perception of the world. This is not to say that they are good, only that they are necessary" (18).

For another well-known reading along similar lines, this time in the classic colonial context, see Homi Bhabha, "The Other Question," *Screen* 24, no. 6 (1983): 18–36, reprinted in *Contemporary Postcolonial Theory: A Reader*, ed. Padmini Mongia (London: Edward Arnold, 1996), 37–54. Amid a barrage of terms taken from psychoanalysis, none of which receives any sustained analysis, Bhabha makes a simple argument, namely, that racial stereotypes in colonialist discourse are always already ambivalent:

"The stereotype is in fact an 'impossible' object" (50). Insofar as it understands stereotypes as part of a psychic process of identification and subjectivization, Bhabha's argument, despite its seeming complications, does not differ essentially from Gilman's.

8. Theodor W. Adorno has likewise asserted the indispensability of stereotypes *in art*; however, his view about stereotypes in the contemporary media is a negative one. In the latter situation, he writes, dependency on stereotypes is really a result of the stultifying culture industry: "Since stereotypes are an indispensable element of the organization and anticipation of experience, preventing us from falling into mental disorganization and chaos, no art can entirely dispense with them. Again, the functional change is what concerns us. The more stereotypes become reified and rigid in the present set-up of cultural industry, the more people are tempted to cling desperately to clichés which seem to bring some order into the otherwise ununderstandable" ("How To Look at Television," in *Culture Industry: Selected Essays on Mass Culture*, ed. with an intro. by J. M. Bernstein [London: Routledge, 1991], 147). This chapter was originally published in *The Quarterly of Film, Radio and Television* 8, no. 3 (1954): 213–35.

9. See Fredric Jameson, "On Cultural Studies," in *The Identity in Question*, ed. John Rajchman (New York: Routledge, 1995), 251–95. Hereafter this work will be referred to as OCC, with citations provided in parentheses in the text. In her detailed study, Rosello also states that she does not believe "it is very useful to argue with stereotypes, to try and confound them, to attack their lack of logic or common sense" (*Declining the Stereotype*, 16). However, the solution she proposes, namely, a way of reading stereotypes that involves the double movement of participation and refusal, of inhabiting while displacing, is fundamentally not different from a deconstructive and defamiliarizing kind of vigilance that places stereotypes "under constant surveillance" (34). Rosello calls this double movement "declining" (playing on both the conventional and grammatical senses of the word): "Declining a stereotype is a way of depriving it of its harmful potential by highlighting its very nature" (11). Although I am impressed with Rosello's scholarship, I do not find her solution a theoretically satisfactory one to the issues I am raising.

10. Erving Goffmann, *Stigma: Notes on the Management of Spoiled Identity* (Englewood Cliffs, N.J.: Prentice-Hall, 1963).

11. Sigmund Freud, *Civilization and Its Discontents* (1930), in *The Standard

Edition of the Complete Psychological Works of Sigmund Freud, trans. under the general editorship of James Strachey (London: Hogarth, 1961), 21:57–145.

12. Jameson's much criticized argument about third world literature as being almost always about "national allegories" can also be understood in the light of these remarks about stereotypes. To that extent, national allegories are stereotypes, and Jameson's reading of third world literature is consistent with his view that stereotypes are inevitable in intercultural relations. See "Third-World Literature in the Era of Multinational Capital," *Social Text* 15 (fall 1986): 65–88. What remains to be debated—and this is the reason so many people have criticized his argument—is, of course, the question of power: who gets to mobilize stereotypes, whose stereotypes matter and become universalized, who becomes invariably stereotyped and ghettoized, and so on. See the next chapter for an extended discussion of national allegories and mimeticism in ethnic self-representation.

13. Jane M. Gaines's remark in a different context may be borrowed as a comment on the liberal solution: "Here the rhetorical flaw is in the assumption that the 'positive' image is not itself also a stereotype—that somehow it is exempted from criticism because it is not pejorative (another problem arising from the situation in which 'stereotype' has become synonymous with 'pejorative' even when stereotypes can as easily be laudatory)" (*Fire and Desire: Mixed-Race Movies in the Silent Era* [Chicago: University of Chicago Press, 2000], 261). Gaines's interesting and suggestive discussion of stereotypy in relation to the films made by African Americans in the Silent Era can be found on pages 258–63 and throughout her book.

14. Rosello, *Declining the Stereotype,* 32, 38.

15. Richard Dyer, *The Matter of Images: Essays on Representations* (New York: Routledge, 1993), 16; emphasis in the original.

16. For a compelling critique of the biases in the Western media that are overwhelmingly in favor of Israel and in discrimination of Palestinians, for instance, see Edward W. Said, "The Ideology of Difference," in *"Race," Writing, and Difference,* ed. Henry Louis Gates (Chicago: University of Chicago Press, 1986), 38–58.

17. Rosemary J. Coombe, "The Properties of Culture and the Possession of Identity: Postcolonial Struggle and the Legal Imagination," in *Borrowed Power: Essays on Cultural Appropriation,* ed. Bruce Ziff and Pratima V. Rao (New Brunswick, N.J.: Rutgers University Press, 1997), 78.

18. Jacques Derrida, *Of Grammatology*, trans. Gayatri Chakravorty Spivak (Baltimore: Johns Hopkins University Press, 1976), 90. For a sustained discussion of the fantastic role played by Chinese writing in Western modernist poetic and theoretical thinking, including Derrida's, see Eric Hayot, "Chinese Dreams: Pound, Brecht, *Tel Quel*" (Ph.D. diss., University of Wisconsin, Milwaukee, 1999). Addressing the invention of "the Chinese poem" by an enthusiast such as Ezra Pound, for instance, Michelle Yeh writes:

> The tendency to see the Chinese poem as a concatenation of concrete visual images with few discursive elements is inseparable from the conception that the Chinese language is "largely pictographic" or ideographic. Such a view, with a long history that goes back to Catholic missionaries in the sixteenth century, is based on the notion that Chinese written symbols are visual embodiments of particular things in nature rather than artificial signs of phonetic import. Despite efforts by sinologists—for example, Peter Boodberg, Yuen Ren Chao, and John DeFrancis—and others to dispel the myth, it remains strong to this date, and it is but a short step from seeing the Chinese language as pictographic to seeing Chinese poetry as an unmediated expression of the concrete world of experience.
>
> ("The Chinese Poem: The Visible and the Invisible in Chinese Poetry," *Manoa: A Pacific Journal of International Writing*, summer 2000, 137)

19. The source of this picture is given on the back cover of some editions of the English translation as follows: "The artist's seals and emblems of longevity from a *kakemono* (hanging scroll) by Nikka (19th cent.). Ink on paper. Reproduced from *The Uninhibited Brush* by J. Hillier, with the permission of Hugh Moss Publications, Ltd., London. From the collection of Nick Grindley." See Stanley K. Abe, "No Questions, No Answers: China and *A Book from the Sky*," *boundary 2* 25, no. 3 (fall 1998): 176–77, for brief allusions to the debates around "Chinese writing" in response to Derrida's reading and his notes 15–17 (190–91) for references to various critical works in such debates. Notably, on the cover of the corrected edition of *Of Grammatology* that was issued by Johns Hopkins University Press in 1998, the picture of Chinese writing has been replaced by one from the papyrus of Hunefer, depicting Thoth, the advocate of Osiris, writing on his tablet.

20. For an example of this standard Western view, see Ferdinand de Saussure, *Course in General Linguistics*, ed. Charles Bally and Albert Sechehaye in collaboration with Albert Reidlinger, trans. Wade Baskin (Glasgow: Fontana/Collins, 1974), 25–26.

21. John DeFrancis, *The Chinese Language: Fact and Fantasy* (Honolulu: University of Hawaii Press, 1984), 133. Haun Saussy writes: "It is notable that, despite the decay of many simplistic illusions about the singularities of the Chinese written language, the motif of a *contrast* between alphabetic writing and ideogrammatic writing as modes of representation survives to direct many accounts of the contrasts between 'Chinese' literature and 'Western' literature" ("The Prestige of Writing: *Wen*, Letter, Picture, Image, Ideography," *Sino-Platonic Papers* 75 [1997]: 2–3; emphasis in the original). Saussy's essay offers an erudite historical account of the debates, in Chinese and Western languages, of the intricacies surrounding the notion of "ideogrammatic" writing. See also Abe, "No Questions, No Answers," 190–91 nn. 15–17, for other references to this controversy.

22. Spivak, translator's preface to *Of Grammatology*, lxxxii; emphases in the original.

23. Han-liang Chang, "Hallucinating the Other: Derridean Fantasies of Chinese Script," Working Paper no. 4 (Milwaukee: Center for Twentieth Century Studies, University of Wisconsin, Milwaukee, 1988), 8.

24. The phoneticization and alphabetization of Chinese have been intensified and made irreversible now by the ubiquitous usage of computerization involving the alphabetical keyboard. For an interesting discussion, see Anthony C. Yu, "Enduring Change: Confucianism and the Prospect of Human Rights," *Lingnan Journal of Chinese Studies*, n.s., no. 2 (October 2000): 27–70. Referring to the computer's effects on the functioning of the Chinese language, Yu concludes that "the non-Indo-European has become part Indo-European" (33).

25. For related interest, see David Palumbo-Liu, *Asian/American: Historical Crossings of a Racial Frontier* (Stanford, Calif.: Stanford University Press, 1999), 81–146, for an informative discussion about the habitual readings of exteriors—faces and bodies—in the treatment of Asian Americans by mainstream American society.

26. Abe, "No Questions, No Answers," 185.

27. Slavoj Žižek, "Introduction: The Spectre of Ideology," in *Mapping Ideology*, ed. Slavoj Žižek (London: Verso, 1994), 32 n. 34. Žižek is alluding

to Derrida's *Spectres of Marx*, but his remarks are equally germane to Derrida's utopianist treatment of the "otherness" of Chinese writing.

28. "What appeals to Leibniz, Fenollosa, Eisenstein, and Derrida in Chinese script is what they have found relevant to their own applications. In the jargon of comparative literature studies, this kind of misreading, or mirage, is a common phenomenon when two cultures encounter one another. The value of their readings, therefore, does not lie in their contribution to etymology, but lies, as Derrida puts it in *Of Grammatology*, in their aesthetic breakthrough of the entrenched Western tradition" (Chang, "Hallucinating the Other," 12).

29. Since I have already offered a detailed discussion of the relations among language, writing, and the persistence of political struggles in modern China elsewhere in my work, I will not repeat my arguments here. Interested readers are asked to see the chapter "Pedagogy, Trust, Chinese Intellectuals in the 1990s: Fragments of a Post-Catastrophic Discourse," in my *Writing Diaspora: Tactics of Intervention in Contemporary Cultural Studies* (Bloomington: Indiana University Press, 1993). This chapter was originally published in *Dialectical Anthropology* 16, no. 3 (1991): 191–207.

30. Matthew Turner, "Hong Kong Sixties/Nineties: Dissolving the People," in *Hong Kong Sixties: Designing Identity*, ed. Matthew Turner and Irene Ngan (Hong Kong: Hong Kong Arts Centre Publications, 1995), 26, 29.

31. See also Rey Chow, "King Kong in Hong Kong: Watching the 'Handover' from the USA," *Social Text* 55 (summer 1998): 93–108, for a discussion of the historical circumstances that created Hong Kong's unique position and their implications after 1997.

32. Wildly successful, the cartoons have also been republished in a number of anthologies, including *The World of Lily Wong* (1988), *Quotations from Lily Wong* (1989), *The Adventures of Superlily* (1989), *Postcards from Lily Wong* (1990) (all published by Macmillan Publishers, Hong Kong); *Execute Yourself Tonite!* (coauthored with Nury Vittachi) (1993), *Banned in Hong Kong* (1995), and *Aieeyaaa! I'm Pregnant!* (1996) (all published by Hambalan Press, Hong Kong). All reproductions of *Lily Wong* and other cartoons in this chapter are made with the permission of Larry Feign. Readers interested in seeing more of his work may look up the Lily Wong Website at *www.lilywong.net*.

33. David Feign, letter published in the section "Letters to the Times," *Los Angeles Times*, July 14, 1996, M4. See Larry Feign, *Banned in Hong*

Kong, foreword by Martin Lee (Hong Kong: Hambalan, 1995), for a detailed account of the circumstances leading up to the discontinuation of his strip.

34. Martin C. M. Lee, "One Country, Two Systems—But No Sense of Humour" (an expansion of the letter Lee wrote to the *South China Morning Post* that the newspaper declined to print), in Feign, *Banned in Hong Kong*, 2–3.

35. Feign, *Banned in Hong Kong*, 6.

36. Turner, "Hong Kong Sixties/Nineties," 25; my emphasis. Turner is quoting from the 1984 Joint Declaration, Article 3 [4], [5]; and Annexe I [I], [xiv].

37. The symposium "Cities at the End of Time: Hong Kong 1997," organized by the Pomelo Project, Vancouver, Canada, February 1997. People who were present in the audience would be able to testify to this incident.

38. This information is from David Feign's letter, cited above.

39. "There is no document of civilization which is not at the same time a document of barbarism. And just as such a document is not free of barbarism, barbarism taints also the manner in which it was transmitted from one owner to another. A historical materialist therefore dissociates himself from it as far as possible. He regards it as his task to brush history against the grain" (Walter Benjamin, "Theses on the Philosophy of History," in *Illuminations*, ed. and with an intro. by Hannah Arendt, trans. Harry Zohn (New York: Schocken, 1969), 256–57.

3. Keeping Them in Their Place: Coercive Mimeticism and Cross-Ethnic Representation

1. John Berger, *About Looking* (New York: Pantheon, 1980), 1–26.

2. Berger himself seems hesitant about using the zoo as a symbol (24), but I would like to demonstrate that this symbol has implications that are much too far-reaching to be left unexplored.

3. Fredric Jameson, "Third-World Literature in the Era of Multinational Capitalism," *Social Text* 15 (fall 1986): 65–88.

4. The first and most cited critic to counter Jameson's argument was Aijaz Ahmad; see his "Jameson's Rhetoric of Otherness and the 'National Allegory,' " *Social Text* 17 (fall 1987): 3–25; see also Fredric Jameson, "A Brief Response," *Social Text* 17 (fall 1987): 26–27.

5. Berger, *About Looking*, 21.

6. For arguments about iconophobia in modern and contemporary literary and critical practices, see Martin Jay, *Downcast Eyes: The Denigration of Vision in Twentieth-Century French Thought* (Berkeley: University of California Press, 1993); Nancy Armstrong, *Fiction in the Age of Photography: The Legacy of British Realism* (Cambridge: Harvard University Press, 1999). For a related discussion of the question of (mimetic) literalness in cross-cultural representation and its difficult relation to poststructuralist theory, see part 3 of Rey Chow, *Primitive Passions: Visuality, Sexuality, Ethnography, and Contemporary Chinese Cinema* (New York: Columbia University Press, 1995).

7. See, for instance, Jean Baudrillard, *Simulations*, trans. Paul Foss, Paul Patton, and Philip Beitchman (New York: Semiotext(e), 1983).

8. Dudley Andrew, "The 'Three Ages' of Cinema Studies and the Age to Come," *PMLA* 115, no. 3 (May 2000): 346.

9. Martin Jay, *Cultural Semantics: Keywords of Our Time* (Amherst: University of Massachusetts Press, 1998), 120. The quotation is taken from the chapter "Mimesis and Mimetology: Adorno and Lacoue-Labarthe," in which Jay delineates a set of theoretical alternatives, through the work of Adorno and Lacoue-Labarthe, to the drastic dismissal of the mimetic as found in the influential writings of poststructuralist theorists such as Roland Barthes, Jacques Derrida, Gilles Deleuze and Félix Guattari, Jean-François Lyotard, and Paul de Man.

10. Frantz Fanon, *Black Skin, White Masks*, trans. Charles Lam Markmann (New York: Grove Weidenfeld, 1967), 10.

11. Homi K. Bhabha, *The Location of Culture* (New York: Routledge, 1994), 40, 44.

12. Consider, for instance, Bhabha's criticism of what he calls "image analysis," by which he means the method of reading that considers the literary text (representation) as an image of the given reality (the represented), an image that has to be correctly reproduced and measured against the essential, original meaning. As an alternative to image analysis, Bhabha proposes ideological analysis. See his essay "Representation and the Colonial Text: A Critical Exploration of Some Forms of Mimeticism," in *The Theory of Reading*, ed. Frank Gloversmith (Sussex: Harvester, 1984), 93–122. Given the academic context in and against which Bhabha was writing in the early 1980s, namely, the Leavisian tradition of English literary criticism, his was a much needed intervention.

13. Bhabha, *The Location of Culture*, 49.

14. Mary Louise Pratt, "Scratches on the Face of the Country; or, What Mr. Barrow Saw in the Land of the Bushmen," in *"Race," Writing, and Difference*, ed. Henry Louis Gates Jr. (Chicago: University of Chicago Press, 1985, 1986), 160.

15. See the chapter "Where Have All the Natives Gone?" in Rey Chow, *Writing Diaspora: Tactics of Intervention in Contemporary Cultural Studies* (Bloomington: Indiana University Press, 1993).

16. Albert Memmi, *The Colonizer and the Colonized*, expanded ed., trans. Howard Greenfeld, intro. Jean-Paul Sartre, afterword Susan Gilson Miller (Boston: Beacon, 1991), 85.

17. Gerald Vizenor, *Fugitive Poses: Native American Indian Scenes of Absence and Presence* (Lincoln: University of Nebraska Press, 1998), 41–42; emphases in the original.

18. Louis Althusser, "Ideology and Ideological State Apparatuses (Notes Towards an Investigation)," in *Lenin and Philosophy and Other Essays*, trans. Ben Brewster (London: Monthly Review, 1971), 127–86.

19. Slavoj Žižek, *The Sublime Object of Ideology* (London: Verso, 1989), 43; emphasis in the original. See also his "Introduction: The Spectre of Ideology," in *Mapping Ideology*, ed. Slavoj Žižek (London: Verso, 1994), 1–33.

20. In the case of Asian Americans, Hattori calls this process of interpellation the "model minority discourse." Also making use of Žižek's argument about ideology, Hattori emphasizes that the cultural and social contradictions inherent to the model minority discourse must be understood by way of the work of global capital, which effectively turns racialized bodies into commodities. See his provocative essay "Model Minority Discourse and Asian American Jouis-Sense," *differences* 11, no. 2 (summer 1999): 228–47; the quotation is on 231.

21. James Clifford, "Objects and Selves—An Afterword," in *Objects and Others: Essays on Museums and Material Culture*, ed. George W. Stocking Jr. (Madison: University of Wisconsin Press, 1985), 236–46.

22. For a discussion of the stakes involved, see Linda Alcoff, "The Problem of Speaking for Others," *Cultural Critique* 20 (1991–92): 5–32.

23. Jean-François Lyotard, *The Postmodern Condition: A Report on Knowledge*, trans. Geoff Bennington and Brian Massumi, foreword Fredric Jameson (Minneapolis: University of Minnesota Press, 1984).

24. Michel Foucault, *The History of Sexuality*, vol. 1, *An Introduction*, trans. Robert Hurley (New York: Vintage, 1980), 222.

25. As I wrote these lines, I happened to come across an ad taken out by the organization Chinese for Affirmative Action on behalf of the Los Alamos scientist Wen Ho Lee, who had been shackled and incarcerated in a federal prison by the U.S. government for nine months without bail in spite of the fact that the charges of espionage against him were without foundation. The headline of this ad gives a frightfully literal significance to my suggestion that ethnicity can be seen as a criminal conviction: Lee has been, it states, "Charged with Being Ethnic Chinese" (*New York Times*, August 7, 2000, A23). Lee was subsequently set free in September 2000.

26. See *Dangdai (Con-Temporary Monthly)*, April 1, 1992. The editors of this special issue on Chinese film write: "As Jameson says, all third-world literature, including Chinese literature, is, to put it in a nutshell, political allegory, a product of the political unconscious. *Judou, Yellow Earth, Hibiscus Town*, and *Raise the Red Lantern* are all footnotes" (150; my translation).

27. Robyn Wiegman, "Whiteness Studies and the Paradox of Particularity," *boundary 2* 26, no. 3 (1999): 115–50.

28. Michelle Yeh, "Chinese Postmodernism and the Cultural Politics of Modern Chinese Poetry," in *Cross-Cultural Readings of Chineseness: Narratives, Images, and Interpretations of the 1990s*, ed. Wen-hsin Yeh (Berkeley: Institute of East Asian Studies, University of California, Berkeley, 2000), 122.

29. I borrow the term "fictive ethnicity" from Etienne Balibar, "The Nation Form: History and Ideology," trans. Chris Turner, in Etienne Balibar and Immanuel Wallerstein, *Race, Nation, Class: Ambiguous Identities* (New York: Verso, 1991), 86–106; see, in particular, the discussion on page 96.

30. In his study of Japan, Naoki Sakai perceptively calls this kind of effort to promote an ethnic culture "mimetic": "The desire to identify either with Japan or the West is . . . invariably a mimetic one, so that the insistence on Japan's originality, for instance, would have to be mediated by the mimetic desire for the West" (*Translation and Subjectivity: On "Japan" and Cultural Nationalism*, foreword Meaghan Morris [Minneapolis: University of Minnesota Press, 1997], 52). As my arguments show, this mimeticism fundamental to modern East-West relations is further complicated in the China situation by sinologists' (ideological) insistence that classical Chinese writings are, in and of themselves, nonmimetic in nature.

31. For an informative discussion of the intellectual problems generated by such arguments in the field of ancient Chinese poetry and poetics, see

Yong Ren, "Cosmogony, Fictionality, Poetic Creativity: Western and Traditional Chinese Cultural Perspectives," *Comparative Literature* 50, no. 2 (spring 1998): 98–119. See also Haun Saussy, *The Problem of a Chinese Aesthetic* (Stanford, Calif.: Stanford University Press, 1993), chapter 1, "The Question of Chinese Allegory," for a discussion of the views that sinologists doing "comparative poetics" typically advance to support the claim that Chinese literature is nonmimetic and nonallegorical.

32. A good analogy here is Julia Kristeva's "positive" and laudatory reading of Chinese women by way of the psychoanalytic notions of preoedipality, motherhood, the semiotic, and so forth, in *About Chinese Women*, trans. Anita Barrows (London: Boyars, 1977). For an incisive recent critique of this kind of essentialist reading of ethnic cultures by critics following theorists such as Kristeva, see Tomo Hattori, "Psycholinguistic Orientalism in Criticism of *The Woman Warrior* and *Obasan*," in *Other Sisterhoods: Literary Theory and U.S. Women of Color*, ed. Sandra Kumamoto Stanley (Urbana: University of Illinois Press, 1997), 119–38.

33. Ien Ang, "The Differential Politics of Chineseness," *Communal/Plural* (Research Centre in Intercommunal Studies, University of Western Sydney, Nepean) 1 (1993): 25.

34. Etienne Balibar, "Is There a 'Neo-Racism'?" trans. Chris Turner, in Balibar and Wallerstein, *Race, Nation, Class*, 21–22. It is, of course, conceivable to associate the assertion of Chineseness with what Albert Memmi calls "defensive racism," a racism that is "neither biological nor metaphysical, but social and historical" and based not on a belief in the inferiority of the detested group (in this case, Westerners) but "on the conviction, and in large measure on the observation, that this group is truly an aggressor and dangerous" (*The Colonizer and the Colonized*, 131). In the case of China studies, however, the possibility of such an association is complicated by the fact that many of those who assert the essence of Chineseness as such (who, in other words, take it upon themselves to exercise "defensive racism" on behalf of the Chinese against the West) are themselves Westerners defending and protecting their own orientalist professional investments.

35. One such form is, I think, the genre known as reportage, which, as Charles Laughlin argues, should be dated from the 1930s rather than the more recent Chinese Communist period. See Laughlin, "Narrative Subjectivity and the Production of Social Space," in *Modern Chinese Literary and Cultural Studies in the Age of Theory: Reimagining a Field*, ed. Rey

Chow (Durham, N.C.: Duke University Press, 2000), 26–47, for the intricate relations between style (narrative subjectivity) and politics (the production of social space) in modern Chinese literature since the early twentieth century.

36. Edward Gunn, *Rewriting Chinese: Style and Innovation in Twentieth-Century Chinese Prose* (Stanford, Calif.: Stanford University Press, 1991).

37. Gunn writes: "The new political cohesion in China required predictability in language and writing to build the nation. . . . Style was fixed largely as it existed in politically acceptable works of the late 1940's. . . . In stabilizing writing style to such a degree and greatly expanding the literacy rate, the PRC had to sacrifice the aesthetic value of the unpredictable, whether in the language-specific, metonymic range of regional vocabulary and grammar, or in the more metaphorically charged range of cohesion and disjunction" (*Rewriting Chinese*, 56).

38. For a related discussion, see, for instance, Anthony Kane, "The Humanities in Contemporary China Studies: An Uncomfortable Tradition," in *American Studies of Contemporary China*, ed. David Shambaugh (Washington, D.C.: Woodrow Wilson Center Press; Armonk, N.Y.: Sharpe, 1993), 65–81. Kane recapitulates the idealistic manners in which American China scholars in the early 1970s tried to defend the noble "difference" of PRC literature and art. What these scholars were really defending, he writes,

was the *politics* of contemporary Chinese literature and art while simply positing the existence of the literature and art itself. In the years since the death of Mao and the fall of the Gang of Four, the false optimism of the early 1970s has become the cause of much soul-searching and embarrassment, acknowledged and unacknowledged. Why, many wonder, were many in the field so determined to defend something that in retrospect seems so completely indefensible? . . . The mistake was not in trying to avoid being culture-bound; rather it was that in the process scholars suspended their disbelief to a point where they lost the ability to analyze critically. (69; emphasis in the original)

39. See Yeh's discussion of this type of criticism in "Chinese Postmodernism." See also the chapter "Leading Questions" in my *Writing Diaspora* for a discussion of similar issues.

40. Tomo Hattori, "China Man Autoeroticism and the Remains of Asian America," *Novel*, spring 1998): 217.

41. For similar reasons, Paul Gilroy advocates a political struggle against the massive media spectacularizations of racial and colored identities. See his *Against Race: Imagining Political Culture Beyond the Color Line* (Cambridge: Harvard University Press, 2000).

4. *The Secrets of Ethnic Abjection*

1. Ferdinand de Saussure, *Course in General Linguistics*, intro. Jonathan Culler, ed. Charles Bally and Albert Sechehaye in collaboration with Albert Reidlinger, trans. Wade Baskin (Glasgow: Collins, 1974), 120, 122; emphases in the original.

2. Stuart Hall, "Cultural Identity and Diaspora," in *Colonial Discourse and Post-Colonial Theory: A Reader*, ed. and intro. Patrick Williams and Laura Chrisman (New York: Columbia University Press, 1994), 393–94. This essay was originally published in *Identity: Community, Culture, Difference*, ed. J. Rutherford (London: Lawrence and Wishart, 1990), 222–37. For other examples of poststructuralist discussions of identity, see *The Identity in Question*, ed. and intro. John Rajchman (New York: Routledge, 1995); and *Displacements: Cultural Identities in Question*, ed. Angelika Bammer (Bloomington: Indiana University Press, 1994).

3. See, for instance, the essays on Hall's work in *Stuart Hall: Critical Dialogues in Cultural Studies*, ed. David Morley and Kuan-hsing Chen (New York: Routledge, 1996).

4. Pheng Cheah, "Given Culture: Rethinking Cosmopolitical Freedom in Transnationalism," *boundary* 2 24, no. 2 (summer 1997): 157–97. Cheah's essay can also be found in *Cosmopolitics: Thinking and Feeling Beyond the Nation*, ed. Pheng Cheah and Bruce Robbins (Minneapolis: University of Minnesota Press, 1998).

5. A typical example of this tendency is found in this statement from the call for papers for the *PMLA* special issue "Mobile Citizens, Media States": "As national borders become increasingly problematic in an era of global media culture, categories of citizenship and local forms of identity are becoming more mobile, nomadic, and hybrid" (*PMLA* 114, no. 5 [October 1999], "Special Topic" page).

6. Barnor Hesse, "It's Your World: Discrepant M/multiculturalisms," in *New Ethnicities, Old Racisms?* ed. Phil A. Cohen (London and New York: Zed, 1999), 207.

7. For this reason, David Palumbo-Liu argues (in an essay about the politics of canonizing ethnic literature in American literary studies) that it is necessary to pursue a "critical multiculturalism"—one that is alert to the social problems masked by the liberalist celebration of diversity. See his introduction to *The Ethnic Canon: Histories, Institutions, and Interventions*, ed. David Palumbo-Liu (Minneapolis and London: University of Minnesota Press, 1995), 1–27.

8. Smaro Kamboureli, *Scandalous Bodies: Diasporic Literature in English Canada* (Don Mills, Ontario: Oxford University Press, 1999), 82.

9. For a comparable argument, see Lisa Lowe's critique of how the North American university itself perpetuates the contradiction of protecting Western cultural study "as a largely autonomous domain" while "'democratizing' the institution only to the extent that it addresses the needs of an increasingly heterogeneous student population through the development of business, engineering, technical, and other professionalizing programs" ("Canon, Institutionalization, Identity: Contradictions for Asian American Studies," in *The Ethnic Canon*, 50). Lowe's point is that multiculturalism institutionalized in this manner is simply serving the interests of the capitalist market economy.

10. M. Nourbese Philip, *Frontiers: Essays and Writings on Racism and Culture* (Stratford: Mercury, 1992). 181.

11. See Kamboureli, *Scandalous Bodies*, 162–74, for a similar critique of the work of Linda Hutcheon. "Making room for [other] voices [to be heard]," she writes, "does nothing to change their minority positions" (171).

12. Philip Deloria, *Playing Indian* (New Haven: Yale University Press, 1998), 173.

13. The controversy over illegal immigrants from mainland China in western Canada is a good case in point. Among those who speak up most loudly against these immigrants in Vancouver, according to a report in the *New York Times* (August 29, 1999, Y6), are wealthy Chinese immigrants who are well established and leading comfortably settled lives in the city.

14. For useful discussions of the problematic of (aesthetic) reflection in Marxist theory, see, for instance, Pierre Macherey, *A Theory of Literary Production*, trans. Geoffrey Wall (London: Routledge and Kegan Paul, 1978); and Terry Eagleton, *Criticism and Ideology* (London: Verso, 1978). For related discussions, see Henri Arvon, *Marxist Esthetics*, trans. Helen R. Lane, intro. Fredric Jameson (Ithaca, N.Y., and London: Cornell University Press, 1973); *Marxism and Art: Essays Classic and Con-*

temporary, selected and with historical and critical commentary by Maynard Solomon (New York: Knopf, 1973); and Theodor Adorno, Walter Benjamin, Ernst Bloch, Bertolt Brecht, and Georg Lukács, *Aesthetics and Politics*, trans. ed. Ronald Taylor, afterword Fredric Jameson (London: Verso, 1980), as well as the essays collected in *Marxists on Literature: An Anthology*, ed. David Craig (Baltimore: Penguin 1975).

15. Friedrich Engels, "Letter to Minna Kautsky," in *Marxists on Literature*, 268. See also chapters 8, 9 (Marx's and Engels's letters to Lasalle), and 13 (Engels's letter to Margaret Harkness), all reprinted from Karl Marx and Friedrich Engels, *Selected Correspondence* (Moscow, n.d.).

16. Friedrich Engels, "Letter to Margaret Harkness," in *Marxists on Literature*, 270.

17. David Craig, introduction to *Marxists on Literature*, 22.

18. "Modern immigrant writing is almost exclusively autobiographical in nature. It defies and redefines the boundaries of the genre" (Azade Seyhan, "Ethnic Selves/Ethnic Signs: Invention of Self, Space, and Genealogy in Immigrant Writing," in *Culture/Contexture: Explorations in Anthropology and Literary Studies*, ed. E. Valentine Daniel and Jeffrey M. Peck [Berkeley: University of California Press, 1996], 180).

19. Sigmund Freud, "On Narcissism: An Introduction," in *A General Selection from the Works of Sigmund Freud*, ed. John Rickman, appendix Charles Brenner (New York: Anchor/Doubleday, 1957), 105.

20. "The term [Asian American] is inherently elastic and of fairly recent currency. . . . It carries within it layers of historical sedimentation. Not merely a denotative label with a fixed, extralinguistic referent, it is a sign, a site of contestation for a multitude of political and cultural forces" (Sau-ling Cynthia Wong, *Reading Asian American Literature: From Necessity to Extravagance* [Princeton: Princeton University Press, 1993], 5). Wong offers a useful summary account of the legalist definitions and ramifications of the term in recent United States history. Similarly, David Palumbo-Liu writes that "as it at once implies *both* exclusion and inclusion, 'Asian/ American' marks both the distinction installed between 'Asian' and 'American' *and* a dynamic, unsettled, and inclusive movement" (*Asian/ American: Historical Crossings of a Racial Frontier* [Stanford: Stanford University Press, 1999], 1; emphases in the original). For related discussions, see also Elaine H. Kim, *Asian American Literature: An Introduction to the Writings and Their Social Context* (Philadelphia: Temple University Press, 1982); Sucheng Chan, *Asian Americans: An Interpretive*

History (Boston: Twayne, 1991); *Reading the Literatures of Asian America*, ed. Shirley Geok-lin Lim and Amy Ling (Philadelphia: Temple University Press, 1992); Sheng-mei Ma, *Immigrant Subjectivities in Asian American and Asian Diaspora Literatures* (Albany: State University of New York Press, 1998); Angelo Ancheta, *Race, Rights and the Asian American Experience* (New Brunswick, N.J.: Rutgers University Press, 1998); and David Leiwei Li, *Imagining the Nation: Asian American Literature and the Cultural Consent* (Stanford, Calif.: Stanford University Press, 1999).

21. In *Under Western Eyes: Personal Essays from Asian America*, ed. Garrett Hongo (New York: Anchor/Doubleday, 1995), 5.

22. Julia Kristeva, *Powers of Horror: An Essay on Abjection*, trans. Leon S. Roudiez (New York: Columbia University Press, 1982), 2 (emphasis in the original), 4.

23. Elizabeth Grosz, "Julia Kristeva," in *Feminism and Psychoanalysis: A Critical Dictionary*, ed. Elizabeth Wright (Oxford: Blackwell, 1992), 198.

24. For this important point, I thank the enthusiastic, good-humored audience at the conference on Persistence of Exile at the University of Colorado at Boulder in March 2001, in particular, Michael DuPlessis.

5. When Whiteness Feminizes . . . : Some Consequences of a Supplementary Logic

1. Toril Moi, *Sexual/Textual Politics: Feminist Literary Theory* (London: Methuen, 1985).

2. Moi, *Sexual/Textual Politics*, 86, 87, emphases in the original, quoted with slight modifications in Deborah E. McDowell, *"The Changing Same": Black Women's Literature, Criticism, and Theory* (Bloomington: Indiana University Press, 1995), 161.

3. Ann Douglas, *The Feminization of American Culture* (New York: Avon, 1977).

4. This second-wave feminism is sometimes known as "difference" feminism or "gynocentric" feminism. All these terms designate the turning point at which Western feminists systematically developed women-specific approaches that generated more complex explanations for the problem of women's oppression than the ones hitherto provided by classical Marxist analyses. For a succinct account that highlights feminists in nonliterary

disciplines, see Linda Nicholson, introduction to *The Second Wave: A Reader in Feminist Theory*, ed. Linda Nicholson (New York: Routledge, 1997), 1–5.

5. In opposition to Douglas, Jane Tompkins, for instance, affirms women's sentimental fiction by arguing that literary sensationalism can be a form of political intervention. See her *Sensational Designs: The Cultural Work of American Fiction, 1790–1860* (New York: Oxford University Press, 1985).

6. Andreas Huyssen, "Mass Culture as Woman: Modernism's Other," in *After the Great Divide: Modernism, Mass Culture, Postmodernism* (Bloomington: Indiana University Press, 1986), 44–62.

7. For an exemplary critique of feminist essentialism and its philosophical origins, see Elizabeth V. Spelman, *Inessential Woman: Problems of Exclusion in Feminist Thought* (Boston: Beacon, 1988).

8. The unstable and unstabilizable status of "woman" is, in part, what has provoked some recent debates about the status of women's studies as a field of inquiry. See the essays in the *differences* special issue "Women's Studies on the Edge," edited by Joan Scott, in particular, Kathryn Cook and Renea Henry, with Joan Scott, "The Edge. Interview," *differences: A Journal of Feminist Cultural Studies* 9, no. 3 (fall 1997): 132–55. See also Robyn Wiegman, "Feminism, Institutionalism, and the Idiom of Failure," special issue "America the Feminine," ed. Philip Gould and Leonard Tennenhouse, *differences* 11, no. 3 (fall 1999/2000): 107–36.

9. Charlotte Brontë, *Jane Eyre (1848): Complete, Authoritative Text with Biographical and Historical Contexts, Critical History, and Essays from Five Contemporary Critical Perspectives*, ed. Beth Newman (Boston: Bedford, St. Martin's, 1996).

10. Sandra Gilbert and Susan Gubar, *The Madwoman in the Attic: The Woman Writer and the Nineteenth-Century Literary Imagination* (New Haven: Yale University Press, 1979).

11. Cora Kaplan, " 'A Heterogeneous Thing': Female Childhood and the Rise of Racial Thinking in Victorian Britain," in *Human, All Too Human*, ed. Diana Fuss (New York: Routledge, 1996), 171.

12. Gilbert writes that "Bertha . . . is Jane's truest and darkest double: the angry aspect of the orphan child, the ferocious secret self Jane has been trying to repress ever since her days at Gateshead" ("Plain Jane's Progress," in Brontë, *Jane Eyre*, 492; this essay was originally published in *Signs* 2, no. 4 [summer 1977]: 779–804). In a more recent essay, Gilbert upholds and

updates her previous views by reading Jane Eyre as a Cinderella filled with intense sexual passion. As for Bertha Mason, Gilbert emphasizes her whiteness: "The beautiful but dissolute daughter of a 'Creole' (probably French and Spanish) mother, Bertha is most likely of European descent, although her upbringing in the hot West Indies has led to a tradition of critical speculations that she is racially mixed" ("*Jane Eyre* and the Secrets of Furious Lovemaking," *Novel: A Forum for Fiction* 31, no. 3 [summer 1998]: 360). She then proceeds to read Bertha as a woman driven mad by her excessive and unsatisfied sexual hunger. In thus adopting what in the context of *Jane Eyre* is Rochester's (racist) view of Bertha's sexuality (a view that equates dark-skinned peoples from hot climates with overly sexed natures), Gilbert proves herself, even in the late 1990s, an unswervingly compassionate and loyal wife to the master (in terms of the argument I am making). For a considerably more nuanced discussion of the ambiguity of Bertha's race, see Susan Meyer, *Imperialism at Home: Race and Victorian Women's Fiction* (Ithaca, N.Y.: Cornell University Press, 1996), 63–70.

13. For this argument, see Nancy Armstrong and Leonard Tennenhouse, "Introduction: Representing Violence, or 'How the West Was Won,' " in *The Violence of Representation: Literature and the History of Violence*, ed. Nancy Armstrong and Leonard Tennenhouse (London: Routledge, 1989), 1–26.

14. See Gayatri Chakravorty Spivak, "Three Women's Texts and a Critique of Imperialism," *Critical Inquiry* 12 (1985): 243–61.

15. See also Jenny Sharpe, *Allegories of Empire: The Figure of Woman in the Colonial Text* (Minneapolis: University of Minnesota Press, 1993), 26–53; and Meyer, *Imperialism at Home*, 60–95.

16. V. I. Propp, *Morphology of the Folktale* (1928), trans. Laurence Scott (Austin: University of Texas Press, 1968), 19.

17. Armstrong and Tennenhouse's reading in their introduction to *The Violence of Representation* is responsive precisely to this fact of Jane as a writer; they argue that language and writing are the very means by which Jane empowers and socially reproduces herself despite her utter deprivation. See also Kaplan's " 'A Heterogeneous Thing' " for a discussion of the differences in Brontë's novel between the innocent child protesting against social injustice and the well-seasoned, knowledgeable adult Jane retelling her past.

18. See Daphne du Maurier, *Rebecca* (New York: Modern Library, 1938). There was some controversy over plagiarism regarding du Maurier's

work (raised by the family of a Mrs. MacDonald who wrote a novel called *Blind Windows*, which they claimed du Maurier's story copied). According to du Maurier, the case was legally dismissed (see *The Rebecca Notebook and Other Memories* [London: Gollancz, 1981], 14–15). Du Maurier, who has made references to Emily Brontë and *Wuthering Heights* in her memoirs (*The Rebecca Notebook*, 106–7; 120–21), has not, to my knowledge, indicated any borrowing from Charlotte's work, but the remarkable resemblance of her story to that of *Jane Eyre* speaks for itself. In "*Jane Eyre* and the Secrets of Furious Lovemaking," Sandra Gilbert writes that "*Jane Eyre* is more a romance in the mode of such diversely Gothic descendants as *The Turn of the Screw*, *Rebecca*, and *Wide Sargasso Sea* than it is a 'realistic' novel in the mode of *The Mill on the Floss* or *Middlemarch*" (368). As the present chapter will make clear, I am much less interested in the issue of plagiarism than in what I think are the generic features of prevalent narrative elaborations of whiteness as whiteness undergoes feminization.

19. Although, in the film version of *Rebecca*, Max describes Rebecca as having accidentally killed herself during a quarrel with him, in the novel, he actually confesses to having killed her. Du Maurier clearly registers this sense of complicity on the part of the young wife, the narrator of the tale, in these words: "I had listened to his story and part of me went with him like a shadow in his tracks. I too had killed Rebecca, I too had sunk the boat there in the bay" (Du Maurier, *Rebecca*, 266).

20. "*Rebecca* is the story of a woman's maturation, a woman who must come to terms with a powerful father figure and assorted mother figures (Mrs. Van Hopper, Rebecca, and Mrs. Danvers)"; "*Rebecca* shows the *heroine's* attempt to detach herself from the mother in order to attach herself to a *man*" (Tania Modleski, *The Women Who Knew Too Much: Hitchcock and Feminist Theory* [New York: Methuen, 1988], 46, 50; emphases in the original).

21. The strongest evidence for this is found in the character of Mrs. Danvers, who is fiercely defensive about her lost female idol. (See Rhona Berenstein, " 'I'm Not the Sort of Person Men Marry': Monsters, Queers, and Hitchcock's *Rebecca*," *Cinéaction!* 29 [1992]: 82–96, and Robert Samuels, *Hitchcock's Bi-Textuality: Lacan, Feminisms, and Queer Theory* [Albany: State University of New York Press, 1998], 45–57, for discussions of the lesbian implications of Mrs. Danvers's affections and the circulation of feminine desire.) By her doctor's account, when Rebecca

went secretly to see him about what she thought was a possible pregnancy, she did so under the name Mrs. Danvers.

22. In *Rebecca*, in the scene in which Max de Winter makes his confession, the young woman's entire demeanor changes as she discovers, for the first time, that her husband never loved Rebecca. This discovery gives her the strength to help him because the other woman is, at this point, clearly out of the picture—as the common enemy against whom husband and wife will now unite. Du Maurier's text reads as follows:

> The rest of me sat there on the carpet, unmoved and detached, thinking and caring for one thing only, repeating a phrase over and over again, "He did not love Rebecca, he did not love Rebecca." . . . Something new had come upon me that had not been before. My heart, for all its anxiety and doubt, was light and free. I knew then that I was no longer afraid of Rebecca. I did not hate her any more. . . . Maxim had never loved her. I did not hate her any more. Her body had come back, her boat had been found with its queer prophetic name, Je Reviens, but I was free of her forever. . . . I was not young any more. I was not shy. I was not afraid. I would fight for Maxim. I would lie and perjure and swear, I would blaspheme and pray. Rebecca had not won. Rebecca had lost.
>
> (Du Maurier, *Rebecca*, 267)

23. Insofar as I think that even a strong woman character such as Jane Eyre is ultimately subordinate to men, my reading departs from the critical tradition of protofeminist arguments, made in the 1980s by critics such as Tompkins, about sentimental fiction (see Tompkins, *Sensational Designs*). The reasons for my departure should, I hope, be clear from my arguments throughout this chapter.

24. Moi, *Sexual/Textual Politics*, 69.

25. Marguerite Duras, *Hiroshima mon amour: Scénario et dialogue* (Paris: Gallimard, 1960); idem, *Hiroshima mon amour*, trans. Richard Seaver (New York: Grove, 1961). References to Duras's text cite the English translation.

26. Alfred Cismaru, *Marguerite Duras* (New York: Twayne, 1971), 149.

27. Propp, *Morphology of the Folktale*, 20–21. Propp's morphology has been modified and critiqued by various structuralist theorists, among whom is Claude Lévi-Strauss, who argues that the empirical discovery of functions is insufficient for a generic understanding of the folktale as a form (or as a completed kind of narrative). See Lévi-Strauss, "L'analyse morpholo-

gique des contes russes," *International Journal of Slavic Linguistics and Poetics* 3 (1960): 122–49; and idem, "La structure et la forme: Réflexions sur un ouvrage de Vladimir Propp," *Cahiers de l'Institut de science économique appliquée* 99 (March 1960). My purpose in referring to functions is different here; I am primarily interested in demonstrating the detectable continuities between the Anglo-American and French narratives and not in developing an entire metanarratological model.

28. Leslie Hill, *Marguerite Duras: Apocalyptic Desires* (London: Routledge, 1993), 31.

29. Deborah N. Glassman, *Marguerite Duras: Fascinating Vision and Narrative Cure* (London and Toronto: Associated University Presses, 1991), 27.

30. Hill describes this "elevating" in the following manner: "Place names in Duras function consistently—particularly, say, in *Hiroshima mon amour*—as shorthand ciphers for a series of catastrophic events that have somehow broken loose from the confines of geography and history" (*Marguerite Duras: Apocalyptic Desires*, 97).

31. Duras's emphasis might also have been a response to the fact that Alain Resnais, her collaborator, was originally commissioned in 1958 to make a short documentary on the atomic bomb. He decided he could not do so and instead proposed an alternative that led to the Japanese-French coproduction of *Hiroshima mon amour*, with Duras as the writer of the screenplay.

32. Sharon Willis, *Marguerite Duras: Writing on the Body* (Urbana: University of Illinois Press, 1987), 59.

33. See, for instance, Glassman, *Marguerite Duras: Fascinating Vision*, 24–33, for a lucid discussion of the gender and existential implications of Duras's uses of visual representation as opposed to language and narrative.

34. Insofar as this racing and/or ethnicizing of representational statuses is a priori, Duras's placement of the Japanese in factographic referentiality is not categorically different from, for instance, Julia Kristeva's placement of Chinese women in the so-called preoedipal stage (see her *About Chinese Women*, trans. Anita Barrows [London: Boyars, 1977]). What is common to both cases is the perfunctory, theoretical simplification—that is, primitivization—of the nonwhite other, in contrast to the psychical and textual complexity that is copiously endowed on the white subject.

35. Sherene H. Razack's comments on complicity are worth citing at length:

An attention to complicity has not strongly emerged in feminism because, for the most part, we continue to avoid any inquiry into domination and our role in it when we confront issues of difference and diversity. Instead, each of us feels most safe in these discussions anchored in our subordinated position by virtue of our being of colour, disabled, economically exploited, colonized, a lesbian, or a woman. . . . Knowing the difficulties involved in confronting our own role in systems of domination, we may find that being anchored on the margin is more preferable. Yet, if we remain anchored on the margin, the discourse with women subordinated to ourselves stops, and various moves of superiority, notably pity and cultural othering, prevail. We become unable to interrogate how multiple systems of oppression regulate our lives and unable to take effective collective action to change these systems.

(*Looking White People in the Eye: Gender, Race, and Culture in Courtrooms and Classrooms* [Toronto: University of Toronto Press, 1998], 132).

36. Nancy Armstrong, "Captivity and Cultural Capital in the English Novel," *Novel: A Forum on Fiction* 31, no. 3 (summer 1998): 373–98.

37. Susan Gubar, "What Ails Feminist Criticism?" *Critical Inquiry* 24, no. 4 (summer 1998): 878–902.

38. Razack, *Looking White People in the Eye*, 169–70.

39. For a comparative discussion of this situation by way of political philosophy, see the analysis of the problematic of injury in Wendy Brown, *States of Injury: Power and Freedom in Late Modernity* (Princeton: Princeton University Press, 1995).

40. See Robyn Wiegman, "What Ails Feminist Criticism: A Second Opinion," *Critical Inquiry* 25 (winter 1999): 362–79.

41. The final version of this chapter has benefited from discussions I had in spring 2001 with participants in my undergraduate seminar "Vision and Narration" at Brown University and with participants in Professor Panivong Norindr's graduate seminar on postcolonial criticism at the University of Southern California.

Postscript: Beyond Ethnic Ressentiment?

1. Frantz Fanon, *Black Skin, White Masks*, trans. Charles Lam Markmann (New York: Grove Weidenfeld, 1967), 47–48.

2. Rey Chow, "The Politics of Admittance: Female Sexual Agency, Miscegenation, and the Formation of Community in Frantz Fanon," *Ethics Af-*

ter Idealism: Theory–Culture–Ethnicity–Reading (Bloomington: Indiana University Press, 1998), 55–73. This essay was originally published in *UTS Review* 1, no. 1 (1995): 5–29.

3. Max Scheler, *Ressentiment*, new ed., trans. Lewis B. Coser and William W. Holdheim, intro. Manfred S. Frings (Milwaukee: Marquette University Press, 1994). Scheler's discussion of Nietzsche draws on *The Genealogy of Morals*. Whereas Nietzsche associates *ressentiment* with Christianity, however, Scheler offers a very different—a much more positive—reading of the latter.

4. As some critics have pointed out, such *ressentiment* must also be understood as simultaneously homosocial and homophobic in nature. See, for instance, Diana Fuss, "Interior Colonies: Frantz Fanon and the Politics of Identification," *diacritics* 24. nos. 2–3 (summer–fall 1994): 20–42; and Kobena Mercer, "Decolonisation and Disappointment: Reading Fanon's Sexual Politics," in *The Fact of Blackness: Frantz Fanon and Visual Representation*, ed. Alan Read (Seattle: Bay, 1996), 114–25. In envying and repudiating the women of color's sexual access to white men, Fanon, it would seem, implicitly desires these white men also and yet cannot imagine (or must repress the possibility of) a black man having the same kind of access to them.

5. John Pomfret, "China Halts Plans to Publish Ha Jin's Award-Winning Novel," *Ithaca Journal*, June 24, 2000, 3B. The report was reproduced from the *Washington Post*.

6. Fanon, *Black Skin, White Masks*, 18.

7. See my discussion of Zhang in the chapter "The Force of Surfaces," in *Primitive Passions: Visuality, Sexuality, Ethnography, and Contemporary Chinese Cinema* (New York: Columbia University Press, 1995).

8. Cai Guoqiang won one of three international prizes for his installation at the Venice Biennale in 1999. The work was a reconstruction in clay of an icon of class struggle in the People's Republic during the 1960s, a sculptural tableau entitled *Rent Collection Yard*, which depicted the ways a cruel landlord exploited his peasants. Cai was criticized in the Chinese press for being a "green card artist" and a "banana man" (yellow on the outside, white on the inside), who had illegally appropriated and infringed on the copyright of the original collective artwork. Most of all, he was accused of "pandering to malicious Western misconceptions . . . scoring easy points by mocking the excesses of Mao's Cultural Revolution" (Erik Eckholm, "Cultural Revolution, Chapter 2," *New York Times*, August 17, 2000, B1, B6).

9. In 2001 Gao Xingjian, the mainland Chinese writer who is a French citizen, became the first ethnic Chinese author to be awarded the prize. Amidst celebrations of Gao's achievement in various Chinese communities, including Taiwan and Hong Kong, the habitual *ressentiment* was almost immediately marshaled against him and his works by the mainland Chinese government and some mainland Chinese critics.

10. Aijaz Ahmad, "Jameson's Rhetoric of Otherness and the 'National Allegory,' " *Social Text* 17 (fall 1987): 5.

11. Garrett Hongo, introduction to *Under Western Eyes: Personal Essays from Asian America*, ed. and intro. Garrett Hongo (New York: Anchor/Doubleday, 1995), 19–20; emphasis in the original. The best example of an Asian American writer who was, on achieving general recognition, accused of selling out is Maxine Hong Kingston. For exploratory accounts of the debates around Kingston, see ibid., 17–22; King-Kok Cheung, "The Woman Warrior Versus The Chinaman Pacific: Must a Chinese American Critic Choose between Feminism and Heroism?" in *Conflicts in Feminism*, ed. Marianne Hirsch and Evelyn Fox Keller (New York: Routledge, 1990), 234–47; and Sau-ling Cynthia Wong, "Autobiography as Guided Chinatown Tour? Maxine Hong Kingston's *The Woman Warrior* and the Chinese American Autobiographical Controversy," in *Multicultural Autobiography: American Lives*, ed. James Robert Payne (Knoxville: University of Tennessee Press, 1992), 248–79.

12. Indeed, a Chinese translation has already been published in Taiwan. See Ha Jin, *Dengdai*, trans. Jin Liang (Taipei: Shibao Wenhua, 2000).

Index